Let's Cook FOR OUR CAT

Written and Illustrated
by
Edmund R. Dorosz, B.S.A., D.V.M.

"Merry Christmas" (1995)
Mom

"Our Love for ever."
Doug, Max & Martha.
XXXX
OOOO

Cover Art: Our "Fluffy" as a kitten

Our Pet's books: Let's Cook For Our Cat, Let's Cook For Our Dog and dog prints of the original watercolours are available.
For ordering details refer to the back of the book.

Let's Cook
FOR OUR CAT

Let's Cook FOR OUR CAT

Copyright © 1995 by **Edmund R. Dorosz**, B.S.A., D.V.M.

Permission is granted to reproduce sections of
Let's Cook For Our Cat, including recipes.
Please credit Our Pet's Inc, Let's Cook For Our Cat
and the author upon publication
Reproduction of the Art work is prohibited.

First Edition June 1995

I.S.B.N. 0-9696884-1-7

Canadian Cataloguing in Publication Data
Dorosz, Edmund R.
Let's Cook For Our Cat
Bibliography: p
Includes index
1. Cats — Food 2. Cats. I. Title.

1995

Published and distributed by
Our Pet's Inc.
P.O. Box 2094
Fort Macleod, Alberta, Canada
TOL OZO

Printed and bound in Canada by Friesens

CONTENTS

Acknowledgements 8
Note To Readers 9
Introduction 11

PART ONE Nutrition and Nutrients 14
Our Pet's Basic Nutrition 16
Our Pet's Basic Digestion and Absorption 27
    The Digestion Tube 28
    Pancreas and Liver 35
Water 38
Energy 41
Proteins 44
Fats 48
Carbohydrates 52
Vitamins 56
    A 59
    D 62
    E 63
    K 65
    B's 66
    C 72
    Antioxidants 73
    Vitamin Summary 75
Minerals 77
    Calcium, Phosphorus, and Magnesium 80
    Potassium, Sodium and Chlorine 85
    Iron, Zinc, Copper, Vanadium, Silicon
    and Molybdenum 86
    Chromium, Manganese and Selenium 89
    Nickel, Iodine, Cobalt, Sulfur and Fluorine 90
    Mineral Summary 91
Toxic Elements 94
Recommendations
    Water, Protein, Fats, Carbohydrates,
    Vitamins and Minerals 95

PART TWO Commercially Prepared Cat Food 102
Cat food: Yesterday, Today and Tomorrow 104
Kinds of cat food 110
Advantages and disadvantages 111
How to shop for prepared cat food 112
    Reading the label 114
    What's In A Label 117
Types of Commercial Cat Food 126
Home Evaluation
    Cost 130
    Container and Contents 131
    The Home Feeding Trial 133
Guidelines for Feeding
    What Should We Feed Our Cat? 138
    Classifications of Cat Food Available 139
    How Should We Feed? 140
    How Often Do We Feed? 140
    How Much Do We Feed? 144
Exercise 147
Summary 149

PART THREE Getting Started 151
Basic Feline Differences 152
Evaluating Table Scraps 156
Equipment 161
Ingredients 162
Health Food Store Ingredients 170
Nutrient Comparisons of Ingredients 172
Understanding the Measurements 174

PART FOUR Recipes 175
Traditional Recipes 181
Natural, Health Conscious, Organic Recipes 189
Price Conscious Recipes 203
Gourmet Recipes 211
Special Individuals 219

Overweight and Obesity 221
Underweight 227
Sick and Convalescing 228
Mothers 231
Kittens 236
Sick Kitten Care 240
Orphans 241
Neutered Individuals 245
Seniors 246
Needs For Special Breeds 252

PART FIVE Nutritionally Related Problems 253
Appetite 257
Digestive System Problems
    Mouth and Dental 259
    Halitosis, Bad Breath 261
    Stomach 261
    Liver 264
    Pancreas 265
    Yellow Fat Disease 266
    Retinal Degeneration 266
    Vomiting 267
    Diarrhea 268
    Constipation 271
    Flatulence 275
Food Intolerances and Allergies 273
Behavior Problems 278
Skin Problems 279
FUS, Feline Urological Syndrome 283
Summary 285
Going on Trips 286
   Appendix 288
   Glossary 290
   Index 297
   Recipe Index 300
   Additional readings 302
   Author profile 304

ACKNOWLEDGMENTS

I would like to thank my wife Sandra for her support and my children Sean and Sarah for putting up with my dreams for this kind of a book for years. I have to mention our tan siamese cross "Max" and black tabby "Indy" for being the tester of my recipes. Thanks as well are extended to Rhonda Henke, Sandy Irvine of By Design Services, Jim Beckel of Friesen Printers and David Poulsen, author and English Instructor for their professional assistance.

I acknowledge my late parents, E.C. Dorosz for always praising my art productions and encouraging me to higher education, and Stephanie Dorosz for her artistic genes, love of cooking and recipe collection.

Lastly, I would like to acknowledge my students and veterinary patients who inspired my interest in practical nutrition and "Kittle", our calico that was with us for 15 years, always tough, independent and neat: a character.

NOTE TO READERS

This book is an educational and informative guide for feeding our cat. The recipes have all been tested and no harm can be encountered if the directions are followed. One single recipe should not be the sole source of food over any length of time. Variety is best.

All cats are different. If a particular cat should have a problem in which nutrition may be involved, use the information in this book to assist in a diagnosis and/or treatment. For the final diagnosis I encourage you to discuss the ideas presented with your cat's veterinarian.

The Goals of this book are

- To present as simply as possible an understanding of our pet's basic nutritional requirements for an active and healthy life.

- To evaluate commercial cat foods so that informed shopping decisions can be made.

- To provide recipes prepared from fresh ingredients found in our kitchens.

Since we feed our pets every day and every individual pet is different, it is up to us to determine if our pet is being adequately looked after. There is an old saying that "Nutrition is in the eye of the Feeder". The feeder must observe the pet and make adjustments to the diet based on those observations.

It has been my goal to simplify cat nutrition so that we can all understand what we are doing when we feed our cat. With this basic knowledge, we can apply it to the art of cooking for our cat. However, when we simplify, many details are eliminated and exactness suffers.

You will not find many Do's and Don't's, Must's or Must Not's in this book. I have deliberately stayed away from this. I have been in this business long enough to develop grey hair by having someone prove me wrong when I have made a rigid statement. There are many examples in everyday life that were gospel yesterday but not today. We've heard no bones, no table scraps, no vitamins or mineral supplements are necessary; cats don't need vitamin C and the list goes on. Many times in my professional career as a practicing veterinarian, I have been proven wrong when giving strict advice for animal nutrition and health.

I believe that there are those of us in advisory professions who get in a rut. We tend to give yes-no answers to questions when maybe the solutions are more grey than black or white.

When dealing with animal nutrition and health, many factors are involved as each animal and situation is unique. Feeding and animal care is an art as well as a science. Some of us are better at the art than others. The final picture is the health and well-being of our cat.

I have attempted to explain as simply as possible with words and pictures many aspects of nutrition and feeding so that we can make knowledgeable decisions on what is best for our pet. We live with our pet everyday and are the ones who must make these decisions.

Nutrition is a big part of health, but if a medical problem is suspected, we should seek good veterinary medical advice.

Good luck, and remember we should watch and listen to our cat as he or she will tell us what is right for it. It is up to us to be smart enough to understand what our cat is telling us.

INTRODUCTION

SIAMESE

Like a queen
or maybe a baby
you stare at me
your gaze baleful
mysterious as the moon

How you fill
my universe
with beauty
I feed you
I brush you
but still you elude me

Your spell. . .
daily new
My wonder. . .
never done

Leona Flim

This is a book about feeding our cat: what foods our cat needs and why, as well as how to observe the signs of poor nutrition and how to correct the problems.

If we own a cat we should know how to feed and look after it. It has become our responsiblity to do this properly. Feeding our cat is the most important thing we do as cat owners, especially those of us with confined cats that cannot roam the neighbourhood.

"Cats are what they eat and cats eat what they are."

Cats are what they eat. Cats eat food to provide themselves with energy and nutrients to build and repair body parts. Good wholesome food with the right nutrients will grow healthy kittens and maintain them as healthy adults.

Most of the cat's body is constantly being worn out and replaced. This requires food to replace these tissues. Not eating the right foods will quickly become apparent. The cat's attitude, eyes, hair coat and stools will change. On the other hand, adequate amounts of the right food will result in a healthy, happy and active cat. Cats are what they eat.

Cats eat what they are. Cats are carnivores. Cats are flesh eating mammals. These particular animals that we have recently domesticated have hunted live prey as their sole source of food for millions of years. They have not changed. Our domesticated house cat is a flesh eating carnivore.

This is what this book is about. How to feed our cat and why.

This is a book about cat nutrition: what foods our cat needs to be healthy and what happens if these foods with their nutrients are not supplied.

A cookbook for cats? Why not? There are thousands of cookbooks for people and very few for our pets.

In North America and Europe we spend billions of dollars every year on pet foods that are prepared, processed, and packaged great distances from where they will be eventually eaten. What happened to feeding fresh people food to pets and where are the recipes for preparing people food for our pets?

Prepared commercial pet food looks like wonderful stuff: handy, simple, and available. However, it is not perfect. If we are to feed our cat properly, a basic knowledge of feline nutrition and a little effort are required.

Before we get started, we should review our pet's basic nutritional requirements and understand what we are doing when we feed our cat. We must also appreciate the cat's digestive system and how it is different from other animals and our own. As with any topic, knowledge is our greatest tool.

Commercially prepared cat foods are available to us today, so we should take full advantage of them, know what we are buying and understand the pitfalls.

The recipes in this book were developed and tested with appreciation of the differences between us: human and cat. The recipes can be prepared with ingredients that we are familiar with and can be modified if we should so desire. Remember that cooking is an art as well as a science. No one single diet or recipe should be the sole source of food over any length of time. "Variety is the spice of life," for all of us. Variety also helps to insure that all nutrients are present.

We must always remember that cats, like people, are individuals and what is good for one may not be good for another. Recipes and commercial cat foods are developed for the average individual and we must always ask, "What is average?" We also assume that the cat we are feeding is normal and healthy. If we have an individual that may have some abnormality, perhaps he or she should be under veterinary supervision.

This is a book for the cat, with sections on nutrition and nutrients, commercial cat foods, recipes that we can prepare and nutritionally related problems. I hope that you have as much enjoyment feeding your cat as I had in writing and illustrating this book.

PART ONE Nutrition and Nutrients

"Dietary management is the lifelong daily control of nutrient intake to meet the changing unique requirements of both healthy and diseased pets, in order to maximize the quality and length of life."

Hills, *Small Animal Nutrition.*

Nutrition does not have to be difficult to understand and yet, when we look around at the human species, we may conclude that very few of us understand even the basics. We are going to discuss the basics of nutrition and how it applies to the cat, and then, with this knowledge, we will be able to feed our pet.

What is nutrition? Nutrition is the consumption of food of sufficient quality and quantity that will permit an animal to reach and maintain a body condition of which it is genetically capable within its given environment. Another way to define nutrition would be to say it is the digestion and processing of foods into substances that the cat's body can use. Nutrients are the substances that the cat requires for living. In other words, we are going to discuss foods: how, why and what they do for the cat's body.

When animals are provided with the proper nutrients in adequate amounts they will attain their inherited potentials.

In this section we will further define nutrition, discuss digestion and absorption, outline the basic nutrients and then specify how we can provide foods with these nutrients, thus enabling our pets to achieve good health.

For us to provide our pet with an adequate diet, we must have a basic understanding of the cat's nutritional requirements and the food sources of these requirements. As owners of the modern cat, we are in total control of what and how much our cat will eat, as compared to a cat in the wild who can wander and pick its own food. Since our cat totally depends upon us and has no choice, we should have some understanding of nutrition.

In other words
- what are the requirements for activity, growth and play?
- what foods contain these requirements? and
- how do we provide these foods in adequate amounts?

Perhaps we have not really thought about it in this manner. If the food that we feed our pet does not meet these requirements, trouble is just over the horizon.

For a cat's food to fulfill these requirements the food must
- be palatable,
- supply enough energy for the particular daily energy needs
- have the proper nutrients in the correct amounts and balance for adequate growth and repair of tissues
- be digestible and utilized by the cat.

With these four must's, we feed our pet everyday and keep her in a state of good health.

When is our cat healthy? We, as the sole providers of food and shelter, have taken on the responsibility of maintaining this individual in a state of good health. What are the signs?

Some signs of good health and nutrition are
a good appetite,
proper weight,
alertness,
glossy haircoat,
regular urination and defecation,
and vigor.

OUR PET'S BASIC NUTRITION

"Quality of nutrition is the greatest single factor in determining the quality of one's life."

Dr. Thomas McKeown

For us to feed our cats properly, we must have some basic understanding of their make-up. Cats, *Felis domestica*, are the small domesticated cats that belong to the feline family or *Felidae*.

It is believed that our cats were first domesticated about eight thousand years ago and were put to work protecting man's granary stores of grain from mice and rodents. The ancestors of our pet cats originated from arid, almost desert type areas. Fossil findings tell us that the early peoples of Cyprus and Egypt had these small cats.

Cats need water but are able to conserve more and get along with less than dogs. Cats take much of their water from the prey they eat and are able to concentrate their urine output.

All *Felidae* are flesh eaters or carnivores. They all have sharp strong teeth, typical of predators, and sharp retractile claws. They walk on their tiptoes for silent stalking of prey and have whiskers and eyes adapted for night hunting. Their ability to smell and hear is very good. All of these traits have served them well for millions of years as hunters.

Other members of this family are the lions, tigers, leopards, lynxes and jaguars. Our domesticated cat and the other wild members of the cat family are carnivores. Carnivores are those mammals of the scientific order *Carnivora* which not only includes cats but also dogs, bears and weasels. Carnivores, for millions of years, have eaten the flesh of other animals.

This was their complete and balanced diet. They obtained all their required nutrients from the prey which they would have consumed almost in its entirety.

Carnivores are occasional feeders as opposed to herbivores that are continuous feeders. Watch a cow or horse and it seems to be continually eating. Its type of diet requires much more processing and digesting before it can utilize the nutrients. Carnivores, by contrast, eat foods that are easily digested as well as being highly concentrated, allowing them to go for extended periods of time without food.

Some carnivores, such as dogs, eat other foods besides flesh, such as cereals and other plant products. They had access to these when they ate of the stomach and intestinal contents of their prey. Today some people refer to dogs less as carnivores and more as omnivores, meaning individuals that can consume a variety of foods besides just flesh or meat and organs. For cats, however, the general consensus is that they are more of a true carnivore and must have a diet primarily of meat and fat and less plant matter. More on this later.

Because animal flesh was the diet of cats for many years, their digestive systems are especially suited for this with some basic differences from other animals. For example, their teeth are sharper, intestines shorter and livers larger than herbivores. Eating habits were also different among the ancestors of today's cat; they ate occasional big meals containing primarily animal protein and fat. In between these big meals, they rested and nibbled.

The cats of prehistoric time as well as our modern domesticated and wild cats eat the flesh of their prey which may include the complete carcass. Almost everything was consumed: hair, bones, organs and the contents of the stomach and intestines. By consuming everything, they had access to vegetables, cereals, fruits and berries.

In addition they obtained all of their required nutrients such as vitamins and minerals that may not be present in flesh alone. Often the prey of the cats was a herbivore that ate strictly plant matter, and its stomach would be filled with partly digested plant material. The wild cats, however, seem less interested in eating of these stomach contents than wild dogs.

We have to remember this when we feed our cat cereals and vegetables. We must keep these to a minimum and partially cook or grind this type of food, so that the cat is better able to digest it, thus getting the most benefit with the least problems.

Vomiting appears to be more difficult for most cats than for dogs. By ripping, tearing and then swallowing with very little chewing, large pieces of tough gristle and fragments of bones can be swallowed. Vomiting then would be an asset as this material could be brought back up and be either chewed and reswallowed or discarded. Having this natural ability to vomit prevented a lot of problems, so we should not become too upset if our cat occasionally vomits. If, however, our cat should persistently vomit, something could be wrong and a visit to a veterinarian may be called for.

Cats by nature do a lot of grooming thereby swallowing a lot of hair. This consumption of hair may be beneficial in that the hair can wrap around any sharp objects such as small, sharp bones from the prey that the cat had eaten such as birds and mice. On the other hand, this hair may become a problem so the ability to vomit up balls of hair prevents these from becoming troublesome if they should become too large and continue down the intestinal tract.

The eating habits of the cat for millions of years did not change much. With domestication and confinement, our modern cat does not have to hunt for her next meal. However, she cannot pick and choose. She must eat what we give her. The cat has become totally dependent upon us. Not that long ago, the domesticated cat was fed table scraps and whatever she could pick up from her wanderings about the neighborhood. In the last seventy-five years, the commercially processed pet food industry has evolved, which offers the modern cat owner a wide variety of totally prepared food. Modern science has discovered and identified many nutrients. We know a lot about nutrition though we still have a lot to learn.

Of all the domesticated animals, the North American feedlot steer is the most researched and studied animal. The chicken, hog and dairy cow would be next as far as being extensively studied. When we look at the amount of research done on the domesticated cat and dog, it is quite limited in comparison.

It seems that every day we hear something about an unknown nutrient or how we should or should not eat a known one. Taurine is a good example of a nutrient that we have just recently learned about that is required by cats. We must always keep this in mind when feeding our cat today. Maybe we ought to be more flexible in what we give our cat to eat, so that she is not missing something that modern science has not yet discovered.

The cat's body is a wonderful, complex organism with great abilities to adapt. Some individuals may not adapt. With the many changes to the cat's environment, we are now seeing "diseases of domestication and confinement." We are seeing nutritional and behavioral problems in our confined cats. Some feel that the cat should be fed a variety of foods, including fresh food, as opposed to a constant diet of processed food. Then her diet will be more like it was before we changed her environment.

"My ideal petfood includes four elementary concepts: variety, moderation, suitable for human consumption and fresh food daily."
                                                    Carol Barfield

Modern veterinary training, in my opinion, is quite limited in the field of nutrition and tends to place greater emphasis on pharmacology or drug therapy. Thank goodness we have many life saving pharmaceuticals available today. Also, I believe that we tend to treat the symptoms of disease more than we do the causes of illness.

I believe an underlying cause of many diseases and problems with our cats is poor nutrition. By correcting the nutrition with the proper nutrients, many of these conditions can be eliminated.

We are in the best position to determine if our cat is healthy because we see our pet every day. If we see signs such as poor appetite, poor hair coat, or lack of vigor, poor nutrition may be the cause. Cats are great creatures of habit and can easily develop a taste for one particular food which can lead to problems. It is our duty to beware of these signs of poor nutrition and make corrections.

The basic food requirements for the cat can be broken down into six main groups of nutrients. In order for the cat to function, these must be present in varying proportions depending upon the individual's particular needs. These basic requirements are the same for all animals as well as for us.

The six main groups of nutrients are

- Water
- Proteins
- Fats
- Carbohydrates
- Vitamins, and
- Minerals.

Foods have some or all of these nutrients in them, and cats need these nutrients in varying amounts on a regular basis.

Another item we may put on the list that is not really a nutrient is fibre. The ancestral and wild cats obtained their fibre from the hair and feathers of the prey that they consumed. Our modern cat does not have access to this material, so we include fibre in another form such as undigestible plant matter. This then acts as the fiber part of the diet.

Nutrient requirements will vary with such things as age, breed, activity and temperament. Each cat is an individual with specific requirements; therefore, the amounts will differ.

Differences may not be that great between two cats, but over time may become obvious. For example, if we fed two cats of different size the same diet everyday, one may become overweight and the other may lose weight. From this simple example, we can see the obvious. One cat was getting too much to eat and the other not enough, for their individual requirements.

When all of the required nutrients are provided in the correct proportions we say that the diet is "complete and balanced".

The picture on the next page will illustrate how these groups of nutrients maintain this balance.

Balanced Requirements

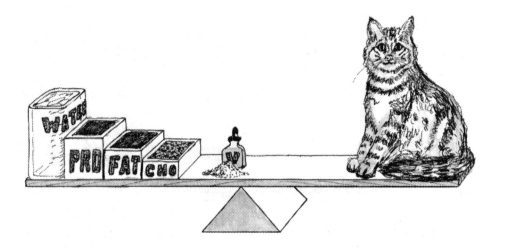

Water
 Protein
  Fat
   Carbohydrate

Vitamins
Minerals

Cat
fed for
one week

From the picture on the previous page we see how the cat is balanced on the teeter-totter with the six nutrients: water, protein, fat, carbohydrate, vitamins and minerals.

In the picture the nutrients are placed on the teeter-totter in order of importance, with water being out on the end, then proteins on to vitamins and minerals near the centre. This is not to say that vitamins and minerals are less important, but if we should take water away from the cat, she will suffer very quickly. However, a shortage of a vitamin or a mineral may take months to result in a noticeable difference in the cat.

The size of the containers of the various nutrients on the teeter-totter roughly illustrate the amounts of each that would maintain an adult cat with normal activity. If we could fill the water container with water, the protein container with pure protein, the fat container with pure fat, the carbohydrate container with pure carbohydrate, and the vitamins and minerals accordingly, this cat would be fed for a week. Unfortunately, it is not that simple; however, this is a good model to remember.

You will note that the carbohydrate container is not very large in comparison to the protein and fat containers. This is to illustrate the fact that the cat is more of a true carnivore and carbohydrates are not a large part of its diet.

How are things different? First, the size of the containers will vary with the cat on the other end. If the cat is a growing kitten, for example, the protein container will have to be larger, because a growing kitten requires more protein for the growth of muscles and other tissues. Vitamins and minerals will also have to be increased as the kitten will need more for bone growth. If the cat on the other end of the teeter-totter is a nursing Queen with a litter of kittens to feed, she will require greater amounts of highly concentrated energy, so we would make the protein and fat containers bigger.

We would make the protein, fat and carbohydrate containers smaller if the cat was neutered or overweight, because we would want to lower the energy amounts fed so that this cat would maintain her weight and not gain.

Another problem with this model is that foods, with few exceptions, are really mixtures of nutrients. For example, a piece of meat contains water, protein, fat and some vitamins and minerals. A slice of bread is mostly carbohydrate with some proteins, vitamins and minerals. Few foods contain only one nutrient.

Because foods are mixtures of nutrients, the cat's digestive system must break down the foods eaten into the various groups. Once the foods are separated into water, protein, fat, carbohydrate, vitamins and minerals, the process continues so that the nutrients will become acceptable for her use.

The other consideration when dealing with foods and the different amounts of nutrients in them comes into play when we attempt to calculate the daily requirements. We must go to charts of foods that list the average nutrient content and then balance what the cat can eat with what she needs. If each of the foods contained simply one nutrient, this calculation of diet balancing would be easier.

This has been a very basic introduction to nutrition. The six food requirements of water, protein, fat, carbohydrate, vitamins and minerals provide the cat with everything she needs. Foods containing the right amounts of these nutrients must be eaten by the cat to balance with her particular body needs.

Once eaten, the food will be broken down and processed into usable forms for the many cells of the cat's body.

This, very simply, is cat nutrition.

The illustration on the next page depicts the eating habits of the wild and ancestral cats. It really was feast or famine. Much activity and exercise was required in hunting their prey. After capture they would feast, sleep and be quite inactive. During this time their body stores were replenished. As time passed and they became hungry again, they would have to become active again to search and hunt for the next meal. Our cats today may hunt very little and feast every day. This not only limits their choices but also reduces the amount of exercise that the cats may get.

Because cats eat a lot of fat in their diet, they are able to sleep often and go without eating for long periods of time. Fat, as we will discuss later, contains over twice as many calories of energy as the other energy supplying nutrients: protein and carbohydrates.

Later when we discuss water and the cats' exceptional ability to conserve water we are again reminded of their ancestral background. The early cats lived in semi-desert, arid parts of the world, so water conservation was important. Their hunting habits were such that they hunted at night when it was cooler and the various prey that they hunted for food were active. This allowed the cats to sleep during the hot days and not expend much energy or lose much water. Further to this, their bodies became adapted to night hunting.

Later we will also discuss fat and how important it is to the cat. Fat being a highly concentrated form of energy gave the ancestral and wild cats of today a reserve of fuel so that they could survive for days without eating, should hunting for something to eat be unsuccessful.

These are all traits that our modern domesticated pet cats have, which we must take into consideration when we feed and look after them.

Eating Habits of Wild and Ancestral Cats

FAMINE
Hunter, hungry and active

FEAST
Sleep, full and inactive

OUR PET'S BASIC DIGESTION AND ABSORPTION

Digestion is all the processes in which consumed foods are prepared within the cat's digestive system to be absorbed and used by her many cells. Food is required by the cat to furnish energy for body activities and for the building and repair of tissues. All foods, with the exception of water and minerals, are organic. Organic foods come either directly or indirectly from plants which have stored energy acquired from the sun. The cat obtains this energy directly if she consumes plant material and indirectly if she consumes animal products. Once consumed, the food material must be digested or broken down into usable forms before being absorbed for her own use.

The digestive process occurs within the cat's digestive system. This system is basically a tube with a few attachments or organs that break down the consumed food into usable forms. Food enters at one end of the tube and, as it passes through, is transformed into absorbable products. The undigested is eliminated out the other end. This tube has adapted itself over millions of years to digest the cat's food.

Each part of the digestive system fulfills a specific task in the processing of the foods that enter the tube. The basic functions of the system include

- the secretion of digestive enzymes,
- the movement of food materials, and
- the absorption of nutrients.

Our domesticated pet cats are quite small and relatively uniform in size as opposed to dogs which come in all sizes from the very small to the giant breeds. Cats don't vary much so we can set some standard quidelines for the amount we feed.

We shall discuss the parts of the digestive system and the duties each part performs.

The Digestion Tube

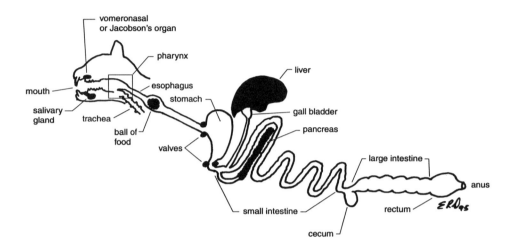

Mouth

The mouth includes lips, tongue, teeth and salivary glands. The lips and tongue enable the cat to pick up and handle food, and the teeth, by tearing and chewing, provide some mechanical breakdown.

The tongue has rough spines which help to clean meat off of bones as well as being an aid in grooming. Kittens have a row of spines along the outside edge of their tongues which helps them hang on to their mother's nipple when they nurse. The tongue can also taste, so that undesirable foods and objects will not be swallowed. Taste buds are located on the tongue in different areas for this purpose.

The young cat will have twenty-six deciduous or baby teeth which are replaced to end up with thirty permanent teeth in the adult. The six incisors we see across the front of the upper and lower jaw are flanked by the two large canines. Molars are those teeth further back inside the cheeks. The large canines are used to grab and hold prey. Molars act as scissors for cutting.

Because cats are carnivores and basically meat eaters, their teeth serve them well as not much grinding is required.

The salivary glands add saliva to the food which starts the digestion process, especially in kittens. Saliva is also a lubricator which makes the swallowed food slippery, so that it will easily slide down the esophagus on its way to the stomach. Saliva also acts as a solvent, cleaning out the taste buds so that tasting of other foods can continue later on.

On the roof of the cat's mouth is the vomeronasal or Jacobson's organ. It is about one cm. long and is a smell organ. This explains our cats' behavior when they open their mouths and their tongues seem to be flickering with a concentrating look in their eyes. They are using this organ to identify some smell.

Pharynx

The pharynx is the area of the throat between the mouth and the esophagus. Here, a flap, or valve, allows food to be swallowed when ready. The rest of the time, during breathing, air moves back and forth to the lungs.

Esophagus

The esophagus is a tube between the pharynx and stomach that is normally flattened except when a ball of food is being swallowed. Mucus is produced in this muscular tube, making it slippery. As the ball of food reaches the stomach, a muscular ring relaxes and the food enters the stomach. The ring then tightens preventing food from coming back up.

Stomach

The stomach is a bag or pouch that is actually an enlargement in the digestive tube where food is stored and digestion started.

The cat's stomach is quite small - something to consider when feeding. When empty, the stomach is the size of a quarter or fifty cent piece so that two tablespoons at a meal would fill it. Not very much.

Digestion begins with the actions of gastric juices, primarily enzymes, hydrochloric acid and mucus. These special organic chemicals go to work breaking down the food into usable forms. Enzymes, for the most part, are made by the pancreas and small intestine. The stomach also contains hydrochloric acid that helps in the digestion of food and may kill bad bacteria that could cause disease. Like the mouth and esophagus, mucus is also produced by the stomach wall. It lubricates and protects the lining of the stomach. We know that if an animal is under a lot of stress for a long time, too much acid may be produced and the walls may be eroded. These erosions or ulcers to the stomach wall can be troublesome.

Basically, the stomach is a storage and digestion organ where very little absorption takes place although some absorption of water and simple sugar or glucose may take place via tiny blood vessels in the walls of the stomach.

The mixture of food and gastric juices in the stomach is called chyme, and at various intervals this mixture is "squirted" into the beginning of the small intestine, where digestion will continue.

The cat's stomach will empty between meals, unlike the herbivore's stomach - such as the cow or sheep, where food may remain for several days before moving on. Within the herbivore's stomach, bacterial action starts on the plant material that the cow or sheep has eaten starting the digestive process. Because of the cat's animal flesh and fat diet, little if any bacterial action takes place here. These differences remind us that the cat is a carnivore and is built accordingly.

Small Intestine

The small intestine is a muscular tube that receives food from the stomach. It is here that the final phases of digestion and absorption of nutrients takes place. It has been said many times that the lining of the small intestine is one of the most remarkable organs of the body because of all the functions that it performs.

For the most part, digestion is completed in the beginning of the small intestine, and absorption in the last part. Chyme that was squirted from the stomach came from an acid environment and is now in an alkaline or basic environment that allows for a different type of digestion to take place. Here, in the small intestine, digestion will be completed with the aid of many different kinds of enzymes that originate primarily from the lining of the small intestine and pancreas. The pancreatic enzymes arrive through a tube or duct that empties near the front of the small intestine. Three main types of enzymes are at work in the small intestine breaking down protein, fat and carbohydrate.

Near the duct from the pancreas there is another duct that secretes bile from the liver, which also helps in the digestion of fat. This bile duct comes from the gall bladder and liver where bile is recycled and stored.

As the muscles of the small intestine push and pull the digesting food along, enzymes, bile and other secretions are doing their respective jobs in breaking down the food material. When nutrients become available in a usable form, they are absorbed through the walls of the small intestine. The inside wall of the small intestine is not a smooth surface but rather a surface of many hills and valleys called villi. These villi provide up to seven or eight times more surface area for the absorption of nutrients.

Wall of the Small Intestine

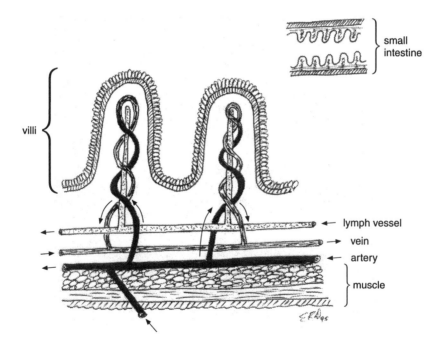

As the nutrients become acceptable for absorption, they are picked up by the blood and lymph. The majority of the nutrients are taken by the blood to various locations in the cat's body to be further processed or used directly.

Lymph is the fluid of the lymphatic system, another transportation system in the cat's body primarily involved with the fighting of disease. An example of something being absorbed by this system would be the absorption of antibody proteins in a kitten. These antibodies are present in the mother's milk, ready for use by the kitten to fight disease until she is able to make her own.

Foods that do not need to be broken down much are digested and absorbed quickly; more complex ones will take longer and some will not be digested at all and will be passed out as feces.

This is a very simple explanation of the complex process by which nutrients contained in foods make their way to the cells of the cat's body. As with any simplification, many facts and details are omitted, but it is important to realize that the small intestine is a very important and complex organ.

The small intestine of the cat is quite short compared to that of other animals. The length is about three and a half times the length of the cat's body. Because the cat is a carnivore, her intestine can be short as the food she has eaten for millions of years is relatively easy to digest. Other animals, such as cows, which are herbivores or vegetarians, have a very long intestine. The cow's diet consists of coarse plant materials that are very hard to digest. The longer intestine allows for more room and time to digest this material. Furthermore, the cow has four stomachs and must rely on small microorganisms such as bacteria to help in the breakdown and digestion of this plant material.

Large Intestine

Next, the food moves into the large intestine. Most of the digestion and absorption has already taken place. As its name suggests, the diameter of the tube is larger than that of the small intestine. Valves open and close between the two, and near this junction is a small pouch called a cecum. This pouch is the equivalent of the appendix in people. In herbivores the cecum is quite large and important as it permits the plant food to stay longer in the digestive system, thus allowing further microbial digestion. In the cat, however, the cecum is quite small and non-functional.

The main role of the large intestine in the cat is to absorb and conserve water. If a cat is short of drinking water for some time or has lost water due to exercise, illness or hot weather, her stools will be hard and dry. This is the result of her body conserving as much water as it can. There is also a great amount of mucus production in the large intestine to lubricate and protect the walls from this dried out fecal material.

Rectum and Anus

The rectum is the end of the digestion tube and is the storage facility for all undigested material. This undigested material, feces, is stored here until a time is suitable for removal through the last valve, the anus.

We have discussed, once again in very simple terms, the digestion tube, a tube that takes in swallowed food at one end and as the food is pushed along its length, is where digestion and absorption of nutrients take place. We note that there are major differences between the digestive systems of carnivores, or predominantly meat eaters, and herbivores, or plant eaters, which we must remember when feeding our cat.

In addition to this digestion and absorption tube, there are two very important organs: the pancreas and the liver. The pancreas and the liver, along with the stomach and the small intestine, are the central digesting and processing machinery involved in the conversion of food to a form that can be utilized by the cells of the cat. Before we leave the digestive system, we must discuss these two very important organs.

Pancreas

The pancreas is a gland situated near the beginning of the small intestine. It performs two main functions: the production of digestive enzymes and the formation of two hormones, insulin and glucagon, which are involved in regulation of blood sugar.

Enzymes are internal organic catalysts. These chemical substances are made in the pancreas and are able to stimulate a specific chemical reaction without themselves entering into the reaction or undergoing any change. Enzymes are present in tiny amounts and can either promote the breakdown of complex organic compounds or stimulate the formation of other compounds. Each enzyme has one very specific function that it performs.

Many enzymes have been discovered and identified to date, and there are probably still more to be discovered. The digestive enzymes are manufactured primarily in the pancreas and small intestine. An example of an enzyme produced in the small intestine is the enzyme lactase, which acts upon the milk sugar lactose. Lactase reduces or breaks down lactose in milk into simpler sugars that the kitten can utilize for energy. There is less lactose in the nursing kitten's milk than in cows milk, and since lactase may not be present in the adult cat, giving cows milk to a cat can cause diarrhea. The kitten may not have enough of this enzyme and the adult may not have any, so cows milk is passed only partially digested and is fermented by bacteria in the large intestine. Yogurt, on the other hand, can be digested and is a good protein source for the young and adult cat.

The other function of the pancreas is the production of insulin and glucagon. These two hormones regulate the amount of blood sugar, called glucose, circulating in the blood.

Insulin makes the glucose in the blood and tissues more readily available for use as energy by the cells. Without insulin, blood glucose levels rise because the cells are not willing to use the glucose. This disease from lack of insulin production by the pancreas is called diabetes mellitus (mellitus meaning honey, or sweet). When cats have this problem, they are excessively thirsty and frequently urinate as their bodies attempt to lower this high blood sugar level.

The other hormone made by the pancreas is glucagon. Glucagon functions in the breakdown of liver glycogen, or animal starch, to glucose for energy. This will be discussed further in the section on carbohydrates.

Liver

The liver is the largest gland in the cat's body and is essential to life. The large size is due to the cat's carnivorous diet. A large liver is required to metabolize the high concentration of protein and fat.

This important complex organ and gland is made up of a group of specialized cells whose main purpose is to release certain substances and to separate and eliminate other substances. Some of the functions that the cat's liver performs are

- the formation and storage of animal starch (glycogen)
- the secretion of bile (for fat digestion)
- the detoxification of poisons
- the breakdown of uric acid and the formation of urea (from protein digestion) and
- the breakdown of fatty acids (from fat digestion).

The liver is also involved in the storage of vitamins, the destruction of old red blood cells and the formation of blood proteins. As we can see from this long list, the liver is a complex and important organ. It is believed that the liver is also a site of hormone production for the regulation of the complex digestive processes.

The large liver of the cat is kept busy digesting the food she has eaten and processing the nutrients into a form that her cells can use.

In summary we have looked at the digestive system as a modified tube with two accessory organs, the pancreas and the liver. Whole food is taken in at one end; the "good stuff" is taken out and the rest passes through.

We must, however, appreciate how important and complex the digestive system is. We must also appreciate that the cat is a carnivore and her digestive system has suited her well on this type of diet for millions of years. That is, her teeth are primarily for tearing and ripping; she has the ability to vomit easily; her intestines are short and her liver is large and effective.

All of these characteristics have given the cat the ability to live and survive on her predominantly animal flesh diet. These are all considerations we must bear in mind when we feed and cook for our cat.

We shall now discuss the food groups and nutrients in greater detail with regard to body functions, food sources and deficiency problems, always keeping in mind our cat's specialized nature.

WATER

> *"Water is undoubtedly the single most important nutrient necessary for the proper function of all living cells."*
>
> *Nutrient Requirements of Cats,*
> The National Research Council

Water is the most important nutrient of all. Without water life cannot continue. Let's look again at the illustration.

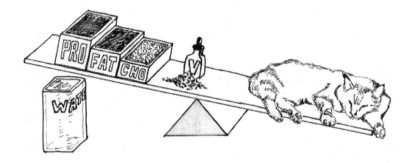

The body of the adult cat is approximately sixty per cent water. If the cat loses ten per cent, it is in big trouble and a twenty per cent loss results in death. The cat can get by for a long time without the other nutrients but not without water.

Our domestic cat has a remarkable ability to concentrate its urine and conserve water - something it has inherited from its desert ancestors. However, it still requires water. The cat normally should get water from the food she eats as well as from drinking to meet her own requirements. A cat may not drink much if she is on a canned cat food as this contains seventy per cent water or more; however, a dry cat food is only around ten to twenty per cent.

We may see our cat drink from the toilet bowl, aquarium or from a puddle out in the yard. This may be because she likes the taste and she simply finds the water in her own bowl not to her liking, perhaps because of the soap we used to wash the bowl or some other reason such as the chemicals that the drinking water may have been treated with.

Fresh water should always be available no matter what kind of a food - canned or dry, that she is on. We should make the effort to keep the bowl clean and rinsed of any soap residue. This is especially important if we are feeding our cat mostly dry cat food.

Greater than sixty per cent of the cat's total body weight is water, but the daily amount required will vary greatly. It will vary with the individual cat, her environment and her activity. If, for example, she is very active and the weather is hot, then much more water is consumed, because water is needed for the cells as they burn up energy and also for the removal of heat. If a mother is nursing kittens, she needs more water, as would a cat sick with fever, diarrhea or kidney disease.

Other things to consider are the temperature and the mineral content of this water. Too warm or too cold may discourage the cat from drinking as much as she needs. Water with a lot of minerals can lead to kidney and bladder stones. More on these conditions later when we discuss FUS or Feline Urological Syndrome.

How do we know if our cat is not getting enough water? She will have hard, dry, foul-smelling stools, and if more serious, she will show signs of dehydration. Her eyes will become sunk into their sockets, her nose becomes dry and she may look and ask for water. If we should pinch the skin on the side of the neck of a short-haired individual, it would stay in a fold for several seconds. These are all signs of serious dehydration, and we should have her looked at by a veterinarian as soon as possible.

Severe dehydration can occur with sickness such as fever, diarrhea or heat stroke. Young kittens are especially vulnerable to dehydration and may be so dehydrated that water given orally may not be enough, and intravenous fluids may be necessary if the kitten is to live.

Water fulfills many needs for the cat. Water is an excellent solvent and is the main component of blood. It provides transportation for blood, nutrients, antibodies and waste. Temperature regulation such as heat loss due to evaporation and removal of heat from internal organs out to the skin surface is another function that water provides. Lastly, water is essential for digestion and urine production. We cannot overemphasize the importance of water.

Water is obtained from the consumption of liquids, solid foods and chemical oxidation. When foods are digested and metabolized within the cat's body, some water is produced. For example the oxidation of 100 gm of protein will yield about 40 gm of water, 100 gm of carbohydrate 55 gm of water and 100 gm of fat about 100 gm of water. All of these sources provide her with the water that she requires to maintain her body stores.

Normally water is lost through the lungs (expired air), skin, milk, feces and urine. The cat's skin doesn't perspire like ours, so when she is hot she will pant to get rid of excess heat. Heat can be lost through the pads of her paws as some perspiration occurs here.

Always have clean fresh water available for the cat, especially when her environment is hot.

Cats by nature are active at night and sleep during the day. In their wild ancestral desert home, the nights were cool and the days were hot, so much daytime activity was avoided. Also their prey was inactive during the day but would come out at night, so they could be hunting when it was cooler. Cats drink both during the day and night whereas dogs tend to drink during the day, so water should be always available.

When a cat drinks water or milk it curls its tongue backwards and ladles the liquid into its mouth to be swallowed.

ENERGY

"Any substance can be designated as food if it can be used by the cat as a source of energy, a body builder or as a regulator of body activity."

Ernest H. Hart & Allan H. Hart, B.V.Sc.

As we have discussed previously the cat is a strictly adapted carnivore, an individual that is metabolically "lazy" and is unable to survive without eating animal products.

A cat eats to fulfill her energy requirements. The food she eats contains stored energy that originates from the sun. She obtains this energy indirectly when she eats animal products and directly if she should eat plant material. Plant material takes more effort to digest and metabolize, and the cat by being a strict carnivore eating animal products, is referred to as metabolically lazy. Animal products are easier to digest and metabolize.

The food the cat has eaten, containing this stored energy, is first digested and absorbed by her digestive system. Later it is metabolized or changed within the many cells of the cat. In the cells, energy is used or released. This metabolism, be it either a breakdown process or a building process, occurs within the tissues and results in energy used for heat or work.

Energy is required for many things:

- to maintain body temperature,
- for vital activities;
- heart beating and blood circulation,
  - breathing,
  - all internal body functions such as digestion,
- for the growth and repair of body tissues and
- for muscular activity, like running and play,

Energy is the "bottom line" and like water is an essential item for all living things.

Nutrients, such as proteins, fats and carbohydrates, all supply energy. The unit for measuring energy is the calorie. Some foods contain more calories than others and some none at all. For example a unit of fat has 2.2 times the number of calories as the same unit of protein or carbohydrate. Only proteins, fats and carbohydrates contain energy or calories. Water, vitamins and minerals do not.

The amount of energy or calories required per day by an individual cat will vary. Each individual cat has different energy requirements and the number of calories needed everyday will vary:

- Age; young require more than old
- Breed; large cats require more than small cats
- Pregnancy and lactation increases energy requirements
- Intact; more than spay or neutered - due to less activity
- Activity; running more than sleeping
- Environment; Cold more than warm surroundings
- Emotion; excitement, worry more than calm and relaxed.

For example a young, active and pregnant female outside during the winter, would require many more calories than an old neutered male living in a warm apartment. This is an extreme example but illustrates the point that caloric requirements vary with the individual cat in the particular circumstance.

The cat eats only until her energy requirements are met; then she will stop. For an average adult cat this is about 250 to 280 kcal a day. If these calories of energy come from a balanced diet containing the other essential nutrients of protein, fat, vitamins and minerals, she will be fine. If not she is headed for trouble.

We have heard the term "empty calories"; these are foods such as sweets, for example, that supply calories of energy but nothing else, no protein, no vitamins and no minerals. These types of foods only supply energy.

Because a cat eats to fill its energy requirement first, the common worry is that she may not be getting enough of the other required nutrients, such as protein from the diet before she has eaten her daily requirement for calories and stops. If this should continue for any length of time, she will become deficient.

In formulating diets, the first consideration is balancing the available energy content of the food with the daily energy needs of the particular cat.

Energy, like water, is very important and if the intake is inadequate, the cat will soon start losing weight as her body stores are being used. However, if the energy intake is more than the cat requires for her daily needs, her body will store the excess as body fat and save it for another time when she may be short.

There is the balance: not enough results in weight loss, and too much results in gain. If either of these situations continue for long, the outcome is starvation or obesity.

PROTEINS

> *"Protein metabolism is unique in the cat and is manifested by the unusually high maintenance requirement for protein as compared to the dog."*
>
> Lon D. Lewis, DVM, PhD, Mark L. Morris, Jr., DVM, PhD and Michael S. Hand, DVM, PhD
> *Feeding Dogs and Cats*

Proteins are the building blocks for the cat's body as well as providing energy. These building blocks are used for literally all the cells of the cat's body. The cat's liver also has an enzyme system that requires a constant supply of protein to be used in energy production or glucose.

Proteins are also the most complex molecules found in nature. Things like hair, claws, muscle and hormones are classified as proteins. Proteins are made up of simpler compounds called amino acids. Of these amino acids, twenty-three have been known to modern science for some time. Thirteen can be manufactured in the cat's body from digested protein, while the other eleven, called essential amino acids, must be present on a regular basis in the food that the cat eats. This list is changing as modern science learns more.

The essential amino acids for the cat are

arginine	lysine	tryptophan
histidine	methionine	valine
isoleucine	phenylalanine	taurine
leucine	threonine	

A diet must have several different proteins in it to be sure that the cat gets all the amino acids she needs. Foods such as meat, fish, eggs and dairy products contain large amounts of the essential amino acids. Vegetable source proteins may be short of some essential amino acids, so it becomes important to feed animal source proteins or a combination in order to ensure that all the essential amino acids are present.

Proteins are quickly digested or broken down into the simpler amino acids. These are then absorbed and go either to be broken down further in the liver to glucose for energy or to the cells of the body to be used for growth or repair. Newly-made proteins in the body are classified into structural or functional proteins. Muscle would be structural and insulin functional. Unlike carbohydrates and fats, proteins are not stored in the cat's body for very long. In an adult cat that is "stable", not gaining or losing weight, the amount of protein eaten will be equal to the amount removed or excreted as waste. This is called Nitrogen Balance. An exception to this would be a growing kitten that would be using more protein to grow muscles and other cells. Other examples would be a nursing queen or a cat getting over an injury. Any excess protein not used for growth or repair and energy will end up as body fat or removed as waste.

Because of this nitrogen balance and the fact that proteins not used cannot be stored, it is important that the cat eat enough quality protein for her unique needs on a regular basis.

There are many different things that proteins do in the cat's body. They are involved in the formation of cells, muscle, tendons, hair, skin, internal organs, hormones, enzymes and antibodies. Proteins form the bulk of the organic compounds in all cells. They are used in the formation of new cells and the repair and restoration of cells that already exist. Protein not used for new cells or repair of other cells is broken down in the liver, kidney and muscle into energy or waste. The energy can be used or stored as fat, and the waste, ammonia, is excreted in the urine. (Cats require dietary arginine in order to detoxify ammonia.)

Some protein is used for energy as is fat and carbohydrate, but fat and carbohydrate cannot be used as protein. Protein must be eaten as protein. And this protein must be animal source protein.

Some of the cat's own body protein - such as muscle tissue - can be used as a source of energy during starvation for a short period of time but will result in permanent damage or death if prolonged. In other words the cat's body is consuming itself and not its reserves as with body fat. To repeat again, protein must be regularly present in the diet.

Signs of deficiency include poor growth or weight loss and a depressed appetite. Milk production drops, the hair coat is rough and dull in appearance and antibody production is decreased. These can all result either from not enough high-quality protein or from a lack of a specific amino acid.

For example, taurine is an amino sulfonic acid that helps prevent blindness, reproductive problems and heart failure. Taurine is found in mice, clams, tuna, cod, chicken, meat and eggs. A whole mouse contains 2440 mg/kg of taurine (*Taurine in Feline Nutrition* by Mark Sunlin, Natural Pet July/Aug. 1994) There is very little to none in plant material, so taurine is added to many commercial cat foods that contain vegetable or plant ingredients. Cats, for centuries, obtained this vital amino acid from mice and various prey.

A cat's daily diet must contain enough of the right kind of protein if she is to survive and be healthy. The amount of protein a cat will need every day will depend on how well the protein can supply her needs for amino acids and energy. The ability of the protein to do this is called Biological Value. Foods of high biological value are those with many of the essential amino acids present in them. Eggs and fish meal have a high biological value, for example, and foods like rice and wheat gluten have a low biological value.

When buying commercial cat food, look to the label and the first four ingredients listed should contain at least two sources of High Biological Value protein such as meat, fish, poultry or cheese.

Animal source proteins are the best, telling us again that the cat is a strict carnivore. Some of the plant material, for example, the gluten meals, can cause problems. Gluten meal is the residue from processed wheat, corn and other grains. These can cause intestinal problems, such as gluten enteropathy or difficulty for foods being absorbed by the cat's intestine.

This basic knowledge about the cat's unique nature becomes important in balancing the cat's requirements for protein. Check the label for adequate protein.

Minimum protein percentages should be:

- Dry Food   30 to 35 %
- Canned   10 to 12 %
- Semimoist   22 to 26 %

If we are feeding our cat home made meals, we must have enough animal protein and fat present. We do not have to worry about overdoing it as the cat is well equipped to utilize these nutrients, as it has for millions of years, to the extent that it can eat a diet of only animal protein and fat without any or very little carbohydrate. A common mistake is that we may not give enough.

Protein is an important nutrient that must be eaten regularly and cannot be replaced by anything else. And the high quality proteins are the animal source proteins.

Based on what we have discussed so far with regard to the cat's ancestral history and body makeup having been adapted to a strict carnivore diet over millions of years, it is my opinion that to feed a cat a strictly vegetarian diet is impossible and cruel. It is impossible in that the cat cannot get all of its required nutrients from vegetables alone but must have enough animal source ingredients. This in my opinion is also the highest form of cruelty. It is un-natural.

FATS

Fats provide energy. This nutrient fills other needs but the primary one is as a concentrated form of energy. Within the body, fat can be stored to be used as energy later if the need should arise. Cats have a remarkable natural ability to digest and utilize high levels of fat in their diet. Like protein, animal source fats are best again because they are natural.

Dietary fat that ends up as body fat provides padding for organs such as the heart, kidneys and eyes, as well as giving contour, or shape, to the cat's body. Fat is also very good insulation against cold temperatures. It also influences diet acceptance or palatability in that it contains volatile fatty acids or flavours. Fats can also go rancid when they combine with oxygen from the air - this is called oxidation and will turn off a cat. More on this later when we discuss commercial cat foods.

The principal function, however, other than for energy, is the part that fats play in the production of substances vital to the internal workings of the cat. Fat comprises a major part of the walls of all body cells, especially brain and nerve cells. Fat is also necessary in the digestion and processing of other nutrients, particularly proteins.

Fat in a cat's diet serves many functions:

- Provides a source of concentrated energy
- Supplies essential fatty acids
- Acts as a carrier for fat soluble vitamins
- Adds palatability or taste

The fat soluble vitamins A, D, E and K are stored and carried by fat, both dietary fat and body fat.

All fats are made up of triglycerides. Triglycerides are three fatty acids and a unit of glycerol. Different fatty acids give a fat its particular characteristics. There are dozens of fatty acids known to us today and we classify them into two basic groups:

- Saturated, or hard fats from animal sources, such as lard and butter,
- Polyunsaturated, liquid, or soft fats from vegetable sources.

Cats can utilize fats from either animal or plant sources. The digestibility of fats will vary with the source and the processing. Cats seem to do better on animal fats rather than plant fats maybe because of their strict carnivorous nature.

The fatty acids linoleic, linolenic and arachidonic are considered to be essential, in that they cannot be manufactured in the cat's body. They must be eaten. Linoleic and linolenic can come from plant sources but arachidonic acid must come from animal fat. These three fatty acids make up the base for the production of other fatty acids that are important to her everyday life.

Among the vital substances made in the body from the essential fatty acids are a group of organic substances called Prostaglandins. Lately, in human medicine, it is thought that Prostaglandins and faulty fatty acid metabolism may have something to do with many of man's chronic health problems such as heart disease, cancer, allergies and obesity. We may learn that this is also true in cats.

Fat eaten by the cat is broken down by enzymes into fatty acids and glycerol. After absorption, the fatty acids are either used to manufacture vital substances or to build or repair cell walls. The glycerol is used for energy.

Good high quality fat sources are the soft animal fats such as chicken fat or bacon grease and butter.

The average cat's diet should contain between twenty to forty per cent fat. As much as sixty-five per cent of the cat's caloric needs can be given in the form of fat. Remember that fat has 2.2 times the amount of energy or calories as compared to protein or carbohydrates.

With cats that tend to put on weight or become obese, lowering the fat intake must be considered.

Minimum amounts to look for on commercial cat food labels are

- Dry food should be at least 15 %
- Canned food should be at least 3 %
- Semimoist should be at least 8.5 %

A cat deficient in the essential fatty acids will have coarse brittle hair, dry rough skin, impaired growth and loss of muscle tone. Hair loss with crusting skin may also occur especially on the abdomen, inside the thighs and between the shoulder blades. The cat is also more prone to illness and disease.

Fat in the food is the cat's source of energy as well as providing the other requirements. Animal fats contain all the essential and non-essential fatty acids and are highly digestible and easily metabolized by the cat. Vegetable oils can be used to some extent but not exclusively because of the cat's special need for arachidonic acid which she cannot make from linoleic acid like the dog. Arachidonic acid is present in animal fats.

For long term glossy coat and soft pliable skin, the diet needs the animal fats. Again, as with all good things, too much is not good.

All excess fat consumed will be stored in the form of body fat. These stores are available for the cat to use later when starvation or food for energy is not available. We have said before that proteins and carbohydrates can also be converted to body fat stores as well. Something we must note is that the cat's body will go on storing or saving this energy as fat continually. The cat will get "fatter and fatter" as she saves more and more. There seems to be no limit to how obese a cat can get.

In other words, too many calories end up in fat. For every 3000 - 3500 excess calories consumed, the cat would put on about one pound of body fat. To remove body fat and have our cat lose weight, the intake of calories must be lowered to below the daily requirements so that body stores will be used instead. If the cat requires more calories due to a lot of exercise, for example, these reserves will be used up faster.

Simply put, "calories in should equal calories out". The cat should be fed enough calories to supply her daily needs. Any more than that requirement will end up as body fat. Any less and the cat will use body fat and lose weight. Too rapid a loss of body fat can sometimes result in problems, so a weight loss program should be done gradually. When lowering the caloric intake, we must be careful not to eliminate or reduce the other nutrients, especially the fat soluble vitamins A, D, E and K.

Fat is an important nutrient performing many important functions as well as being a powerful energy fuel.

Fat has received a lot of publicity lately, being blamed for many problems in people, but as with so many things, we must look at the whole picture. To isolate one nutrient out of many without regard for the interaction of all in a living body in a particular environment, is often a mistake.

CARBOHYDRATES

"There is no known carbohydrate requirement for the cat, although commercial diets containing 40 per cent or more are well utilized."

The National Research Council
Nutrient Requirements of Cats

Carbohydrates are the main source of energy, or calories for many mammals, including people. Carbohydrates are of plant origin and include vegetables, fruits, pulses and grains. We know that the cat has lived for millions of years as a carnivore eating very little carbohydrate, except when she ate the stomach contents of her prey. The cat can get all of her energy from protein and fats, with very little coming from carbohydrates.

The ancestral and wild cats ate "second-hand" carbohydrates when they ate the stomach and intestinal contents of their prey. Our modern cats today get to eat more carbohydrate type foods because they are included in the commercial cat foods.

Why are carbohydrates or cereals and vegetables in commercial cat foods? One reason is that these ingredients are cheaper than animal proteins and fats, not only cheaper to purchase but also cheaper to process and preserve. Such ingredients do provide some nutrition for the cat as well as providing fibre or bulk.

We have learned that many carbohydrates can be used by the cat. We have also learned that it is important to break down these foods before we give them to the cat. For example, grains and vegetables should be cooked or baked first to aid digestion. Large amounts of raw carbohydrates may lead to diarrhea and flatulence as they are not digested and are subject to fermentation by bacteria in the large intestine.

Simple carbohydrates are called sugars and the more complex are starches. They are also called monosaccharides and polysaccharides. Saccharides are sugar molecules, mono meaning single, and poly meaning many. A list, with examples, may help explain.

Monosaccharide	single sugar	glucose, fructose (fruit sugar)
Disaccharide	two sugars	sucrose (table sugar,) or glucose and fructose,
Polysaccharide	many sugars	starches (potatoes)

Polysaccharides, or starches, are several chains of single sugars interlinked one with another. The digestive system with its enzymes must break these down into single sugars before they can be absorbed and utilized by the cells. Microorganisms, like bacteria, help in this breakdown of starches in herbivores such as the cow and horse. Cats, not having a digestive system suited for these microorganisms, cannot digest many of these starches and so they pass on through. This material, we refer to as fibre or roughage.

Fibre can be polysaccharides such as cellulose which makes up the main structure of plant cell walls and is almost impossible for the cat to digest. This fibre can bind water and adds bulk to the stools.

The wild cat obtained her roughage or fibre from the prey that she ate, by consuming the whole animal or bird, including the hair and feathers. This acted as the "fibre" part of her diet which could "bulk-up" the feces and also protected the intestinal walls from sharp things such as fragments of bone. The hair, feathers and other similar material formed a coating to the stool, protecting the intestinal walls from these sharp pieces.

Let's get back to digestion of carbohydrates. Sugars and starches that are consumed must first be broken down to single sugars, such as glucose, before the intestine can absorb this material. Once it is absorbed through the walls of the intestine, blood picks up the glucose and transports it to where it can be

- Used by the cells directly for energy,
- Converted in the liver to glycogen (animal starch)
    then stored as liver glycogen. or
    stored in the muscles as muscle glycogen,
- Converted in the liver into fat and stored on the body as body fat, or
- Excreted through the kidneys.

Glucose is usually the only simple sugar circulating in the blood. The liver is very important at this point in that it can take glucose and store it for a while or convert it to glycogen or fat. The liver can also convert these back to blood glucose if the need for energy should arise later.

Muscle glycogen, the stored form of glucose in the muscle, is used only by the muscles and cannot go back to the liver to be recycled. As the glycogen is used in the muscles, one of the by-products formed is a substance called lactic acid. If there is a lot of this material formed, for example after a big work out, the cat will be stiff and sore. Only after the lactic acid is either sent back to the liver, or converted back to glycogen by more blood glucose, will the stiffness subside.

The liver is the main storage organ for blood glucose. If a cat is starving the glucose would last for about twenty-four to forty-eight hours, and then body fat would have to be converted back to blood glucose and energy.

These body reactions that we have just discussed are all referred to as metabolism. Glucose, or blood sugar, is the main form utilized for energy in the cat's body and glycogen, or animal starch, the main storage form.

The amount of blood glucose circulating in the cat's body is regulated by hormones. If there is too much, the pancreas will release insulin which will make the cells accept more glucose. If there is still too much, it may be removed by the kidneys and excreted in the urine. If the blood glucose is too low, a condition called hypoglycemia, the adrenal gland will release adrenalin (as well as glucagon from the pancreas) to activate the liver to release more glucose or to make more from its stores of liver glycogen.

This "shot" of adrenalin and the resulting quick burst of energy is very important for the "Fight or Flight" mechanism and the cat's ultimate survival if she should be confronted with danger or when trying to catch tonight's dinner.

All cells require energy, as we have said, and brain cells are no exception. If anything, the brain is especially vulnerable to low blood glucose levels. Glucose can readily pass from the blood to the brain. We know, for example, that if we feel tired and listless, we can get a quick "lift" by eating a chocolate bar. The sugars in the bar are quickly absorbed into the blood and transported to the cells of the brain for energy. This is also true with the cat, so if we have an active cat and she appears listless between meals, maybe a small treat is in order.

In feeding our cat vegetables, cereals or other carbohydrate type ingredients, we have to remember who we are feeding. These have to be processed in some way so that our cat can get some benefit from them. Mashing, cooking or aging in some fashion prepares these foods for the cat's unique digestive system.

VITAMINS

Vitamins are vital organic food substances necessary in small amounts for normal metabolism and growth of the cat. Vitamins help regulate the chemical reactions that protect cells and aid in the conversion of food into energy and living tissue. Everyday we hear more about these vital substances and how they are involved in many areas of nutrition. Vitamins are similar to enzymes, in that they are present in very small amounts as they perform their metabolic functions, but differ in that they are not produced in the body. They must be in the diet.

Scientists have so far identified thirteen of these organic substances that we call vitamins. In 1911, a scientist named Hopkins realized that there was something else present in foods besides proteins, fats and carbohydrates that were required for health. He referred to these nutrients as "accessory food factors". The next year, Funk discovered a nitrogen factor in yeast and rice polishings that cured beriberi (a muscular paralysis, seen in people eating a diet high in polished rice.) This he called vitamine (life amine) later to be called Vitamin B1 or Thiamine. Accessory food factors, or vitamins, were soon realized to be essential nutrients.

The vitamins were given letters of the alphabet and classified into those soluble in fat: A, D, E, and K, and those soluble in water: B and C. Later it was discovered that there was more than one substance involved with some of these so they were given numbers, for example, B_1, B_6, B_{12}. I am sure there are more to be discovered and identified in the future.

After their discovery, vitamins were used to prevent deficiency problems such as scurvy, beriberi and rickets. Today's scientists are looking at the use of vitamins in maintaining optimal health and maybe preventing some diseases.

Some of the latest vitamin research in human health has to do with the antioxidant properties of Vitamins: E, C and beta carotene (vitamin A base). Antioxidants are able to deactivate harmful substances such as free radicals. Free radicals are chemically reactive substances that have combined with oxygen when the body is exposed to things as x-rays, sunlight, tobacco smoke, car exhaust and other environmental pollutants. Free radicals can damage DNA, alter chemical compounds, corrode cell membranes and kill cells outright. Scientists think this kind of damage leads to cancer, heart and lung disease and cataracts. By consuming natural antioxidants that will attach themselves to the free radicals, making them harmless, perhaps we can prevent some diseases. Another benefit may be in delaying the many problems associated with aging. A lot of the human vitamin research can apply to the cat and we will be hearing more.

Questions that arise when feeding our cat include does she need vitamins? and is she getting these vitamins? Yes, cats require vitamins just as we do. Many years ago she obtained her vitamins from the various animals that she hunted and ate. However, as we stated earlier, her diet and environment have changed radically. Now that she is limited to processed foods, other questions must be asked. For example, what does the heat of processing do to the vitamin content of the original food ingredients? What does the addition of preservatives do to the vitamins? Should we be feeding a variety of fresh foods so that she gets the vitamins that she requires, both known and unknown to modern science.

Could there be other important factors involved in the way nutrients act within the cat's body that are still unknown? We also have a cat in an environment that has chemical products, from car exhaust to carpet shampoos, that are totally new to her. In other words our modern cat has a limited diet and different surroundings to contend with. On top of all of this she has no choice!

What are the cat's vitamin requirements? There are tables and recommendations made from studies of cats fed different diets. As with people, feeding recommendations are made for the average individual, in average conditions. The recommendations are for the prevention of vitamin deficiencies, but as we had stated earlier, scientists are now looking beyond this and using vitamins for treatment.

It has been stated that, in general, the vitamin requirements are related to the intake of energy. If energy intake is increased, then vitamin intake should increase. A growing kitten or a nursing queen, for example, would require more energy and also more vitamins. Older cats do not need as much energy but they still require their vitamins even more.

The amounts of vitamins consumed and actually utilized by the cat may vary greatly depending upon many factors. For example, several vitamins are unstable, and their destruction may be promoted by light, heat, oxidation, moisture, rancidity or certain minerals. It is important to note, however, that feeding excessive amounts of some vitamins will cause overdoses. Vitamins are an interesting and ever-changing topic with recommendations on requirements changing everyday.

To feed our cat today we should have a basic understanding of vitamins: what they do, what foods contain them and how we can suspect a shortage. With this knowledge we may be better equipped to evaluate our cat's diet and her health.

We are going to list the individual vitamins with information on what that vitamin does in the body, what signs we may see if the vitamin is deficient or overdosed and some food sources.

Vitamin A

Vitamin A has long been known to be an important vitamin in human and animal nutrition. Generally speaking, vitamin A is important for epithelial cells. These cells are responsible for the internal and external surfaces of the body, including skin, eyes, lungs and uterus.

Vitamin A promotes growth as well as healthy skin and hair and fertility. It also is essential for the eyes, ears, immunity and digestion, basically anything that involves epithelial tissue.

Deficiencies of vitamin A will show up as a loss of appetite, weight loss, dry skin, hairless patches, eye problems and tearing, sensitivity to light, low fertility and generally poor growth and development. Night blindness is a common condition from a lack of sufficient vitamin A. The old saying "eat carrots if you want to see in the dark," has some basis in scientific fact, as the yellow pigment or carotene in carrots is necessary for us to manufacture vitamin A. Cats cannot do this.

For many years livestock people have been aware of the importance of vitamin A for their farm livestock. Most farm animals make their vitamin A from green grass, but during the winter when green grass is not available, they must be supplemented.

Vitamin A, or retinol is only found in animal products and is made from carotenes or the yellow pigments in plants. Beta cartotene is the most important carotene and is water soluble. Cats cannot convert beta carotene, the plant source ingredient, into vitamin A as we can so must get their vitamin A directly by eating it from an animal source.

Because vitamin A is fat soluble and can be stored in fat, excess can be toxic unlike the water soluble vitamins that are not stored.

The best food sources of vitamin A for the cat are all kinds of liver, kidneys, egg yolks, butter and fish liver oils. The beta carotene in dark green leafy vegetables, yellow and orange vegetables and fruits, as we have said, cannot be used by the cat for the production of vitamin A, so feeding these foods do not benefit the cat from the vitamin A stand point.

Cats have relatively high requirements for vitamin A. The average healthy cat should get at least one to three thousand IU (International Units) of vitamin A a day.

As we continue to go through the food sources for the vitamins, liver will be listed as a food source for all the vitamins. Some nutritionists call liver the "perfect food" for this reason. One of the first things eaten by the wild carnivore is the liver of its prey. So they know this as well. We will list many recipes with liver as an ingredient but must always beware not to feed too much, as excesses of the fat soluble vitamins can cause serious problems. Too much vitamin A, for example, can lead to impaired vision, skin rashes, hair loss and liver damage, as well as joint problems involving the neck, back and legs. Kittens may have shortened leg bones as the excess vitamin A impairs their growth.

Cats can very easily develop a taste for liver and some fish, so we must be careful not to let them eat these foods to the exclusion of a variety of foods.

If we feed liver everyday to our cat, it should not be more than one quarter of the total daily diet. A complete meal of liver should be limited to only once or twice a week. We want our cat to get the benefits of this "miracle food", but too much of a good thing is harmful.

Foods containing sodium nitrite can deplete vitamin A, and feeding mineral oil can deplete all the fat soluble vitamins A, D, E and K, as well as the minerals calcium and phosphorus.

To summarize, vitamin A is an important essential vitamin that the cat must get from animal sources. Beta carotene, one of the main ingredients for the production of vitamin A for us and other animals, cannot be used by the cat. Too much vitamin A is trouble, and not enough will show signs of poor growth, dry skin, eye problems and lung and reproductive problems.

Vitamins work in harmony with each other; for example, the full benefits of vitamin A are achieved when the diet includes the B complex vitamins, vitamins D and E, calcium and zinc.

Vitamins, in general, are required in such small amounts that the signs of a deficiency may take some time before we suspect a problem. Unlike the situation with the other nutrients, a cat may carry on for a long time on limited amounts of some vitamins before we are able to suspect a problem.

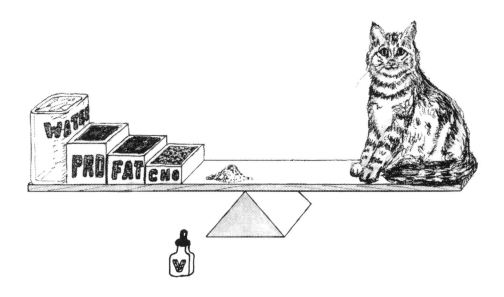

The balance drops only slightly when we remove the vitamins.

Vitamin D

Vitamin D, another fat soluble vitamin, is a vital factor in calcium, phosphorus, and magnesium metabolism of the cat. These four are essential for the formation of bones and teeth. The cat will get its vitamin D from its diet and can make vitamin D in its kidneys as well as from sun exposure or the ultraviolet rays acting with skin oils. The relationship between Vitamin D, calcium and phosphorus is quite delicate with regard to the amounts of each. Too much of one or the other or a shortage of any one can throw this relationship off and problems will arise.

Conditions like rickets, soft bones, enlargement of joints and late appearing and malformed teeth can take place in growing kittens. Older cats will show signs of bone pain and broken bones. New mothers may have eclampsia, a form of paralysis, shortly after queening, all related to vitamin D, specifically D_3.

Oversupply, called hypervitaminosis D, because the cat cannot get rid of excesses, may produce uneven distribution of calcium in bones as well as calcium deposits in abnormal places such as some joints, muscle, lungs, kidneys, heart and blood vessels. Too much vitamin D may appear as fatigue, vomiting, diarrhea and death. Vitamin D is a fat soluble vitamin that can accumulate so we must not overdo it.

Vitamin D is present in liver, butter, fatty fish, fish oils, egg yolks and fortified milk. Commercial labels may list additives such as calciferol, ergocalciferol or cholecalciferol which are the "big words" for vitamin D. The average healthy cat requires from fifty to one hundred IU's per day of vitamin D.

Vitamin D, calcium and phosphorus are crucial in growing kittens. Kittens grow so fast that these three nutrients become very important. If you are raising kittens, the correct balance for these three nutrients is important so seek professional assistance in formulating their diets.

Vitamin E

Vitamin E is actually a group of compounds called tocopherols. Tocopherols are all fat soluble and their absorption from the intestine depends upon digestion and absorption of fat. Vitamin E also functions with the mineral selenium. Both of these are involved in muscle growth and repair and as antioxidants.

As we discussed previously, living tissues are sensitive to the damaging effects of oxygen and other oxidizing substances called free radicals. Oxidation has occurred when food spoils - goes rancid - or when metal rusts. Nature, in its wisdom, has provided substances to protect cells against the effects of oxidation. They are the antioxidants. Vitamins E, A and C are some examples of nature's antioxidants.

Vitamin E has to be eaten on a regular basis because unlike the other fat soluble vitamins, it is not stored for long. The recommended minimum daily allowance is five to fifteen IU for an average cat. This vitamin is destroyed by food processing, high temperatures, iron and mineral oil. Food labels having vitamin E added may appear as alpha tocopheryl acetate.

As an antioxidant, vitamin E protects the cat against chemical pollutants and toxins in its environment as well as slowing down the aging process and strengthening the immune system. It also aids in correcting skin problems and boosting fertility and works with other nutrients to maintain a healthy cat.

Some forty years ago it was observed that vitamin E was involved in the prevention of pansteatitis, yellow fat disease or steatitis. Steatitis - inflammation of body fat - was found to occur in kittens and cats fed diets of raw fish and especially red tuna in the absence of vitamin E. These cats would be sore and cry in pain when petted as a result of this condition. Generally, a vitamin E deficiency in our cat will appear as a combination of a loss of appetite, listlessness, general soreness and fever due to the inflammation of body fat.

We should avoid feeding our cat a complete fish diet, especially tuna in any great amounts for this reason. Cats that are tuna fish " junkies " will have skin problems, generalized body soreness and nervous and/or aggressive personalities.

Vitamin E is found in liver, wheat germ, most vegetable oils, nuts, seeds and broccoli, as well as egg yolks.

Prevention of vitamin E deficiency can be achieved by avoiding raw fish, red tuna and commercial cat foods containing red tuna. If feeding fish to your cat, be sure that enough vitamin E is supplemented to counteract for the steatitis condition.

City cats or cats living in environments with industrial pollutants should be fed adequate amounts of vitamin E and selenium as well as the other antioxidants vitamin A and C for protection from these materials. These pollutants can form those free radicals which are now considered a cause of many disease conditions in us as well as in our animals.

Many fats and oils when combined with oxygen and exposed to heat and light are oxidized and become rancid. This can also happen inside the cat's body. Vitamin E, an antioxidant, can retard this process, by acting as a preservative. It is nature's way of preserving fats and oils from going rancid. This is why we see vitamin E on labels of "natural cat food" as opposed to ethoxyquin or BHT chemical antioxidants that are added to most commercial cat foods. More on this in the section on commercial foods and additives.

To summarize, Vitamin E plays a big role as an antioxidant and free radical fighter. Deficiencies result in muscular dystrophy-like conditions in kittens and reproductive problems in the adults. Too much vitamin E may cause stomach upsets. As with all supplementing, get professional advice when giving a lot.

Vitamin K

Vitamin K (Menadione) is important for the production of blood clotting factors. Factors, especially one called prothrombin, clot blood if the cat is cut or injured. This is another fat soluble vitamin that a cat can normally manufacture within its intestine from the foods that are eaten.

A deficiency of vitamin K is quite rare and can produce bleeding disorders. Sometimes newborn or premature kittens will be supplemented with vitamin K.

Vitamin K is given to a cat that has been poisoned with warfarin, an anti-coagulant and common rodent poison. Warfarin, prevents the rodent's blood from clotting, eventually killing them. It is critical to keep warfarin or poisoned mice and rats away from cats.

As said before, Vitamin K shortages are rare. Overdosing with mineral oil or extended treatments with sulfa-containing medications may induce deficiency. Bloody diarrhea may be the first sign and requires an immediate trip to the vet's office.

This concludes our discussion of the four fat soluble vitamins, A,D,E, and K. Because these four are fat soluble, we must be careful that the cat does not get too much. This can happen if a cat develops a taste for a particular food and we only give her this one food. Exclusive diets of liver or fish are good examples. If we only fed liver or fish, it would not take long before the cat would be in trouble from too much of a good thing. The old saying; "if a little is good a lot should be better", is not true.

As with all the vitamins, we must be sure that the cat has enough, however, to supply her needs. Vitamins, unlike water and energy, will take some time before we might suspect a deficiency.

B Vitamins

The B vitamins are a group of essential nutrients with many common characteristics. They are all water soluble and usually found in the same foods, including brewer's yeast, liver, meat, whole grain cereals and vegetable proteins. Being water soluble, they are required everyday. Chemically the B vitamins are distinct, but their functions are quite similar. Rarely would we see a deficiency of just one but rather a combination of several. Cats have a high requirement for the B complex of vitamins on a daily basis. B vitamins are generally involved with muscle, skin and blood.

Vitamin B_1 [Thiamin]

Thiamin was one of the first vitamins discovered, in connection with beriberi and people eating polished rice. Vitamin B_1 is found in the cat's skeletal muscle, heart muscle, brain, kidneys and liver. Any deficiency will result in deterioration of these tissues. Thiamin plays an important role in energy production and carbohydrate metabolism, as do all the B vitamins.

There are a number of naturally occurring anti-vitamins of thiamin called thiaminases that can modify thiamin and lead to signs of deficiencies. Foods like raw fish, shellfish, ferns, bacteria, yeast, and fungi have thiaminases. Heat will destroy these anti-vitamins so it is recommended that we cook fish before feeding it to our cat.

Signs of thiamin deficiency in the cat include general weakness, vomiting, unsteadiness, especially of the hind legs, acute heart failure and death. Foods containing thiamine include brewer's yeast and bran. Because thiamin is a water soluble vitamin, we do not have to worry as much with overdosing as we do with fat soluble vitamins previously discussed. Thiamine toxicity have been seen in dogs. So, as with all vitamins, a little is fine; too much may be trouble 0.2 to 1.5 mg per day is the recommended minimum.

Vitamin B_2 [Riboflavin]

Riboflavin was first discovered in the 1930's and plays an important role in manufacturing enzymes in the liver. Enzymes are important in the metabolism of carbohydrate, protein, and fat.

Vitamin B_2 is closely related to Vitamin B_6 and both are found in liver, kidney, cooked fish and brewer's yeast. This vitamin will deteriorate in these foods when the foods are exposed to light; however, heat or oxidation will not affect it.

Deficiency may result in loss of weight, muscular weakness in the hind legs, dermatitis, hair loss, red, tearing eyes and cataracts. Riboflavin is important for growing kittens, pregnant and nursing queens and tomcats as well as older cats.

The recommended daily minimum for an adult cat is 0.2 to 1.5 mg. More may be necessary for cats in stressful situations or on a high fat diet.

Vitamin B_3 [Niacin]

Niacin deficiency has long been known to cause pellagra in man and in other animals including the cat. Besides an inflamed tongue, the cat will show weight loss, loss of appetite, foul breath and blood-stained drooling from the mouth. Bloody diarrhea may be another sign that this vitamin is lacking.

Vitamin B_3, as with the other B vitamins, is important in the formation of certain enzymes involved with carbohydrate metabolism such as insulin, as well as for the production of important hormones. Dogs and people can make niacin from the amino acid tryptophan; however, the cat cannot. The cat must ingest its niacin preformed. Additives seen on labels might include nicotinic acid, niacinamide or niacin.

Recommended daily intake is 2.7 to 7.5 mg of niacin. Over supplementing has been known to cause itching.

Foods sources include liver, brewer's yeast, kidney, wheat germ and egg yolks. Cats particularly susceptible are those with a poor protein intake or those on antibiotics or medications containing sulfa.

Vitamin B_5 [Pantothenic Acid]

This B vitamin is important in the production of antibodies, those specialized white blood cells that fight disease. Vitamin B_5 has the same general duties in the metabolism of energy and hormone production as the other B vitamins.

Foods containing pantothenic acid are liver, kidney, egg yolk, wheat germ, bran and green vegetables. 0.5 to 1.5 mg per day is the minimum recommended daily intake.

Stressful situations such as pregnancy, surgery or recovery from illness are all aided by the ingestion of the B complex vitamins.

> *"Vitamins B_5, B_6, and B_9, otherwise known as pantothenic acid, pyridoxine, and folic acid, are the SWAT team protectors of your cat's immune system."*
>
> Dr. Jane R. Bicks, D.V.M.
> *The Revolution in Cat Nutrition*

Medical people tell us that with the B vitamins deficiency signs will show up as mental changes first, signs like irritability, nervousness and insomnia, for example. This is something that is seen with humans. We may also be observing these signs in cats, and they may also be from a deficiency of the B vitamins.

Vitamin B₆ [Pyridoxine]

Vitamin B_6 plays a major role in the metabolism of proteins and fats. Cats on high protein diets require more Vitamin B_6. Cats have four times the requirement for B_6 of dogs. B_6 is important with several body chemicals involved in the brain and has been associated with mood and behavior in humans. B_6 works with vitamin B_{12} for healthy red blood cell production and with B_5 and B_9 in antibody production.

Good food sources include brewer's yeast, liver, kidney, heart, meat, fish, egg yolk, whole grain cereals, bananas and nuts. Cottage cheese is low in vitamin B_6. 0.2 to 1.5 mg per day is the recommended amount for an adult cat.

This vitamin, like the others in the B complex, is easily destroyed by food processing such as cooking, sterilization, canning and time in storage. Because these vitamins are quite unstable, the cat needs to get them every day. The best sources are the fresh foods listed or reputable commercial preparations that have these vitamins added after processing.

Deficiencies result in loss of appetite, slow growth and weight loss. Epileptic type convulsions, skin inflammation and hair loss have also been seen with vitamin B_6 deficiency.

Vitamin B₉ [Folic Acid]

Folic acid is closely linked to vitamin B_{12} and is essential in the workings of the nervous and immune systems. This vitamin is destroyed by cooking and deficiency symptoms are generally the same: weight loss, anemia, shortness of breath and pale skin. Sulfa-containing medications tie up this vitamin.

Food sources are the same as for the others: brewer's yeast, the organ meats, egg yolk and leafy green vegetables. Dairy products contain little Folic acid.

Vitamin B$_{12}$ [Cyanocobalamin]

Vitamin B$_{12}$ is only found in animal tissue. This vitamin plays an important role in the manufacture of red blood cells. Deficiencies appear as anemia, or thinning of the blood, due to a decrease in the number of red blood cells circulating in the body. Red blood cells carry oxygen to all of the other cells. If their numbers are down, the skin around the eyes and mouth will appear pale and the cat will tire easily.

Good food sources are liver, organ meats, meat and to a lesser extent, fish, eggs and cheese. Stores of vitamin B$_{12}$ can last for some time.

Biotin

Biotin is a lesser known B vitamin, and deficiencies appear as a scaly skin condition and hair loss in the cat. Biotin is present in the organ meats, brewer's yeast, egg yolk and whole grain cereals.

Raw egg whites have a protein, avidin, which binds biotin making it ineffective. If we were to feed our cat the odd raw egg, this would not be a problem, but if we should feed a lot for some length of time, she could develop a Biotin deficiency.

A cat on antibiotics or sulfa drug treatment for an extended period of time may also show deficiencies of biotin.

Choline and Inositol

The last two of this water soluble group of B vitamins are involved with the cat's liver in the metabolism of dietary fats. These also assist the liver to eliminate toxins and drugs from the cat's body. The food sources are the same as for the others; deficiencies appear as fatty liver disease and rough scaly skin.

To summarize, the B complex of vitamins which include thiamine, riboflavin, niacin, pantothenic acid, pyridoxine, folic acid, cyanocobalamin, biotin, choline and inositol are all distinct yet similar. They are all water soluble and therefore are subject to destruction from food processing, cooking and heat. Learn to recognize the B vitamins when reading the labels of commercial cat foods and understand that they have to be added after because they were destroyed originally. Being water soluble, they are required everyday in that they are not stored but excess is eliminated through the urine - B_{12} is the exception. Several also are not available to the cat if she is on antibiotics or sulfa-containing medications.

All work together or are dependent on one another for healthy skin, immune and nervous systems or for the production of red blood cells. They all play a very important role in the overall health of our cat, especially for the stressed cat.

Deficiencies of one, several or all will appear in the forms of poor growth, weight loss, skin problems or general poor health and greater susceptibility to disease. A well-balanced and complete diet containing the foods with the B vitamins is best; this may include a daily portion of liver or kidney (not more than a quarter of the total diet.) Brewer's yeast and egg yolk once or twice a week can supply most of these vitamins.

If we suspect a B vitamin deficiency, we should consult with our veterinarian. Using the B vitamin supplements that are made for people is not recommended. Most have fifty to one hundred mg. per tablet which is far too much for the cat, so use those vitamin preparation specifically for cats. Natural foods are best.

Many pet owners feed their pets (including horses) the B complex of vitamins or brewer's yeast as an internal insect and flea repellent. This must be fed for some time to be effective. The claim is that the mosquitoes and fleas are discouraged or put off by the smell that the cat gives off.

Vitamin C [Ascorbic Acid]

Lack of vitamin C in humans has long been associated with a bleeding disorder called scurvy. This was a problem of the British Navy in the seventeenth and eighteenth centuries when sailers didn't have access to fresh fruits and vegetables or raw adrenal glands. Due to the amount of publicity that vitamin C has received today regarding the common cold as well as the prevention and treatment of many disorders, it has become the most widely consumed nutritional supplement.

Popular consensus is that the cat produces her own ascorbic acid or vitamin C. Some studies have shown that there may be a big variation between individuals, especially during times of stress resulting in many veterinarians prescribing vitamin C.

For all of us, vitamin C is essential for the formation of collagen, a cementing substance, that binds the many cells of connective tissue. Collagen is found in skin, tendons, bones, teeth and joints of all kinds. It is also in blood vessels and muscles. Vitamin C then becomes important in wound healing and repair of tissues.

Vitamin C is alleged to be beneficial in many conditions such as allergies, cataracts, diabetes and cancer prevention. Another important function is related to the immune system and stress.

Most fresh fruits and green vegetables, liver, kidney and raw adrenal glands are good food sources. Being water soluble, vitamin C is lost or destroyed quite easily. Prolonged cooking and exposure to the atmosphere quickly reduces vitamin C in foods. Slicing, reheating, and exposure to baking soda adds to its destruction.

Many claims have been made about Vitamin C. Some are founded and more are still to be proven. Heavily processed cat foods have driven out the water soluble vitamin C. Because of this and the particular environment that our cats live in today, I believe that adding vitamin C to the feline diet is appropriate.

Antioxidants

With all of the talk lately of antioxidants in our own diet, it is appropriate to expand our discussion of them in our cat's diet.

What is an antioxidant? First we must discuss oxidation which simply is combining with oxygen. The rusting of metal and the brown spoilage of fruit or butter going rancid are examples of oxidation, the combining with oxygen.

Oxygen is essential for basic cell function in cats, humans and most animals as we all know. However, oxygen can also produce toxic substances and these highly reactive substances, called "free radicals" can combine with other molecules in the body that can be destructive.

> *"It is now becoming evident that free-radical reactions in mammalian systems are probably responsible for such diverse physiological processes as inflammation, aging, drug-induced damage, degenerative arthritis, alterations in immunity, cancer and cardiovascular disease."*
>
> Dr. Stephen Davies & Dr. Alan Stewart,
> *Nutritional Medicine*

There are protective substances that counter this oxidation process and they are the antioxidants. These substances protect the cells against the oxidative process.

Some of the common antioxidants that we know of are vitamin A, vitamin E, vitamin C, selenium containing amino acids, and several enzymes such as glutathione reductase. These substances plus others that are being discovered can, for example, prevent fruit from spoiling or fats from going rancid. More important, however, is the protection that these antioxidants provide inside the body.

Natural pet food manufacturers are using the natural antioxidants vitamin E and C to preserve pet foods instead of preservatives such as ethoxyquin which is a very effective fat preservative. BHA and BHT are also antioxidants that have been used to prevent the fat in pet foods from going rancid in storage. Controversy has arisen over the years with regard to what these preservatives do to the animals that eat them over an extended period of time.

Antioxidants are becoming more important in our modern environment. Excessive oxidation or oxidative stress can develop from many sources. Nutritional deficiencies, disease, stress and heavy metal pollutants from our cat's environment can increase the amounts of free radicals in the cat's body that we are now learning are very destructive. Combined with a diet of refined or processed foods which may have removed many of nature's known and unknown antioxidants that would normally offer protection, it is no wonder that we see more chronic diseases such as cancer in our cats.

Environmental poisons such as insecticides, pesticides, herbicides, preservatives, taste enhancers and colors as well as polluted air and water that our cat eats, breathes and drinks are increasing the load of free radicals that our cat's body must deal with.

To help our cat deal with this, the argument can become quite convincing for feeding fresh foods and supplementing with vitamins and minerals.

The particular substances that we know offer antioxidant protection for the cells are vitamin A (the cat cannot utilize beta carotene), vitamin C, vitamin E, selenium, zinc, manganese and copper. Other antioxidants are being discovered and researched. For example, it is thought that the herb Thyme contains many antioxidants. We are going to hear more in the future about antioxidants and how free radicals cause disease.

Vitamin Summary

To conclude this section on vitamins, I would like to give my own observations on vitamin supplementation. There is no doubt that the cat requires vitamins, some more than others, as we have discussed. The question then arises: is my cat getting all the vitamins she needs? We have been told by human nutritionists that if we eat a balanced diet with the proper amounts of fresh foods, we do not require vitamin supplements. Yet we take vitamins ourselves and see other people doing the same. We have been told either by our veterinarian or cat food manufacturers that if our cat eats such and such balanced, complete cat food, extra vitamin supplementation is not necessary. Why do cats then respond to fresh foods and vitamin supplements?

I have observed many times a dramatic change in cats fed additional vitamins and minerals who were on well known, high quality cat food. I have seen cats, particularly older cats, change dramatically between visits to the veterinary clinic to the point that I didn't recognize them. These individuals were coming in with ailments ranging from persistent coughs to rough, shaggy hair coats and once put onto vitamin supplementation improved dramatically.

Most cats today do not get fresh food but rather processed and preserved foods, in which the vitamins may have been destroyed or made unavailable to the cat.

All cats are individuals in different environments which greatly vary their requirements. We are the best judges of whether our cat is receiving her requirements. We are told to "listen to your body" when referring to ourselves; we must do the same with our cat. Observe her body and she will tell us when she is deficient. We only have to be smart enough to read the signs. If we suspect a deficiency, a look at the diet and a trip to the veterinarian, or animal nutritionist may be in order.

Vitamin Summary

VITAMIN	SOURCE	FUNCTION	DEFICIENCY or EXCESS
A	animal sources liver, egg yolk fish oils	epithelial tissue skin, eyes, reproductive	skin sores, night vision, reproductive problems, excess: pain on handling, bone malformation
D	animal sources liver, egg yolk fish oils	bones, teeth, calcium/phosphorus balance	rickets, soft bones, broken bones, eclampsia, malformed teeth
E	liver, egg yolk, wheat germ oil, seeds, broccoli	muscle, selenium antioxidant	musclular dystrophy, steatitis, reproductive problems
K	egg yolk, yogurt	blood clotting	bleeding disorders
B's	liver, grains brewer's yeast	muscle, immunity, blood, nerves, skin	unthrifty, weak, poor condition
B_1	brewer's yeast	muscle, brain	thiaminases, weakness
B_2	liver, kidney	muscle, skin	dermatitis, tearing
B_3	liver, bran	metabolism	tongue, breath, itching
B_5	liver, egg yolk	antibodies, stress	sick, slow recovery
B_6	liver, meat	proteins & fats	slow growth, hair loss
B_9	organ meats	nerves, immunity	anemia, weight loss
B_{12}	animal tissue	red blood cells	anemia, tire easily
C	organ meats, fruits/vegetables	immunity, collagen wound healing	sick, slow recovery scurvy

MINERALS

Minerals are inorganic substances found in the atmosphere and on the earth's crust. Some of these elements are found in animal tissues and many are considered essential to life as animals cannot live without them and cannot manufacture them. Minerals do not yield energy to the cat but are necessary for life, so are essential nutrients. Minerals are important for strong bones and teeth and with proteins and fats are essential in the construction and maintenance of soft tissues. They also play a role with many enzyme systems and serve to keep the cat's body fluids in a state of osmotic equilibrium or simply in a state of fluid balance.

The four elements: oxygen, hydrogen, nitrogen and carbon are required by the cat, as with all of us, and are present in the air we breathe and the foods we eat. These, we take for granted are present in tissue and are required by all living beings.

For our purposes we shall discuss those minerals that are present in animal tissue in lesser amounts than the first four. Minerals are classified as essential which means that if they are excluded from the diet, problems will result and if supplied, the problem is corrected. Scientists have named nineteen such minerals. Another eight they have called beneficial, saying that life is possible without them. As well there are another twenty or thirty elements that are found in tissues and these have been called contaminants by some experts.

With further scientific research we are going to hear more in the future about minerals. We shall deal with the major essential minerals, commonly called macrominerals, and microminerals (may also be called trace minerals). Macro and micro depends on the concentration of a particular mineral found in the body. Those greater than iron are macrominerals and those less are microminerals. We shall briefly discuss some of the contaminants.

The macrominerals: calcium, phosphorus, magnesium, potassium, sodium and chlorine are required in relatively large amounts every day by the cat. These minerals are involved in the structure of bones, cells and body metabolism. Often they work in harmony with other elements or nutrients to perform a specific body function.

We must realize the harmony that exists in the cat's body with the many complex interactions of all nutrients all playing in tune to the same symphony.

The microminerals: iron, zinc, copper, manganese, iodine, chromium, selenium, molybdenum, cobalt and sulfur are required in lesser amounts by comparison and have important roles in metabolism. Others, like silicon, nickel and florine, may be put into this list as science improves the means to measure them and their benefits can be documented.

Generally the requirements for the minerals are within an estimated range. These estimates have been established from experimental feeding trials done with cats and other species. Certain states such as growth, lactation and muscular effort increase the demand for minerals. Put another way, as energy requirements increase so do mineral requirements. Genetics or inherited differences regarding specific minerals may also be a factor.

Improper supplementation or a poor diet can cause mineral imbalances and excesses. The proper absorption is influenced by such things as vitamins and other minerals. Minerals interact with each other, which can be good or bad. Essential minerals can interact with toxic elements which may lead to problems. Excesses of other nutrients such as some vitamins and amino acids may lead to deficiencies. For example, an excess of vitamin C may lead to a copper deficiency.

Because minerals are required in such small amounts, with roles that are quite subtle, deficiencies may take a long time to be noticed. With new and improved testing methods, many of these can be detected early.

We know a lot about minerals, as with vitamins; however, there is still a lot to learn. Our modern cat lives in a totally different situation than her wild and ancestral cousins. Not only is her environment different, but the foods we give her are different. Many are proccessed and fortified with additives.

When we deviate from the natural state with regards to the foods that the cat ate and the environment that she has lived in for thousands of years, we start to see problems.

An example is calcium. The presence of calcium is high in bones and low in meat or flesh and organ meats. When we eliminate bones from the modern cat's diet and continue to give meat and organs, such as liver, a calcium imbalance develops. In other words the bones provided the necessary calcium to balance the diet.

We do not give bones to our pets today so they are deprived of this natural source of calcium, phosphorus and magnesium. We don't give bones because we are afraid of the sharp ends which may perforate the stomach or intestines and rightly so. The wild and ancestral cats or the domesticated cats that eat mice and birds obtain intestinal protection and fiber from the hair and feathers that they consumed. This material would wrap around these sharp objects to protect the digestive system - the modern day "hair ball".

Today we replace fiber with plant foods such as cellulose and lignin to bulk up the stool; however, the intestinal protection is not replaced so we do not give bones. Bone meal is the alternative.

When our modern cat gets in trouble today, a question we should ask ourselves is "what have we changed from the cat's natural state and why?" The answer to the problem may lie in going back to the natural way.

We have to consider the whole picture and it seems that once we change something, a chain reaction of events starts in motion in which many things are altered.

We are going to discuss each of the minerals separately, briefly describing what each does, what deficiency signs may appear and some good food sources.

Calcium

Calcium is one of the macrominerals required by the cat, primarily for bones and teeth. Over seventy per cent of the minerals in the cat's body are calcium and phosphorus and ninety-nine per cent of the calcium is in the bones and teeth. Lesser amounts are used in the body fluids for blood clotting and muscle and nerve function. Calcium is also important in the regulation of blood and milk formation. In the cat's body, calcium, phosphorus and vitamin D are closely related and must be considered together.

Of particular importance is the ratio between calcium and phosphorus which should be near 1 : 0.8 or 1 part of calcium to 0.8 parts of phosphorus. More of one or the other will affect the availability of the other creating an imbalance — an excess ties up the other mineral. For example, a diet with a lot of lean meat, which is low in calcium, requires a supplement such as bonemeal. Most bonemeal preparations are thirty per cent calcium to fifteen per cent phosphorus.

Many things can affect the calcium status of the cat besides the ratio. A deficiency of vitamin D, excessive phosphates, magnesium, zinc, manganese and oxalates (rhubarb) can lower the absorption of calcium. Low iodine also affects calcium.

Certain foods can also make a difference. Foods such as bran and unleavened bread contain substances called phytates that can bind calcium and make it unabsorbable. Large amounts of undigested fat also can reduce the availability of calcium which is an important consideration in a nursing queen's diet.

Sufficient amounts of energy and adequate protein are required for calcium absorption. However, a high protein diet will increase the loss of calcium through an acid urine.

Many things can affect the calcium status; therefore, one should not start supplementing minerals, especially calcium and phosphorus "willy-nilly" as this can just make things worse. If you suspect a calcium deficiency, as with any mineral deficiency we shall discuss, we should take our concerns to our cat's veterinarian so that the problem can be corrected.

The total diet including everything that is eaten must be analyzed. This must be done for all the nutrients in order to get the complete overall picture and find where the problem may be. The problem may be from not enough of something or too much of another or the combination of one to another nutrient. If we should decide to give a particular supplement such as calcium, for example, without consideration for the complete nutritional picture, we may just be making matters worse.

Good food sources of calcium are milk, cheese, canned salmon, sardines, green vegetables and bone meal. Remember — the adult cat may not be able to digest milk or cheese so consider yogurt instead.

Signs of calcium deficiency are often combined with a phosphorus and vitamin D imbalance. Kittens may exhibit bowing of the legs (rickets), slow growth and a poor appetite. Signs in the adult may include irritability, loss of muscle tone, temporary or permanent paralysis and the earliest signs of osteoporosis.

Cats on acidulent diets - to promote excessively acidic urine to prevent bladder stones (see the section on FUS) may lose too much calcium through their urine resulting in a calcium deficiency as well.

Osteoporosis (porous bone, "bone softening") may occur in the jawbones, skull bones, ribs and finally the long leg bones. Teeth may detach, with receding gums, painful joints, and easily fractured limbs, all due to a depletion of bone minerals.

The most common problem when calcium is deficient is the result of an increase in the release of parathyroid hormone. This hormone coming from a small gland near the thyroid causes calcium to be removed from the bone stores which can in turn lead to skeletal problems such as lameness, bone pain and fractures.

Another calcium, vitamin D (D_3), problem is eclampsia, sometimes called milk fever. This condition may be seen soon after a queen delivers her kittens and starts to lactate or produce milk. The queen will stagger and seem to be paralyzed and be unable to move and if not treated will go into a coma and eventually die. Eclampsia is due to the sudden demand for milk calcium placed upon the queen's body. This sudden drain on the calcium stores, taking away calcium from the rest of her body, causes the problem. Since the calcium ion is required by the muscles to operate, the muscles go limp and the queen appears paralyzed. She must be treated with intravenous calcium as quickly as possible to correct this condition if she is to live.

Eclampsia is due to a combination of several things including Vitamin D_3, calcium, phosphorus and the parathyroid gland. If a queen is known to have this condition with every litter she should be under veterinary supervision with regard to her diet - decreasing the calcium and treating with Vitamin D_3, well before she is to queen - so that eclampsia may be prevented.

Excess calcium can lead to kidney failure, constipation, abdominal pain and deposition of calcium in sites outside bone. These deposits occur in soft tissue, like muscle, especially where tendons attach. If our cat is getting a lot of cottage cheese or milk on top of her commercial cat food, phosphorus may have to be added. Supplementing must be done with care and it is advisable to get professional advice in this regard.

200 to 400 mg of calcium per day is the recommended minimum requirement for an adult cat from all her food sources.

Kittens in certain circumstances may require calcium, phosphorus and vitamin D supplementation and this should be done with everything being considered. Factors such as the stage of growth, amount of mother's milk, exercise, environment and total diet composition must be considered so that the requirements are met to ensure optimal growth without imbalances from excesses. An all meat or all organ diet, such as liver, will result in an imbalance because these are low in calcium and high in phosphorus. Prevention is the best route.

Phosphorus

Phosphorus is closely related to calcium in both nutrition and metabolism. Like calcium, phosphorus is involved in the formation of bones and teeth - where eighty-five per cent is present - and is necessary for the working of every cell in the cat's body. Magnesium and the B vitamins are also interrelated with phosphorus function.

Food sources are meats, heart, milk, bonemeal, poultry, eggs, fish and legumes. The phosphorus in grains is only fifty per cent available because it is combined with phytic acid which is not digested. Phosphorus is quite plentiful in meats and organ foods; however, if these should be fed exclusively, an excess is created over calcium leading to problems. The signs will be those of calcium deficiency.

Deficiencies of phosphorus are less common and appear as those of a calcium imbalance but can also lower the cat's resistance to infection because phosphorus is involved with the immune system and white blood cell performance. Low phosphorus has also been observed to lower reproductive performance in animals.

As has been said before, calcium, vitamin D and phosphorus work together and any deficiency or excess of one or another will often produce similar signs.

Magnesium

Magnesium is abundant inside cells and is closely linked with calcium and phosphorus metabolism. Most of the magnesium is found in the teeth and bones of the cat. The rest is found mainly in the cells. In the cells, magnesium is essential for the movement of sodium, potassium and calcium in and out of the cells and for temperature regulation. The vitamins C, E and B complex work better when sufficient magnesium is present. All are involved in maintaining the internal environment of the cat's body so that all body functions work in harmony.

Deficiencies are rare; however, excesses have been linked with an increase of struvite or the urine crystals that may form, causing certain types of lower urinary tract disease in cats. More on this in the section discussing FUS (Feline Urologic Syndrome).

Food sources are shrimp, sardines, ground nuts, bonemeal, whole grains and green vegetables. Supplementation should be done with professional guidance because of the involvement of calcium and phosphorus.

The minimum daily requirement of an adult cat is four to eight mg. per day.

Potassium

Potassium has received a lot of attention in human nutrition of late with regard to its relationship to high blood pressure. Presently, most reputable commercial cat foods have adequate amounts but if a cat is on prolonged medications, such as diuretics, has persistent diarrhea or is under a lot of stress, potassium supplementation may be required.

Cats on low potassium diets have exhibited poor growth, restlessness, muscular paralysis, tendency to dehydrate and abnormalities of the heart and kidneys. Potassium is present in every cell of the cat's body and is required for the correct working of the heart, muscles and nervous system. It works in conjunction with sodium and the ratio of these two is important for the functioning of all cells.

Beef, poultry, fresh fruits, vegetables and whole grains are rich in potassium.

Sodium and Chlorine

These two minerals, or common salt, are considered together. Sodium is essential for the maintenance of the cat's body fluids and blood pressure. With potassium, the correct fluid environment of the cells is maintained so that the cells can function. Cats on a high meat diet will obtain their sodium from meat; however, as we feed more vegetable type foods, which are low in sodium, some salt is added. There is adequate salt in all commercial cat foods. Sodium is lost through sweat or perspiration.

Cats do not sweat or perspire much as compared to us, so they do not lose the same amounts of sodium that we do. Sweat contains a lot of salt, hence its salty taste. Because cats do not lose much salt, it is not as important as ingredient in their diets as it is for us. However, in hot weather with excessive exercise, salt is important.

In developing recipes for the cat, salt is often excluded. Food sources are table salt, meats, shellfish, bacon and grains.

Signs of deficiency are fatigue, retarded growth, dry skin, loss of hair, poor reflexes and increased susceptibility to heat prostration.

Iron

Iron plays a main role as an oxygen carrier in red blood cells and muscle. Its other role is in the composition of some enzymes. Deficiencies will be related to anemia such as listlessness, fatigue and poor growth in kittens.

Foods rich in iron are red meats, liver, and egg yolks. Vegetables are poor sources of iron and overboiling vegetables can reduce their iron content by as much as twenty per cent. Whole grains inhibit iron absorption and vitamin C improves absorption. Growing kittens and pregnant queens require more iron. If kittens are maintained on an all milk diet for an extended period of time, they may become iron deficient. This may be due to the lack of sufficient iron in the milk.

Cats in the wild obtain most of their iron from the flesh and bones that they consume. Iron excesses can result in unthrifty cats.

Zinc

In the past few years zinc has been given a lot of attention in human nutrition and is appearing to be quite an important nutrient. Zinc deficiency in cats has been known for some time to be the cause of hair loss, thickening of the skin, poor growth, weight loss and poor appetite. Other conditions include delayed sexual maturity, immune deficiencies and poor wound healing. Zinc has been shown to increase the blood levels of thymulin in humans - for the T cells of the immune system.

Best food sources are muscle meats, oysters, liver, egg yolk, split peas, garlic, wheat germ and brewer's yeast. The availability of zinc is influenced by iron, manganese, selenium and copper, and excesses of zinc can disturb these as well. Processing foods and a diet high in soy meal have been shown to reduce the zinc content.

If a zinc deficiency is suspected, supplementation can be tried in that reasonable amounts have not been shown to be harmful and if the condition improves, zinc may have been the problem. Too much zinc can result in anemia as iron and copper are tied up.

With the extensive studies in human nutrition, we shall hear more in the future about the trace minerals that may or may not apply to cats.

Copper

Copper is another of the essential microminerals. It is involved with iron and the blood's ability to carry oxygen. Copper is also contained in a number of enzymes, especially those involved with brain metabolism and the production of elastin and collagen - substances found in joints and scar tissue. Deficiencies produce anemia, aneurysms, bone fractures, abnormal wound healing, reproductive failure and impaired immunity. Copper deficiency can also result in hair depigmentation. Copper deficiency can be mistaken for iron deficiency and is associated with the utilization of vitamin C. Food sources include oysters, kidney, beef and liver.

Vanadium

Vanadium is being considered of value in preventing heart disease and cancer in man. Many human vitamin-mineral supplements contain vanadium today and we may hear more in the future with regard to the cat.

Silicon

Silicon appears to be an essential element. Silicon is similar to carbon but much stronger in chemical bonds and appears in the structural material of cartilage, tendons, skin, arteries and cornea of the eyes.

Molybdenum

Refining foods reduces its molybdenum content so we may see more deficiencies in the cat. It and copper interact together so copper deficiencies may involve molybdenum.

Chromium

Chromium is an essential trace element and is necessary in blood sugar control. It has been shown to be important for the action of insulin and the regulation of normal blood sugar levels. Deficiency signs appear as clouding of the cornea of the eyes, sugar in the urine, and elevated blood sugar. The best food source is brewer's yeast.

Manganese

Manganese is found in bone, soft tissues, liver and kidney and is necessary for growth of the uterus in the female. Deficiencies include disc and joint problems, birth defects, reduced fertility and poor growth. Excess manganese may reduce fertility and has been shown to produce albinism - a total lack of skin and hair pigment in Siamese cats. Egg yolk, leafy green vegetables, whole grains and tea are rich sources of manganese.

Selenium

Selenium has long been known to be essential in animal nutrition. Vitamin E and selenium are important in muscle growth and as antioxidants. Dandruff and ringworm have been effectively treated with selenium shampoos so selenium appears to be essential for skin and hair tissue.

Good food sources are grains grown on soil containing selenium. Excessive intake is toxic producing weight loss, vomiting, weakness and pulmonary edema. Excesses have been observed in livestock on soils containing high levels or from industrial wastes. Symptoms include hair loss, brittle hooves, tooth decay, poor appetite and weight loss.

Nickel

Nickel is involved in glucose metabolism and insulin's effectiveness on blood sugar. It is being evaluated in people with reference to heart attacks, strokes and allergies. We may hear more later of the value of nickel in feline nutrition.

Iodine

Cats require small amounts of iodine for the prevention of goiter. Goiter is the enlargement of the thyroid gland situated in the neck. The thyroid gland is instrumental in the regulation of growth so as iodine becomes deficient, the gland enlarges to compensate. Hypothyroidism, goiter, unexplained weight gain, reproductive failures, delayed shedding of deciduous teeth, hairlessness, dullness and drowsiness can all be signs of lack of iodine.

Excesses may be more of a concern than deficiencies. Foods such as dairy products, meat, fish, poultry, cereals and grains contain iodine. Excessive feeding of seaweed and kelp may also result in skin problems from too much iodine.

Cobalt

Cobalt is an essential trace element closely associated with vitamin B_{12}. It is required for healthy blood, in particular hemoglobin, the oxygen carrier in blood. Cobalt is required for the production of vitamin B_{12} so a deficiency of either one could be seen as anemia and listlessness. Liver, organ meats, eggs and dairy products are good sources.

Sulfur

Although sulfur is present in all living matter and essential for life, little is known about deficiencies. It is present in all proteins and especially in the two amino acids, methionine and cysteine. It is also present in some enzymes and some vitamins. Since these amino acids cannot be made in the cat's body, it is believed that the sulfur is obtained primarily from the foods of animal sources. Some plants like onions and cabbage contain sulfur as well. If a cat is on an adequate animal protein diet, sulfur is not a concern.

Fluorine

Fluorine, or Fluoride, has received much publicity in human medicine for its ability to reduce tooth decay. This is probably true for the cat. Excess has been shown to cause mottling of the tooth enamel in the cat.

Mineral Summary

To summarize this section on minerals, we have discussed those minerals that modern science considers to be essential to life. Actual requirements for most minerals have been studied, documented and deficiencies identified.

Cats in the wild have survived for millions of years in their particular environment with their particular diet. The cat of today has a different environment and a different diet so mineral supplementation has become important.

Ideally, the diet should be the source of vitamins and minerals but with current means of processing, refining and preserving foods, questions of mineral losses and availability are to be asked.

Need for supplementing minerals has many considerations, one of which is the diet. Other concerns are age, sex, drug therapy, exercise, hormone status (spayed or neutered) and local environment.

If a mineral deficiency should be suspected, the individual cat, her diet and her environment must be evaluated by professional people trained in the areas of health and nutrition. The whole picture must be evaluated before a diagnosis is made and corrections initiated.

Hit and miss supplementing with minerals may do more harm than good.

The purpose of this section is to help make the cat owner aware of what is known with regard to minerals as nutrients, and appreciate that it is not a simple black and white issue.

For all practical purposes, a well-prepared commercial cat food or a diversified home-prepared feeding plan with variety and fresh ingredients should provide all necessary minerals. Exceptions, as we discussed, may occur with those cats under stress or taking medication for long periods of time. Another exception might be giving calcium and phosphorus to growing kittens with poor milking mothers.

Now and in the future, I believe there is a place for most individual cats to be given a multiple vitamin-mineral supplement, especially today's cat. As we have said before, our modern cat is in a chemically stressful environment and may not be as well-prepared to counteract these stresses with the refined type of diets that it eats today. Some of the nutrients that offer defense may be lacking or at too low a level to adequately protect the cat.

Mineral Summary

MINERAL	SOURCE	FUNCTION	DEFICIENCY or EXCESS
Calcium	bonemeal, dairy products	bones & teeth with vit D & P	rickets, soft bones, eclampsia, deposits
Phosphorus	meats, eggs dairy products	bones & teeth reproduction	as calcium, reproductive problems, poor immunity
Magnesium	bonemeal, grains, shrimp	with calcium & phosphorus	poor bones & teeth bladder stones
Potassium	meats, grains fruits & vegetables	body functions	poor growth, dehydration, heart & kidney problems
Sodium & Chlorine	meats, salt	body functions	poor growth, unthrifty
Iron	meats, liver	blood, muscle	anemia, fatigue, poor growth
Zinc	meats, liver	hair, skin	hair loss, skin problems
Copper	beef, organ meats	blood, joints	anemia, poor wound healing
Chromium	brewer's yeast	with insulin	high blood sugar
Manganese	egg yolk, grains	bones, tissues	disc & joint problems
Selenium	grains, liver	with Vit E.	hair loss, tooth decay
Iodine	meat, fish, kelp	thyroid gland	goiter, hair loss, dullness
Cobalt	liver, eggs	blood with B_{12}	anemia, listlessness
Sulfur	meats, fish	all tissues	poor growth

TOXIC ELEMENTS

In this technological age we are using many minerals for purposes that make our lives more convenient. Some of these metals have concentrated to such an extent in our environment that they have become toxic or poisonous. In particular, lead, aluminum, mercury and cadmium are elements of concern. These metals were always present in our environment but with certain industrial and household use, they have concentrated and are now causing problems for life. They combine with the free radicals that we discussed earlier in the section on antioxidants to cause destruction to the cells. This is a concern for us and our pets. These metals can concentrate in the cat's body over time. Since our cat is much smaller than we are - about one tenth the size - less can be tolerated. Our pets live in the same environment as we do, so it is appropriate to briefly discuss these elements.

Lead

Lead has been known to cause stillbirths, learning problems, cancer, heart disease, depression, immune problems and death. It is in our environment from gasoline exhaust and lead based paint, to dust and dirt. In the body, lead interferes with other trace elements, for example, zinc, which can become deficient. Nutritionally we can help reduce some of the effects by feeding foods rich in vitamins A, C, E and selenium, zinc, calcium, iron, magnesium and other nutrients.

Aluminum

Aluminum seems to affect the central nervous system and bone metabolism, with possible links to Alzheimer's disease in man. Sources include aluminum cookware, processed cheeses, table salt, white flour and tap water.

Mercury and Cadmium

Both of these are in our environment. Mercury can concentrate in the foods that we feed our cat and cadmium is quite high in cigarette smoke. Mercury affects the central nervous system and cadmium binds zinc. It is best to be aware of these metals that do harm and try to eliminate them from our cat's environment.

RECOMMENDATIONS

Up to this point we have discussed the science of nutrition; now is time to apply the art of nutrition. Like many things, the feeding and care of animals is an art as well as a science. The "green thumb" in gardening and the "management in the feed bucket" are phrases used to describe the art of gardening and the art of livestock management. This ability to combine the knowledge of the science and the daily application, we call art.

We can dissect and analyze to great lengths, but the bottom line is the application of this knowledge in the everyday feeding of our cat. From feeding trials in controlled environments to computer calculations of balanced rations, it still comes down to the "eye of the beholder". Each cat is an individual with his or her particular needs in a particular situation. We must be aware of all needs and then feed or act accordingly.

Modern science has discovered and identified many nutrients. It has also given us some insight into which ones are required and some recommendations on how much of these nutrients should be adequate. We must realize that nutrition is a changing science and what is advisable today may not be tomorrow.

From various books and lists of tables, we can obtain nutrient recommendations (see Additional readings pg. 302). These are established for the average cat in an average situation, but in reality there may not be such an individual. Studies are continually being done in the science of nutrition looking into the interactions of different foods, the complexities of digestion, the mechanisms of absorption and the final utilization of nutrients. All this is being done for a cat that is in a different world from what her ancestors knew.

Having said this, we must carry on with the knowledge we have now with regard to feeding our cat but be willing to be flexible as new information becomes available. If we get in trouble we can always look back in history and ask ourselves: what did the cats of old or those in the wild do to survive? This is one of the reasons we have discussed the cat's make up and tried to relate it to her diet. We have also compared her to herbivores to illustrate the differences in body structure and diet.

The question now must be asked: How do we combine the science of nutrition with the art of feeding? To answer this question we must first know what is normal for our cat. By recognizing the normal healthy cat, we can then go on to identify what is abnormal. For example, is it normal for my cat to have a cold wet nose, vomit occasionally, shed hair during certain times of the year or have diarrhea after eating ice cream? The answers to all are yes, these are signs of a normal healthy cat. However, there are many signs that can tell us that our cat is not normal and in fact may have a problem.

Signs of Good Health are

alertness and vigor
good appetite and regular formed stools
proper weight and unblemished skin
sturdy, well-developed bones and teeth
full, thick, and glossy haircoat
and bright eager eyes.

If our cat has all of these signs, we are comfortable that all is well. If not, we become concerned and should either take her to the veterinarian, change her environment or take a look at her diet. The cause of the abnormality could be medical, genetic, behavioral or nutritional.

Signs of Ill-health are

irritability, listlessness, depression, hyperactivity,
aggressiveness, incessant crying, biting, lashing out,
poor appetite, fussiness, bad breath,
diarrhea, constipation, foul smelly stools,
obesity, thinness, puffiness, soft body condition,
dull, dry, greasy, smelly haircoat,
red, pale, dry, flaky, itchy skin,
dull, tearing and inflamed eyes.

Any of these signs could be due to improper nutrition. We are told to "listen to our body" and it will tell us if everything is fine. The same is true for our pets. Observe and they will tell us if something is wrong.

The cat will eat foods that smell right, are palatable, have a favorable texture and are free of harmful products that she finds offensive. Generally, cats like their food fresh, whereas the dog doesn't mind it aged. How often have we seen our dog bury some of his food to be dug up and enjoyed at a later date? We must listen to what our pets are telling us and then give them what they need.

Let us go back over the six basic nutrients that we have discussed previously and make some general recommendations. Now the art comes in as we watch and maintain our cat in a state of good health. If we see that this state may be slipping, we adjust our feeding program accordingly, just like the "green thumb" gardener or the "bucket management" livestock farmer.

The nutrient requirements for a cat are fixed for her situation. The amount of food needed to meet these requirements will vary greatly depending on the amount of each nutrient present in the type of food eaten. In other words, providing nutritious foods containing the required nutrients is our goal.

Water

Water is required in the largest amount of all nutrients and should be available at all times. Cats are not avid water drinkers and usually get and use the water in their food very efficiently; however, if the food is dry, drinking water becomes more important. A dripping faucet, a flower bowl, Christmas tree stands or toilet bowls often taste better for some reason so we should be careful not to add fertilizer or disinfectants to the water. Pine needles can be poisonous.

The dish for water does not have to be very large and can be placed near the food dish. I personally think that cool clean water tastes better from a metal or glass dish than a plastic one. Plastic can become damaged and harbor bacteria as well.

We do not have to worry about not giving our cat enough water if we make it available at all times, but we should become concerned if she seems to be spending a lot of time drinking and urinating. This sign may indicate that she is sick and should have a check up. Things like kidney problems, diabetes and fever from infection are the first things that may come to mind.

Remember that cats on a dry cat food, in warm weather, or that are quite active require more water, and the safest thing is to have a dish of clean fresh water available at all times. The growing kitten and the idle adult will drink about two to three times as much water as the amount of dry matter food that they eat. A cat in hot weather, after severe exertion or lactating may drink four or more times the amount of water compared to the amount of dry matter food consumed. The best situation is to offer self-regulated water with free choice access.

If we are worried that our cat is not drinking enough, we may put out bottled water. For a change we may try tomato or clam juice which cats like. Milk is not a good idea as our cat may be intolerant to lactose resulting in diarrhea and more water loss.

Protein

Proteins are the building blocks in foods used for building and repairing the cat's many cells especially muscle, skin and the cells of the immune system. Protein must be of good quality so that the essential amino acids are included to perform these functions for the cat. Excess protein cannot be stored as protein but is stored as fat, never to be converted back to protein. Therefore, protein must always be present in the diet. High quality protein foods come primarily from animal sources. Protein is required in greater amounts by the growing kitten, stressed individuals and the pregnant and nursing mother cat. Lesser amounts are required for the adult and older cat.

An average adult daily intake of three gm of protein per pound of body weight and 8.6 gm per pound of body weight for kittens daily will adequately provide the cat with his or her requirements. Or thirty-two to thirty-six per cent protein in dry food, thirty-four to forty per cent in semimoist and thirty-five to forty-one per cent protein in canned on a dry basis.

The percentage of protein required in the diet will vary with
- digestibility (animal protein easier than plant sources),
- the amino acid composition (especially the essentials),
- the caloric density of the diet (more fat, more protein), and
- the physiological state of the cat (kitten, adult, etc.).

Inadequate quality protein in the cat's diet will appear in the form of poor growth, rough haircoat, anemia, listlessness, drop in milk production, weight loss and susceptibility to infections and toxins from the environment.

We must always be thinking about protein when we feed our cat. She must have it to stay in good health. Excess can be expensive as protein foods are costly and the protein not used for building and repair will be used for energy or stored as fat. In other words, we can supply energy with less expensive foods such as carbohydrates, so feeding excess protein is pointless from an energy standpoint.

Fats

Nature's powerful energy food, fats, not only provides over twice the amount of energy fuel of proteins and carbohydrates, it also contains the tasty flavors that cats enjoy. Just because they taste good, however, is not reason to overindulge.

Because of their acceptable flavor, fats can be used to enhance the palatability of a meal. We must remember to reduce the other energy foods like carbohydrates for if we continue with a high calorie diet, the cat may become overweight.

Fats are required as an essential nutrient for cell structure and vitamin sources so must always be present in the diet. Recommendations vary from eight to twelve per cent crude fat for dry food, ten to fifteen per cent for semimoist and nine to eighteen per cent for canned cat food. The higher levels need not be a concern if adequate protein is also available. Generally the more fat in the diet, the more protein as well. Coarse dry hair, severe dandruff, poor growth, underdeveloped testicles in the male and absence of heat cycles in the female are signs that a cat will show when the essential fatty acids are deficient.

Carbohydrates

We have learned that the cat requires energy and that the ancestral cat obtained this primarily from proteins and fats. We have learned that some of this energy can be provided to the modern cat by feeding her partly processed carbohydrates. By feeding carbohydrate type foods such as the cereal grains and vegetables, we can dilute the protein down in a high meat diet. We can also lower the caloric density (number of calories within a food) of diets containing a lot of fat. On the other hand, by adding carbohydrates, we increase the volume or bulk of the diet.

The amount of carbohydrate we can feed a cat will depend upon the amount of protein and fat she requires in her diet first. After these are met, then the rest of her energy requirements can be made up with carbohydrates. That is usually about forty per cent of the total diet.

Carbohydrate also provides bulk and fiber to the diet; however, we must always remember to either cook, bake or grind grains and vegetables so that she can take advantage of these foods,

Carbohydrates are primarily found in cereal grains, vegetables, and fruits. These are the sugars and starches we discussed earlier. The cat, because of her small digestive system, must not be overloaded with too much bulk from carbohydrates. The wild cat may eat some of the stomach and intestinal contents of her prey which would be predominately carbohydrates so we really haven't changed our modern cat's diet much if we feed her a little processed carbohydrates. The wild and ancestral cats got along quite well without dietary carbohydrates because the right proteins and fats were eaten.

Vitamins and Minerals

These subtle essential nutrients play many different roles in the cat's well-being and good health. As far as the cat is concerned, a multi-vitamin/mineral supplement may be in order if our cat is suspected of having a deficiency. Cats eating only one commercial brand of food with no variety or fresh foods have in my experience benefited from supplementation. Over supplementing, especially of the fat soluble vitamins and minerals, can be dangerous and should only be done under professional guidance.

Giving the antioxidant vitamins of A, C and E daily may have some merit in the future as we learn more about the damage caused by free radicals and pollutants from our cat's environment and diet.

PART TWO Commercially Prepared Cat Food

> MOST PET OWNERS
> Don't
> have much knowledge of nutrition,
> have much experience feeding animals,
> have access to cheap supplies of cat food,
> and
> don't have the time or desire to cook for the pet
> so
> they depend on reliable prepared pet foods.

The Pet Food Industry is a young industry that has grown rapidly into a multi-billion dollar business. Walk into any supermarket and you will see the huge selection of pet foods available. Pet foods of every variety and price are at our disposal. From this huge selection we attempt to read labels and pick what we think our pet might like from the name and pictures on the containers. At the same time we struggle with our subconscious over media ads and watch our budget, always hoping our cat will like our selection.

We have become vulnerable to the market and the media. Are we really wise and informed shoppers when we pick a catfood to take home? With today's technology and knowledge of nutrition, one would have to spend a lot of time studying to stay current. The average pet owner has been left behind in the rush. We must rely on others for guidance. Armed, however, with some basic knowledge we can be informed and wise consumers.

Always remember that the pet food manufactures have a vested interest - they want to sell more pet food. I believe that we are seeing today the long term results of some of these products with the increase in prevalence of obesity, skin and hair problems, kidney failures, behavioral problems and cancers. This, I believe, is due to the long term feeding of processed foods containing additives and preservatives without the protection our cats received from wholesome fresh foods.

In Part One, Nutrition and Nutrients, we covered the basics of cat nutrition including digestion and absorption. Then we went over the six nutrient groups, discussing the nutrient, what it does, where it is found and what can happen if it is missing.

In Part Two we shall take a look at commercially prepared cat foods. This very young industry saw the demand and is supplying products that are selling in the billions of dollars today. We shall list the various uses and kinds of catfood on the market today and discuss the advantages and disadvantages of each, outline how to shop for these products and list guidelines on how to feed them when we get home.

As consumers purchasing these products, we must

- know what our pet requires,
- select a prepared pet food product that supplies the requirements in the adequate proportions,
- be within our budget,
- evaluate it after our pet has eaten it, and
- make adjustments when necessary.

The manufacturers of pet food have spent a great deal of time and money, some more than others, on research and development of their products. Today they are manufacturing and selling pet foods that should be supplying the necessary nutritional requirements from the various ingredients used. Some say these ingredients are really, "left-overs or table scraps" of the people food industry. It is up to us as consumers to evaluate the products and understand what we are buying. These "left-overs" or by-products may become the ingredients for the cat food we buy. Few companies use raw primary product. This costs more to purchase; therefore, the company would charge more for its final product. The less expensive cat foods that rely on by-products for their ingredients may also vary between batches just as price and availability of this type of ingredient vary. The old adage, "you get what you pay for," applies to cat food as well.

CAT FOOD: YESTERDAY, TODAY AND TOMORROW

Cats, millions of years ago, hunted for their food just like wild carnivores do today. As cats were domesticated by humans we fed them what we were eating. It was not until the late 1800's that the first commercial dog food was made. In the 1860's, an American, James Spratt, was making and selling Spratt's Dog Cake in England which was a mixture of wheat meal, beetroot, meat and vegetables.

The first dog foods were baked biscuits made from grains. Biscuits could be stored and transported easily without losing food value and, when combined with fresh meat, made adequate pet food. Later dog meal appeared, a by-product of the human breakfast industry. Many of these companies are still making both today. Dried meat was incorporated with the cereal grain meals to make a more complete dog food. Human and dog food processing evolved during this same period with the goal being convenience for the consumer.

Shortly after commercial dog food manufacturing came commercial cat foods. Again the first ones were of the canned type. This was later followed with the dry and semi-dry kinds of cat foods that we have available today.

In order for food to be prepared and kept for long periods of time, the science of food preservation had to be expanded beyond the common means of the day such as salting, drying, and freezing. Canning, developed in the mid 1800's, made canned meat available for people. It was from this industry of canning meat for human consumption that the canning of pet food developed, using the less desirable portions. During this time a Canadian veterinarian, Dr. Ballard, was canning a home made product of his own. His is a household name today.

Canning of pet food lead to sales. This was convenient. Consumers bought, so that by the 1930's nearly two hundred brands of food were available on the market for pet owners. Companies did research and feeding trials to make their products nutritious and tasty and advertised accordingly.

Today, more than eight billion dollars is spent annually on pet food in the United States, $800 million a year in Canada, and $700 million a year in Western Europe. It has been stated that the sales volume of pet food today exceeds the human ready-to-eat cereal and instant breakfast food sales combined.

The pet food industry is big business today. Walk into any supermarket and you will see a whole aisle devoted entirely to pet food. There are over 150 manufactures selling over two thousand brands, ranging from dry and canned to semi-moist pet food. Supermarkets, veterinarians, livestock feed stores and pet stores all sell pet food today.

Because this industry grew so quickly, there have been some growing pains. Regulations and standards had to be developed to catch up to the huge volumes of pet food consumed. Today concerned groups are becoming involved, from food manufacturers and pet owners to veterinarians. For example, the AAFCO (Association of American Feed Control Officials) in the United States is involved in regulating pet food manufacturing. The CVMA (Canadian Veterinary Medical Association) has developed guidelines for manufacturers, with accreditations for those that comply.

For example, the AAFCO defines a complete food "as a nutritionally adequate feed for animals other than man: by specific formula is compounded to be fed as the sole ration and is capable of maintaining life and for promoting production without any additional substance being consumed except water."

The United Kingdom Feedstuffs Regulations (1981) defines "a complete feedstuff, as a compound feedstuff which by reason of its composition is sufficient to ensure a daily ration. A daily ration is the total quantity of feedstuff expressed on a twelve per cent moisture basis, required by an animal of a given kind, age group, and level of production, in order to satisfy its average daily nutritional needs".

The complete food concept developed as pet owners were feeding prepared products as the sole daily meal. If these products were not nutritionally adequate, deficiencies soon became evident in the pets especially the young, fast growing individuals.

Because this industry has grown so quickly, there are many unanswered questions concerning the feeding of these products to our pets. For example, we don't know the long term effects of the preservatives and additives on our pets. Also what happens to these products when they are combined with products in the environment? An example would be the latest free radical concern in human medicine and nutrition. What really happens during the processing of these products to the many nutrients that we know and what about the ones we don't know?

Questions will be answered with time. In time, Government regulations will catch up to the demands of the consumers so that products will improve and more precise labeling will allow us to make better buying choices in the future.

The future for the pet food industry looks very good in that the age group of pet owners from forty-five to fifty-five years of age spend the most on pet food and this group is to increase fifty per cent by the year 2000. Also, the possibility of new markets in other countries around the world bodes well for the pet food industry well into the future.

The pet food business is big business today. We as consumers, have become dependent upon convenience. We are all in a big hurry. Time is a very valuable commodity. We have so many things to do. We don't have time to cook for our cat. " I don't even have time to cook for my family." We have made these statements ourselves or heard them from others.

From this modern situation of limited time and a market for convenience items, the pet food industry has evolved. The industry takes the " table scraps, " those products of the human food industry that we will not eat, for whatever reason, and processes, modifies and packages these by-products into marketable, convenient pet foods.

Dogs and cats historically ate of the table scraps from our tables. Today, with less meal preparation in our homes and more of us eating prepared, quick foods as well as eating out in restaurants and fast food establishments, the availability of home table scraps for our pets has dried up. Enter the pet food industry providing prepared pet foods that enable us to feed our pets without having to rely on left-overs from our table or the chore of preparing something ourselves.

For a pet food to be successful from the manufacturers standpoint, several things must be taken into consideration and these are as listed according to their importance:

- Taste
- Taste
- Cost of ingredients
- Packaging and shell life

Nope, that isn't a misprint. The first two are the most important. If our cat or dog will not eat the prepared food, then we are not going to buy any more and may take it back for refund. On the other hand, if our pet likes the food, we think it is wonderful and will purchase more because "Fluffy really likes Brand X ".

This may be misleading from a nutritional standpoint. We know, for example, that a constant diet of candy and sweets is not good for our children just as a constant diet of liver for our cat is not good. Both will like the taste but a continual diet of these to the exclusion of other foods is a recipe for disaster. So even though these are readily accepted, other foods must be eaten so that all the necessary nutrients are supplied.

Cost and the availability of a constant supply of the basic ingredients is the next big consideration. The by-products, by-product meals etc.- those "table scraps of the food industry" are the main ingredients considered. These are the primary sources of animal proteins. Proteins and fats are the most expensive ingredients both from the standpoint of original purchase but also from a processing and preserving aspect. These ingredients often have to be processed to some degree and later, especially with fats, must be preserved.

The perishability of animal proteins and fats makes them the expensive ingredients. These also are the tasty ingredients. Back to the animals in the wild - animal proteins and fats are their number one food.

Once the cat food has been prepared and processed, it has to be treated with preservatives so that the food will not spoil. This is called shelf life. Packaging is also a consideration not only for containing the food but also for protection in shipping and as a way to advertise the product within.

If a pet food manufacturer should stray away from ingredients containing large amounts of animal proteins and fats, the taste or palatability factor drops and the cat is reluctant to eat it or may totally refuse. Flavor is important. Other ingredients that the cat may like must be incorporated, even artificial flavors or flavor enhancers. These mask those ingredients such as cereals and vegetables that are less expensive to purchase, process and preserve but that the cat is not interested in eating.

Other factors than taste and cost such as the nutritional balance and the texture of final product also have to be considered.

Some factors are aimed at us the two legged buyers. The color and shape of the product (of no importance to the cat), the kind, color and pictures of the packaging are all sales promotion designed to get us to pick this particular brand off the shelf and take it home. Note the various colors of the cans, boxes and bags.

The pet food industry is not only a big business today but quite a technical and cost conscious industry. The industry has played a useful role in utilizing the by-products of the human food industry by providing many good and convenient products for our pets. These products are often quite adequate for our pet's daily needs.

There are limitations that the manufacturers must deal with, one being the necessity to sterilize the ingredients to prevent problems such as food poisoning. Another is the need to preserve the final product to allow for a reasonable shelf life.

The ideal food for our cats would be fresh killed prey everyday and since this is impossible we must work on the next best.

Some thoughts on what the pet foods of the future may be. We are going to see more information on the labels. We may see packages of cat food that we take home and mix with fresh ingredients; this will remove the need for some preservatives and additives and reduce packaging and freight costs. We may see more frozen products - these are less convenient but eliminate the need for preservatives and additives. We will see more specialized, specific cat foods, for example, a food for urban cats living in high pollution dense areas made up of antioxidants like vitamins A, E and C. We are starting to see more raw ingredients such as beef or lamb as opposed to the by-products from the meat processing industry.

KINDS OF CAT FOOD

There are basically three kinds of commercial cat food available to us today: canned, dry and soft-moist. The most popular of these are the canned cat foods. All have the same basic ingredients, usually grains, meat meal, vegetables, dairy products, vitamins and minerals.

Canned foods are sealed in tin-plated steel cans that are heated to sterilize the contents. Various ingredients are used in canned cat food but you will note that they all have a high water, protein and fat content which is the reason that canned cat foods are the most palatable of all the commercial products. Canned foods have about seventy-five per cent moisture.

Dry cat foods today are either expanded, formed into biscuits, or kibbled. The expanded forms are made by mixing the ingredients, cooking then whipping into a homogeneous mass that is then pushed through a die - a plate with holes - and expanded with steam and air into nuggets. The nuggets are then dried and packaged into air tight, usually plastic lined, paper bags or paper boxes. The biscuits and kibble, (biscuits that have been broken up) are made by mixing the ingredients into a dough. The dough is then rolled out, cut into shapes and baked just as we would make biscuits in our own kitchens. Dry foods have about twelve per cent moisture and should be used within three months of manufacturing.

Soft-moist cat foods have a higher water content which gives them the soft texture. However, because of the high moisture content, bacteria and molds will easily grow causing spoilage. To prevent this, preservatives and humectants are added. The common humectants that take up water, not allowing bacteria to use it, are propylene glycol and sorbitol. The preservatives are sugars and syrups, preventing bacterial growth and adding flavor and energy. Artificial coloring is added and the food is packaged in individual cellophane portions. Soft-moist will have from fifteen to thirty per cent moisture and a shelf life of several months.

ADVANTAGES AND DISADVANTAGES

Canned, dry and soft-moist are just different ways to prepare and preserve cat food. Each has advantages and disadvantages that we, as consumers, must evaluate for our needs.

Canned foods have a long shelf life if not opened, are usually highly palatable and are the most digestible of the three, due to more fat and more digestible meat protein. On the other hand, this is an expensive way to preserve food; however, no preservatives need to be added but once opened must be refrigerated. We also may not wish to pay for water as these foods are seventy-five per cent water or more. Since very little chewing is required, our pet's teeth may not remain nice and shiny. The high heat used in the can sterilizing process causes loss to some nutrients and often color additives are present. Of the three, canned cat foods are the most expensive and we cannot leave uneaten food out for too long as it may spoil.

Dry foods are more economical, require no refrigeration and do not spoil after the bag is opened. Because of the hard nature of these foods, the act of chewing is beneficial to the health of the teeth and jaws of our cat. However, dry foods may not have enough fat, and preservatives must be added so that the fat will not become rancid with storage. Also, dry foods may not be as palatable or as easily digested as the others again due to less tasty fat and more cereal or vegetable matter.

We must always supply drinking water because the cat will not get enough from the food alone. The bag, once opened, may become contaminated with insects or mice. Kittens, if allowed to engorge, can bloat when the dry food expands within their little stomachs. Dry foods can be left out in the bowl; thus spoilage is less of a problem.

Disadvantages of soft-moist foods are that some cats may develop digestive upsets and we may not like our pets consuming sugar and preservatives in these large amounts.

Other categories we may see when we purchase cat foods, especially dry and canned foods, are those prepared for particular situations. For example, growth rations for growing kittens, maintenance rations for adults and reducing rations for obese cats are available. There are also dietary foods formulated to be fed to cats with specific diseases, such as a low-salt diet for cats with congestive heart failure. These are called prescription diets.

How to Shop for Prepared Cat Food

As cat owners we have the sole responsibility of feeding our cat. If we don't do it right, the cat will suffer, particularly as she may not be able to roam around the neighborhood and pick up what she may be lacking. In this case our cat has become completely dependent upon us to supply all her nutritional needs. Purchasing the right cat food becomes an important decision. Almost all cat owners in North America have bought a manufactured cat food at one time. Why did we pick the brands that we did? I would suspect probably for the following reasons.

- Taste - palatability, "Our cat eats it!"
- Cost
- Our cat doesn't "smell" or have "loose" bowel movements after eating this brand,
- Media advertising, colorful packaging, conveniences.
- Advice from Breeder, Pet store clerk, Neighbor or Veterinarian.

From my experience and observations, this is how we decide which cat food to buy. Let's be wise shoppers and select the best for our pet within our budget. Buying cat food is like buying any other food or consumer item for the home. We should inform ourselves, select what we need, make the purchase and evaluate what we bought when we get home.

To make a wise selection

- Have a basic understanding of the cat's nutritional needs.
- Read the label, understanding what it says and does not say
- Buy wisely regarding cost.
- Buy and feed our cat what he or she requires.
- Once purchased, open and evaluate the package and contents.
- Test the product by feeding and observing the cat.
- Change or supplement if necessary.

With a basic understanding of nutrition, we can read labels, give table scraps, supplement with vitamins and evaluate our cats performance. A basic understanding gives us confidence that we are doing the right thing. Feline nutrition is much the same as human and other animal nutrition with the few exceptions that we have discussed in Part One of this book. Nutrition is not a difficult science; after all we have been eating for many years.

Read books on nutrition and send for information from the Cat Food companies. Seek out nutritionists and veterinarians with an interest and knowledge in feline nutrition. Ask for their advice.

Cost is a concern for all of us. Remember that the adage "we get what we pay for" applies to cat food like many other things we buy. Quality costs more. In pet food manufacturing, the most expensive part is the ingredients as compared to the packaging and processing. So, if a product appears cheaper, it is probably a good bet that the ingredients were cheaper. Pet food has traditionally been made from the "table scraps" of the people food industry commonly referred to as by-products. These products often are nutritionally adequate for the cat but because we would not eat them ourselves, for whatever reason, they are sold as pet food ingredients. Obviously ingredients that could be used as human food would cost more for the manufacturer.

Reading the Label

When making our selection we must read and understand the label. Those companies that go by the AAFCO guidelines label the foods to a particular format.

The label is a statement made by the manufacturer that contains various claims. By reading the label, we as consumers can learn a lot. We may have to read between the lines on some things, but generally the more information on the label, the more confidence we can have in the product.

The basic AAFCO (Association of American Feed Control Officials) guidelines for the information to be put on the container include

- The product name (a brand name),
- Kind of pet food - Cat Food or Dog Food,
- The net weight (the weight of the product less container),
- Guaranteed analysis, at least the
  minimum: crude fat and crude protein and
  maximum: moisture and crude fiber,
- The list of ingredients in decreasing order of amount by weight,
- A statement of nutritional capability,
- The name and address of the manufacturer or distributor.

These vary between countries. Canadian manufacturers must state the kind of food - dog or cat, the net weight and the name of the manufacturer or distributor.

Other things listed might include the feeding directions, a caloric statement, an ingredient claim (for example, no soy, or all beef), a certified stamp of standards such as the Canadian Veterinary Medical Association seal of standards, and a nutritional need like a kitten claim or specific condition (a heart or kidney diet).

An example of a dry cat food label

Claim	Is guaranteed nutritionally complete and balanced for all stages of a cat's life.
Net weight	NET WT. 10 POUNDS
Feeding instruction	An average cat will normally consume 1/2 to 1/3 of a cup per day.
Calculated Energy	5302 K cal/kg 2410 K cal/lb
Guaranteed analysis	GUARANTEED ANALYSIS: Crude Protein, not less than .... 32.0 % Crude Fat, not less than .... 21.0 % Crude Fiber, not more than .... 3.0 % Moisture, not more than .... 10.0 % Crude Ash, not more than .... 6.5 % Calcium .... 0.82 % Phosphorus .... 0.68 % Sodium .... 0.45 % Magnesium .... 0.07 % Taurine (mg/kg) 1890
Ingredients	INGREDIENTS: Poultry By-Products Meal, Chicken, Rice Flour, Ground Yellow Corn, Animal Fat preserved with BHA (Butylated Hydroxyanisole), Beet Pulp, Meat Meal, Dried Whole Egg, Brewer's Dried Yeast, Fish Meal, Dried Animal Digest, DL-Methionine, L-Lysine, Salt, Potassium Chloride, Choline Chloride, Vitamin E, Ferrous Sulfate, Ascorbic Acid, Zinc Oxide, Vitamin B12, Inositol, Niacin, Vitamin A Acetate, Calcium Pantothenate, Manganous Oxide, Riboflavin, Pyridoxine Hydrochloride, Thiamine Mononitrate, Menadione sodium Bisulfite Complex (source of Vitamin K Activity), Copper Oxide, Cobalt Carbonate and Folic Acid, D-Activated Animal Sterol (source of Vitamin D3), Ethylenediamine Dihydriodide (source of Iodine), and Biotin.
Manufacturer	Name and postal address

This is a label on which the company is telling us about its product. Everything is quite straight forward.

We are told that the manufacturer claims that this food is complete and balanced for all stages of a cat's life. In other words, the formula and ingredients therein have been tested and will sustain a cat with nothing else required.

The net weight of the contents, how much we can expect our cat to eat per day and the number of Calories per kilogram and per pound are stated. The guaranteed analysis breakdown gives the main ingredients and the minerals present. We shall discuss more on this later.

The ingredients are listed in order of amount present with the first on the list being the largest amount present, and so on in decreasing order.

The amount of information given is an indicator in evaluating the contents that the manufacturer is more confident in the quality of its product and is eager to let us know.

This label looks all well and good but is it really telling us everything that we would like to know? There are questions with more answers that could tell us a lot more.

Pet food manufacturers are generally very responsible when it comes to the formulation and labeling of their products. We may have difficulty when we try to compare, but with standardized labeling throughout the industry, this problem may be solved.

Two other goals of a pet food manufacturer are to preserve the food for as long as possible and to add as much economic value as possible to the product.

What's In A Label?

What does a label tell us and what doesn't it tell us? Let's go through the seven items listed previously and comment.

Name

The name is an important marketing concept in that it is hoped that we will first become interested in buying this particular brand and later buy some more. Some names are cute or unusual for this purpose. Other names may be used to depict a flavor such as beef or chicken, as is the case with people food like Italian. Specific names are used sometimes to address a particular nutritional purpose or disease condition, directing these products to individual cats. Examples would be Kitten, Adult, or Kidney or Heart diets. "What's in a name" is important from a marketing stand point and cat food is no exception.

Kind of pet food

The words "Cat Food" or "Dog Food" specify that one is for cats and the other for dogs because the two are different. Cat food has more fat and protein. Cats also have different protein and vitamin requirements, such as vitamin A instead of beta carotene, and cat foods have taurine added - so the formulation is not the same. Although dogs can eat cat food and do well, cats should not be given dog food.

Net Weight

The net weight number tells us the weight of the contents. This figure we can use to comparison shop. By dividing the cost with the net weight, we have a price per pound or ounce, kilogram or gram. Just because the containers may be the same size does not mean that the contents are the same. Another consideration is the moisture content; more water means less dry matter which contains the nutrients.

Guaranteed Analysis

This statement by the manufacturer lists the minimum amounts allowed for the energy nutrients of fat and protein and the maximum allowed for non energy fiber and moisture.

This does not tell us the actual amount of the ingredient or anything about the quality but is a rough guide to the composition. An illustration may help explain how these chemical contents are determined in what is called a proximate analysis.

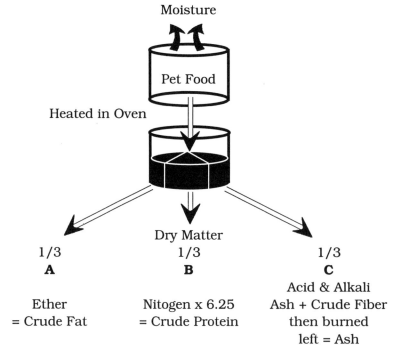

∴ Carbohydrate = 100% - (Fat + Protein + Ash + Fiber + Moisture)

The sample of pet food is placed in an oven and dried to remove the moisture. The remaining dry matter is divided into three equal parts. One is extracted with ether to determine crude fat; another undergoes a nitrogen analysis and the nitrogen content multiplied by 6.25 * to give crude protein and the third is processed in acid and alkali to give ash (mineral) and fiber.

Based on the assumptions that all nitrogen in feedstuffs is as protein and the average nitrogen content of protein is 16%.

Now by adding up protein + fat + ash + fiber + moisture and subtracting from 100 we will get the carbohydrate content.
This proximate analysis is quite accurate for the chemical content of the cat food, but it does not tell us anything about the quality of the nutrients, the digestibility or the individual vitamin, mineral or essential fatty acid content. Let's recall our discussion of protein and how protein is in many things from eggs and meat to corn and feathers. The quality of the protein is valued by its content of essential amino acids and its digestibility.

We should look for:

- canned: at least 10 - 12 % protein, 3 % fat and no more than 77 % water. Ash less than 3 %
- dry: at least 15 % fat, 30 to 35 % protein, no more than 12 % moisture and less than 8% ash.
- Semi-moist: at least 24 % protein, 8.5 % fat, no more than 35 % moisture and less than 7 % ash.

Some manufacturers are listing the minerals such as calcium and phosphorus as well as vitamins.

Ingredients

Initially, canned pet food and later dry meal were the first kinds of commercial pet food available. The canned food was made primarily with meat and meat by-products cooked with barley, wheat, corn meal and some minerals. In the mid 1950's dry petfoods were developed and the main ingredients at that time were corn, soybean meal, corn gluten meal, wheat middlings, meat and bone meal, vitamins and minerals. By the 1970's dry pet food was out selling canned. The early problem with dry food was getting the cats and dogs to eat it. One of the first enhancers for palatability was lypolized white tallow sprayed on the food.

Flavor enhancers have continued to be an important part of this business. Acceptability is important for sales. Even though the cat food is balanced and complete, the cat must eat it.

New technology led to the development of new ingredients which led to new products such as meatballs, formed meat chunks, ersatz meat chunks, soft dry foods, dual phase extruded dry and soft moist products, high protein, high meat and high fat dry cat foods. Some of the new ingredients developed that allowed the production of these products include propylene glycol, for a humectant in soft moist food, textured vegetable proteins in ersatz meat, food starch, gums and colors in gravy products, artificial flavors and colors, BHA, BHT, ethoxyquin and mold inhibitors as preservatives of fat and flours, gums and sodium and phosphorus salts for binders in meatballs. Research and development with new patents are continuing in this field.

As consumer demands influence the market place, the list of petfood ingredients will be changed, some new ones will be added and others will be dropped.

Each ingredient used in making the cat food is listed in descending order by weight with the most listed first, on to the least listed last. Only AAFCO approved ingredient names are used. This can be misleading in several ways.

- Cereal grains may be listed several different times such as ground corn, kibbled corn, flaked corn etc. which in reality is all corn and if called such might be first on the list.

- All-inclusive terms are not particularly descriptive. By-products, what does this mean? For example, poultry by-products could be everything from good quality necks, backs and wings to poor quality heads, feathers and feet.

- Cereal by-products can also vary. Instead of the whole grain, the by-products of milling such as wheat middlings, oat hulls or bran could be the ingredients.

- An ingredient may be included on the list in its dry form which is lighter than if it was weighed wet and therefore can appear further down the list, for example, wheat flour vs meat or liver.

- Pet foods may have a fixed formula list that does not change according to the changing cost or supply of an ingredient. Some may have an open formulation and the contents of the food may change from batch to batch depending on the cost and availability of ingredients. This might explain why our cat may show digestive disturbances when we feed a new bag of the same brand.

- The complete composition of the food may not be listed. Preprocessed ingredients are used and their ingredients may not be on the label. For example, antioxidants may be added to the animal fat or animal by-products before it is added to the cat food.

- Terms like natural, organic, low fat and high fiber must be uniformly defined so that we can buy accordingly.

We should look for

- canned or soft moist food: an animal source protein in the first two ingredients and at least one cereal with a source of calcium (example, bone, chicken, or fishmeal). High meat diets can easily be imbalanced for calcium and phosphorus so calcium is added.

- dry food: an animal source protein in the first three.

Animal based ingredients generally have a higher quality protein with a better balance of amino acids, vitamins and minerals than plant based ingredients.

Vitamins and minerals will be on the list near the end. There is an ongoing debate as to what is better -"natural" or synthetic forms of vitamins and minerals. Vitamins are organic chemicals as opposed to minerals that are inorganic. Simply stated, organic refers to those biochemicals present in nature and derived from living organisms, for the most part containing carbon and hydrogen in their chemical make up. Inorganic are those chemicals such as iron, copper etc. not of organic origin but found in and on the earth and its atmosphere.

Once scientists discovered the chemical make up of vitamins, they were able to duplicate the formula in the laboratory. This then is called a synthetic vitamin because it is man made instead of being made by a plant or animal. From a purely chemical standpoint the two are the same.

The ongoing debate on which is better - the natural source or the synthetic manmade - has many arguments pro and con. The natural proponents suggest that there may be other factors still not discovered by modern science that are required by the animal in some way and are not present in the synthetic. Others say that there is no difference; the formulations are the same so feeding the synthetic is just as good or perhaps better because it is pure. This debate will continue. I believe that the best way to supply vitamins is through the complete food where possible, as opposed to an additive or supplement. However, it may not always be possible for the cat to get enough from the foods, making it necessary for the addition of concentrated forms of the vitamin either from organic or synthetic origins.

We must remember that our cat is living in a different world today with many different chemicals in its environment than what its ancestral cousins had. It may require more of some vitamins than it can get just from its food. An example might be the antioxidant vitamins A, C and E which are currently being studied to determine their role in preventing diseases that may, in fact, be caused by these chemicals.

We also are processing our cat foods today which removes many of these vitamins. With the protecting nature of some vitamins and because some are removed or changed in food processing, it becomes necessary to add vitamins to our cat foods today.

Minerals play an important role in cat nutrition. Often the mineral is present in many different forms. Copper for example, is in electrical wire; however, this particular form cannot be utilized by the cat but something like copper gluconate or cupric sulfate is. This is why we will see these kinds of "big words" listed on the pet food label. These are forms of the particular mineral that can be utilized by the cat. Each form, whatever it may be, also can vary in how well the cat can use it, so continuing research and study is being done to find the best one. Interactions with other minerals and nutrients are also involved so this is becoming extensive research.

Additives also on the list are such things as flavors, flavor enhancers, colors, emulsifiers, preservatives, humectants, anti-oxidants and antimicrobials. Each additive is added for a specific purpose. The primary purpose is either to improve palatability or to maintain and extend shelf life.

These are all purported to be safe. However, again there is an ongoing debate. Several questions are being asked: what are the long term effects after many years of ingestion of these products? Are these additives removed or excreted from the cat's body or do they remain with a residue? What effects do these additives have on the absorption of nutrients and on the cat's cells, organs and behavior in the long term?

The Association of American Feed Control Officials publishes over five hundred animal feed ingredient definitions, with over two hundred of these used in petfoods.

Statement of Nutritional Capability

Statements such as nutritionally adequate, complete or balanced, state that the product when fed as the sole diet without any other food or supplement meets or is greater than the average cat's requirements. Some may be more specific, aimed at one or more of gestation, lactation, growth, maintenance or all stages of the cat's life cycle.

These claims can be made if the food passes certain feeding tests or contains the minimum amount of each nutrient as recommended by the National Research Council (NRC) and is stated as such. The NRC is a government agency that has made statements with regard to the amount of nutrients animals and people require, based on collections of research data in these areas. NRC recommendations may not tell us, however, about digestibility, absorption or utilization of the nutrients and may not indicate toxins or nutrient excesses. The best claims are those that are backed up by feeding trials on fairly large numbers of cats over an extended length of time. The AAFCO has guidelines for these feeding trials so that they are standardized within the industry. Some argue that these are not large enough or long enough.

Two exceptions to these claims are "snacks" and "treats" or that the product should be fed under supervision of a veterinarian.

Watch for these claims and understand the limitations.

Name and Address of Manufacturer or Distributor

Use this address or telephone number to request information regarding ingredients, protein and fat digestibility, vitamins, additives and feeding trials results. Also ask about the quality and consistency of the ingredients. Reputable companies are very interested in offering this information.

The label contains a lot of information with some reservations as we have discussed. In the future we will see more. Much can be learned from the label before we have purchased the product. Labels are becoming more informative, all for our cat's benefit.

You may also see on a label the CVMA, Canadian Veterinary Medical Association, seal of certification. This certification states that the company voluntarily asked to have its pet food certified to meet the standards of the CVMA program. This includes the following:

- The products are tested by the CVMA in a third party laboratory.
- Products must prove with twelve months production that they are capable of meeting a normal pet's nutritional requirements throughout all phases of life.
- Feeding trials are done to ensure that the nutrients in the products are not only present but biologically available or digestible to the animal.
- Once a product achieves certification, it is monitored to ensure that it continuously meets CVMA's high standards for composition, digestibility and palatability.
- Only those pet foods that have met the CVMA standard display the seal of certification.

(This information was obtained from *A Commonsense Guide to feeding Your Dog and Cat*) More information about this program can be obtained from The CVMA Pet Food Certification Program, 339 Booth Street, Ottawa, Ontario K1R 7K1, (613) 236-1162

In my opinion, this is a good program with some limitations. The long-term effects of the additives are not addressed and many of the popular brands sold in Canada today are not in the program. The question arises: is this primarily a marketing tool by providing a national veterinary endorsement that is benefiting our pets for their complete lifetime?

TYPES OF COMMERCIAL CAT FOOD

There are eight types of cat food manufactured and sold:

- Premium brands: veterinary clinics and pet stores
- Gourmet brands: specialty, pet and grocery stores
- Specific Purpose brands: veterinary clinics
- Popular brands: grocery stores
- Private label: grocery stores, feed stores
- Generic brands: feed stores, grocery stores
- Natural Foods: specialty, health food stores
- Treats and Snacks: pet, grocery, specialty stores

Premium brands stress quality and performance. The ingredients used are more selective and constant; therefore, these are the most expensive to buy. The formulation is fixed. Because of better digestibility and nutrient density, less is required per feeding.

Premium brands are also offered for certain life stages such as Growth, Active, Inactive, Lactation or Reducing. Because of this variation in products offered, premium brands are sold through veterinary clinics or pet stores where some direction can be given to the buyers. Generally these brands are not advertised as extensively as the Gourmet and Popular brands.

Approximately twenty per cent of the US pet food dollars are spent on Premium brands. There are no standards on premium brands *per se* when it comes to defining some of the ingredients. For example, what does "chuck steak" or "filet mignon" mean on a label?

Gourmet brands place much emphasis on packaging, consumer eye appeal and media advertising. Designer containers and colorfully labeled, pop-top cans are the norm. The contents are geared to enhance palatability using better quality meats, for example, chicken necks and backs vs poultry by-products such as offals.

Seasoned gravy makes for human eye appeal ("looks good enough to eat") stressing taste, smell and texture. The companies say that these products are more palatable, more digestible, that less is fed and they are more nutritious.

Things to be aware of: if the food is more palatable, the cat will eat more which may lead to obesity if not controlled. More palatable may not necessarily be "more" nutritious - once the nutritional aspects are met for that day, what is more nutritious? The cost per serving or per day to feed our cat to fulfill her nutritional requirements and to maintain an ideal body condition may not be less. We have to compare with other types of cat food in home evaluations to get a cost comparison. These brands are heavily advertised with costly ads. This cost must be recouped through the price of the products sold.

Specific Purpose Brands are primarily prescription type diets. The food is formulated for individual cats with a specific need for or the reduction or increase of a particular nutrient or nutrients. Examples include

- restricted protein for kidney disease and failure
- bland, low fiber for gastro-intestinal upsets
- low calorie, high fiber for obesity and reducing
- low salt for congestive heart failure
- low mineral, restricted protein for bladder stones
- high protein, high energy for growth and convalescing

Some foods may be medicated, for example, with wormer or an oral contraceptive for females. The list can go on and on as consumer demands are met for these types of diets. These are sold only through veterinary clinics under veterinary supervision.

Popular brands are the cat foods that will be advertised in the popular media and sold primarily in grocery stores. They are less expensive and readily available.

The formulations may vary in that a list of possible ingredients that could be used is printed on the label. Variable formulas allow the manufacturer to use those ingredients that come available at the time of manufacture. Popular brands are formulated and targeted at the maintenance level of nutritional requirement. With these popular brands, costs of ingredients, packaging and advertising play a large role in their manufacturing and sale as opposed to optimal nutrition.

Private Label cat foods are manufactured by another company. The particular cat food was made and packaged for another company who will sell it. The label will state this. The manufacturer's name may not be present, only the name of the distributor. Here the prime concern is cost. If a manufacturer can purchase cheap ingredients and make up a cat food for less than its competitors, it will get the tender to package for that distributor. These products are less expensive than the popular brands; however, quality can vary greatly and may not be as palatable or as nutritious.

The Generic type of cat foods are those that are usually produced and marketed locally. They are the cheapest. Private label and generic cat foods are usually manufactured by the same company. They may have a local brand name or "no-name". These products are made with the least expensive ingredients available at the time and may or may not have considered the nutritional aspects other than to have the minimum allowed. The big selling feature here is cost. As we have said before, "we get what we pay for". Poor quality foods fed over any length of time may be harmful and make supplementing necessary. Our cat will tell us.

We may see Natural or Homemade brands in some specialty, pet, health food stores or advertised in magazines. These can be flashfrozen, uncooked or semi-prepared cat foods. They may either be complete and balanced or just ingredients that have to be prepared at home.

If additives are added to the natural brand, the claim is that they are only those that are "natural". An example would be the antioxidant vitamins E and C that are used to preserve the fat instead of a product such as ethoxyquin, a manufactured chemical preservative.

The advantage of this kind of cat food is primarily the absence of manufactured chemical additives and the possibility of loss or alteration of nutrients due to processing.

The disadvantage is a higher cost and a shorter shelf life. The term 'natural' also may be misleading. It should be defined so that we all understand what it means. Natural may mean one thing to some of us and another to others. Balancing the nutrients may have to be done by us and feeding this kind of a cat food may also be less convenient.

Treats and Snacks are basically that. They are not meant to be complete and balanced but rather a tasty food that is highly palatable. These must be fed as such, only occasionally, and not as the sole source of the cat's diet, because they do not contain all the required nutrients.

The various types of cat foods all have their place. They all have their advantages and disadvantages. As an informed and knowledgeable consumer having the best interests of our cat as well as our pocket book in mind, we have to buy what our cat requires and does well on. We also must rely on the reputation of the manufacturer.

Armed with some basic knowledge, this is not that difficult. The bottom line is how well our cat does with regard to the things we have discussed, not only in the short term but also in the many years that our cat is to be with us.

Our cat will tells us which is the best.

HOME EVALUATION

> *"Always keep in mind that often it is only after months (or years) of nutritional deprivation that signs of disease may appear and that the effects of inadequate nutrition can usually never be reversed."*
>
> Terri McGinnis, D.V.M.

Now that we have bought the cat food we start to evaluate it.

Cost

A simple calculation can be done to find out what it costs to feed our cat everyday. When we get home, we should write down the date and price of the cat food. Then we feed the cat food as we always would until it is all gone and note the date. Next we add up how many days our cat took to eat it and divide the number of days into the price we paid. This is the cost of the cat food per day. If we would like to calculate home recipes costs, we can keep track of the ingredients and their prices. We can add this to the price we paid for the commercial cat food before we divide it by the number of days.

Now we have an idea of how much money we are spending per day to feed our cat. We may find that keeping our cat in good condition can be done quite reasonably with good quality commercial cat food. We may not have to feed as much per day as compared to a cheaper lower quality brand.

$$\frac{\text{cost of the cat food}}{\text{days of feeding in bag, box or can}} = \text{cost per day}$$

The amount fed per day becomes the critical factor. Another calculation you may want to try, is to calculate the cost per day of calories fed. Some labels may have the number of calories per cup; then we can calculate the cost from this approach. Either way these are useful exercises in our decisions for purchase. Calories are energy. The most expensive ingredients are proteins and fats.

Containers and Contents

Before we open the bag, can or box, we should look at the container more closely and beware of tears, stains (fat stains from inside) or dents in cans. We might, if we have a fairly accurate scale, weigh the bag or can. Remember, the net weight is the weight of the contents less the container.

If we suspect something is amiss either with the proclaimed weight or contents, we can ask the provincial, federal or state consumers affairs people to have a look at the product. Cat foods are under their jurisdiction. So, if we doubt that the product meets the label statements for ingredients, nutritional claims, moisture content or weight, it is our duty to bring this to the attention of the company and the governing authorities.

Many manufacturers list a toll-free number and a code on the container which identifies where and when it was packaged. If calling, be prepared to quote this code and keep some of the contents in case they or the Government people would like to examine them.

Now we open the bag. Examine the layers of the bag, a multi-layered bag of paper and plastic is preferable to wax paper. The layers are to keep moisture and aroma in, prolonging freshness. The multi-layers add strength to the bag for shipping as well as keeping out insects and mice.

Smell the contents of the bag and evaluate the consistency. We might want to try a little test of our own. Take some of the food and heat it in a sauce pan with a little water. If the smell is offensive or off, maybe another brand should be considered next time. Beware of foreign materials or "moving creatures", all signs of poor quality. Mold also can develop giving the food a musty smell and maybe a white or black dusty coating to the food. Few crumbs should remain once the bag is empty.

With canned food, check for sour, rancid or off odors, but don't be concerned with the dark hole, the result of the air pocket created during canning. Cut through the food and spread it out on a plate so we can observe the contents. Try to identify the contents. Look for undesirable contents such as hair, feathers, sharp pieces of bone, or anything that doesn't look like grain or identifiable muscle, tendon or desirable animal by-products.

When buying soft-moist foods, check the package. Any tears or breaks in the wrapping can dry out and contaminate the food. Again beware of unusual odors or colors. This type of food should be spongy but not feel wet. If we have any doubt, return the product to where we purchased it for a refund.

These are all things that we can do before we give the food to our cat. If something is not right, we should return the cat food. There is a caution that we have for commercial products. They often are processed some time before and one doesn't know what may have happened during shipping and storage. If the package, be it either bag, box, or can, is damaged in any way, beware, as the contents can be altered and serious problems may arise if the food is eaten.

An example of contamination of canned food is botulism. This is a deadly bacterial toxin that can be produced in air tight cans of food. Dented cans may be a warning of this contamination. When we are buying cat food, take time to examine the package or can for tears and dents. Stay away from bargain discounts on old or damaged commercial cat food.

If we are satisfied with our visual inspection, it is time for the ultimate test. Feed our cat. This is the only way to test palatability, protein, fat, vitamin, mineral and fiber content.

Some companies perform feed trials with their products and we can obtain this information by contacting them. However, these trials may be done only on a few cats in a controlled environment. The best is to try it on our cat at home in his or her own environment.

The Home Feeding Trial

When evaluating a particular cat food, feed only this product. Do not give anything else such as vitamin/mineral supplements or table scraps during the test as these could alter the evaluation.

To perform this evaluation we should concentrate on three areas:

- The appearance and condition of the cat,
- The cat's behavior, and
- The stool.

The eyes and skin are two nutritionally sensitive organs that will show signs early when deficiencies arise. So, if our cat has dull, cloudy or tearing eyes or a poor hair coat over an extended period of time, perhaps the diet is the cause.

Appearance and condition of the Cat

Good	SIGNS &	Bad
	eyes	
bright, alert, clear		dull, cloudy, tearing, red
	nose	
cool, moist, clean, soft		hot, dry, hard
	teeth	
clean, white, shiny,		dirty, yellow, foul smelling
	ears	
clean, dry,		inflamed, waxy, foul smelling
	hair	
shiny, soft, clean		dull, dry, dandruff, hair loss
	skin	
soft, pliable,		dry, greasy, inflamed, itchy
	muscle	
firm, developed, defined		soft, lacking
	body condition	
ribby (feel ribs)		obese, pot-bellied, waddling walk
	paws	
smooth, resilient		cracked, sore, nails brittle
	anus	
clean, dry		inflamed, itchy anal glands
	urine	
light yellow, average volume		dark or clear, large amount

Behavior

A healthy, properly fed cat, receiving all the requirements of energy, protein, fat, vitamins, minerals and water will be happy, active and responsive. If we observe any change, we should be concerned. If the cat is irritable, dull, hyperactive, nervous or restless, the cause may be the diet. Also, an increase in the consumption of water, with frequent urinations may be diet related. Any changes in behavior after we start a new diet should be noted. Usually behavioral changes will take several weeks to appear after the cat has been on the new food.

Stools

The cat's stools are also a good indicator of the quality of the diet. Most cats will have from one to two bowel movements a day. More than this may indicate a poor quality diet. A good quality diet and a properly functioning digestive system will yield a small amount of formed, brown firm stools. The small amount tells us that the food has been digested and there is little waste. The smell will be normal.

Colour can also indicate certain foods eaten (liver will be dark, bone meal will be light) and the presence of food dyes. Medical conditions such as internal bleeding or other disease problems can alter the colour of the stools, (see Liver Problems page 264) and the cat should have veterinary medical attention.

Stool quality and quantity can tell us a lot about the food and the cat's reaction to it. The fiber level and digestibility of the food as well as the cat's water intake and general health can be assessed from the stool.

Water intake: If not enough water is consumed, the stools will be dry, hard and may be difficult to pass.

Fiber level: Fiber determines the bulk of the stools. Because it is not digested, a lot of feces would indicate a lot of fiber or poor quality ingredients in the diet. Fiber is an important constituent of the cat's diet. In the wild the cat would obtain fiber from hair or feathers from the various prey that she had captured. Today the manufacturers of cat foods utilize the indigestible cellulose parts of grains for fiber.

Digestibility: High quality animal-source protein, properly processed fat and carbohydrate are efficiently digested in the small intestine. The nutrients are then absorbed, leaving a small percentage of waste. Poor quality food results in undigested material passing into the large intestine where fermentation from bacteria produces gas and loose watery stools. This becomes evident with flatulence and diarrhea. See pages 272 and 268.

Health: If the cat's intestines are infected or infested with worms, the stools will be abnormal. Liver or pancreas problems will also decrease digestion and stools will not be normal.

If something is wrong with the cat's digestive system or the diet is of poor quality or contaminated, the stools may be soft, loose, watery, light-colored or black and smelly. If this continues, the cat should be examined by your veterinarian to insure that the problem is not medical. Try to remember if the cat ate anything unusual or if something changed in his or her environment. Cats, like people, can have food intolerances and allergies to certain foods, food additives or things in their surroundings. See page 273.

From these three basic parameters: body appearance and condition, overall behavior and the stool quality and quantity, we can make a fairly accurate assessment of our cat's health and diet. Any obvious or slight change in any of these three areas should be a concern.

Some dietary deficiencies such as a lack of a vitamin or mineral may take a long time before the outward signs become obvious.

We should continue the evaluation for at least three weeks or more. During this test period we make note of anything abnormal. Itching, an offensive body odor or increased hair loss may be some of the first signs we see. Weight loss combined with an increase in appetite with the same volume fed as before may indicate a poorer quality cat food. If we are feeding the same amount but the cat appears hungry and is losing condition, this may be the result of a food manufactured with poor quality ingredients with fewer digestible nutrients.

If the cat is gaining weight and is in good condition, we may find that we can decrease the amount given per day. This indicates the food is of high quality. Because less is required, the cost per day may be the same or less than the other food even though the cost per bag was more. It is important to calculate the cost per day because this gives us a more accurate indication. In other words if the bag costs us more but lasts longer, the cost per day may be less.

After several weeks of the test, it may become evident that this food requires supplementation. Table scraps with added fat or vitamin and mineral supplements may be required. Fresh food recipes might be something to consider.

Storage

Once a container of cat food has been opened, the contents are exposed to the environment. Canned food, once opened, must be covered and refrigerated to prevent spoilage. Soft-moist is packaged in daily amounts; however, the rest should be kept dry and free from rodents and insects. Dry cat food is best stored cool in a rodent proof, dry, and sealed container. Metal or plastic containers work well.

GUIDELINES FOR FEEDING

"It is impossible to advise exact amounts of food to be given because this is influenced by several factors. Exercise, temperament, breed of cat, climate, all affect the appetite of adult cats as well as kittens."

Juliette de Bairacli Levy
The Complete Herbal Handbook for the Dog and Cat

What Should We Feed Our Cat?

Our cat will tell us the answer. As owners we must feed our cat enough of the required nutrients for the particular stage in life. The right cat food is the one that keeps our cat healthy, happy and in good body condition at a reasonable cost per feeding.

The number one rule is variety. If we start by offering our kittens a variety of food types, brands and flavors, the possibility of them getting all the required nutrients is increased and the chance that they will develop bad eating habits is decreased.

Cats, by their nature, are careful eaters, picking and choosing what they eat. We may say they are finicky but perhaps they are just being careful. They are also creatures of habit so we should develop good habits early by offering variety and not giving in to just one brand or one particular food to the exclusion of others.

All the commercial cat foods on the market today, with few exceptions, can feed our cat to the maintenance level, some for a short time, some for a long time. The maintenance level refers to the number of calories and other nutrients needed to maintain the body weight of a healthy adult cat at rest in a stress-free and comfortable environment. This would apply to most of our average house cats.

Once our cat moves from this type of situation, nutrient requirements change. A growing kitten, a pregnant mother or a sick convalescing individual will require much more.

These individuals we shall discuss later in Part Four. Some commercial cat food manufacturers have made some of their products specifically for such individuals.

Classifications of Cat Food Available

- Maintenance: adult, constant weight, reasonably active
- Kitten: growing, active
- Reproduction and Lactation: mother and nursing
- Less Active: overweight, older, contained
- Special: ill, chronic disease condition

These cat foods are formulated to provide our cats with foods that are more specific to their age or life style.

The average house cat is not too active, growing or living in a harsh environment. Most are free of much stress. This cat will do well on the maintenance diet. If our cat should fit into any of the other classifications, such as a kitten or an over weight, less active individual, then we should look at the appropriate food for that cat.

We said before and must repeat again that all cats are individuals. The variation among cats is great. Cats come in many shapes and sizes and all temperaments. Foods are manufactured and recommended for an average cat. We must feed according to the cat's responses and change if necessary.

Our cat will tell us. She should be content and healthy including all the signs we have discussed but most important she should stay in good body condition, not too fat and not too thin. This again will not only depend upon which food we feed but how much.

How Should We Feed?

Always have clean fresh water available at all times. Feed and water in a quiet place where the cat will not be disturbed. Remember that cats are solitary hunters and feeders - loners that like to eat alone where it is safe and without competition so if we have more than one cat we should set out separate bowls some distance from each other. If a dog is present the cats' dishes should be up or somewhere not accessible to the dog.

The best bowls for water and food are small, shallow and easy to clean. Use non-toxic and non-corrosive materials for the bowls and rinse well after washing with soap or other cleaners. Cats can be very aware of such things that may turn them off.

Use a measuring cup, glass or can to dish out dry food so we can keep track of how much we feed. Warm refrigerated or cold food to body temperature if the cat's appetite is off. If she is fussy, take her food away and try later. Be aware that the cat may be ill. Feed at regular times and avoid snacks. Train the cat; don't allow the cat to train you.

Do not feed before exercise or car or air travel as these can be upsetting. Allow several hours before exercise or travel are planned. Remember, a cat in the wild would lie down and sleep after a vigorous hunt and feast.

How Often Do We Feed?

We can leave food out continuously (free choice), or we can have a scheduled, restricted method of feeding. Each has its advantages and disadvantages, and each will depend upon our cat and our home situation.

Free choice: With free choice (or ad lib), the cat's bowl is filled with food, more than can be consumed in a day and is available at all times. The cat can eat whenever it wants. This is nice in that it takes less work and knowledge on our part.

Dry food is used with this method as canned food would spoil. Having food always available allows the cat to nibble throughout the day which is more natural. Cats, unlike dogs - which may be on a gorge and starve pattern - have smaller stomachs as their hunting patterns are for small rodents and birds.

Some cats may eat too much, however, with this method and obesity can result. Dry cat food has three to four times the calories per bowl of canned food which is over three quarters water. Most cats will self-regulate themselves and maintain a healthy body condition. However, those that put on weight with this method will have to be limited or fed on a schedule.

With free choice feeding, we tend to be less observant and several days may go by with the cat not eating before we realize that the cat has been off her feed. If this was due to illness or diet problems, we may have lost valuable time.

Should we decide to use the free choice method as it may suit our personal situation, in that we may not be home at regular times, there are a few guidelines to follow. When starting, we should feed the calculated amount on the package for one day. When this has been eaten, fill the bowl again. Always have food in the bowl and do not take it away after this. This initial procedure helps to prevent engorgement. Most cats will stop when their appetite is filled.

Some cats just may eat too much and gain weight with food available at all times so will have to be limited. We may purchase cat foods higher in fiber content that will fill the cat with more bulk, thereby reducing the number of calories eaten.

Kittens, mothers and sick cats are best fed on a free choice program which we shall discuss later in their specific section.

Cats, by their nature, eat small amounts often and usually in the evening and early morning - they hunted then when the desert was cool and the natural prey were active. Feeding our domestic cat at these times or having food available all the time then duplicates their old ancestral ways. Eating small meals allows the cat's body to metabolize nutrients at a steady rate.

Scheduled feeding: Here we restrict the amount of food or the time the food is left out. This takes more effort on our part. We have to be there to feed or have someone do it for us. We also have to be more knowledgeable because we are making the decision on how much our cat will eat and when. Having this control, however, we can make our observation with regards to health, appetite, condition and attitude and make changes when necessary.

For an adult cat on the maintenance level, twice a day feeding is believed to be best. Feeding morning and evening gives the cat a shorter time between meals which would not load her digestive system all at once and also limits begging and whining between meals. The anticipation of regular feeding times stimulates her appetite so that she cleans up her bowl.

We can also limit the time that we allow the food to be present. Ten minutes is enough time for a normal adult cat to clean up her daily portion. This is especially important for canned food in that once the can is opened, spoilage can occur due to bacterial or mold contamination. The uneaten portion should be covered - to prevent drying out - and refrigerated.

Expectant cats, nursing mothers and growing kittens should be fed free choice or at least three or more times a day for queens and up to six times for young kittens. These individuals require more nutrients, especially energy, and do not have the stomach capacity to hold enough food at one time to last them very long. By feeding them more often, their greater requirements are met without overloading their systems. More on this later.

These are some guidelines on how often we should feed. Each cat is different and we all have different personal situations. Pick a method that will suit the cat for her requirements and our own time constraints. Train the cat by feeding her to her natural instincts.

This can't happen if we give treats or snacks between meals and soon the cat learns that begging and whining pays off as she has trained us to feed her when she asks. She now loses her appetite at meal time and we wonder why. Worse, this may lead to imbalances in nutrients, as most treats and snacks are incomplete which can result in deficiencies and obesity.

Remember, a healthy cat can fast for a week or more without food but must have water. Fasting or going without food for long periods of time was a natural occurrence in the wild before man came along. If our cat should refuse to eat what we think is an appropriate diet with nothing else offered for two or three days, perhaps a visit to the veterinarian is in order in case something medically is wrong.

Cats in the wild have a regular eating schedule which is primarily at night when it is cooler and the prey are in turn active. They can go long intervals without eating but generally they hunt to eat several times during a twenty-four hour period.

We can get our cat accustomed to regular eating habits and amounts which she will appreciate and respond to.

How Much Do We Feed?

More important - How much will our cat eat? Sit back and take a good look at your cat. See how big he or she is and now imagine that we have X-ray eyes and can see the abdominal contents of our cat. The part of our cat roughly from behind her shoulder blades to her hips and below her backbone contains all her internal organs. Image in this space all the organs including her heart, lungs, liver, stomach, intestines and kidneys plus a few others.

Now try to picture how large her stomach is. It is the small pouch that first receives food that is swallowed. We all know how big a mouse is. One mouse will almost fill the average cat's stomach. Her stomach will hold about a small handful of dry cat food, a small can of canned cat food.

Remember that the part we all may refer to as the cat's stomach is really her whole abdominal cavity which contains all the other organs and intestines and her actual stomach is only a small part of all this.

The food in the stomach is constantly being digested and passed through to the rest of the digestive system, namely the intestines. Either the mouse or bird or prepared cat food will start to move on into the intestines.

The point I want to make is that the cat's stomach is really quite small - a couple of heaping tablespoons of food will fill it. In time - from a half hour to several hours, depending upon the type of food eaten, the stomach will be empty.

Anyone who has a cat has observed this difference when compared to a dog. Some dogs seem to have a huge capacity to eat or engorge a great amount of food and in a very short time.

The cat eats small amounts often. The cat likes its food "fresh-killed" as opposed to aged, which the dog seems to enjoy, so small amounts of freshly opened or new to the bowl is what most cats prefer. This is something that has been natural for them for many generations. This may explain their careful examination of anything they decide to eat.

The ideal amount of food to give our cat is that amount that will keep her in good muscular condition with a thin layer of fat over her ribs.

The correct amount will be that amount that maintains

- body weight at the desired level
- body condition: fat cover, muscle tone and hair coat
- activity level: energy to live and play

It is better, from the health standpoint of our cat, to underfeed rather than overfeed. To use calculations and rules of thumb on the amounts to feed can take away from the prime indicator and that is our cat. How is he or she faring with this cat food and at this amount? The cat tells us how much we should give her.

Try not to fall into the idea that our cat's bowl should be filled with as much food as we would eat. Our cat is around one-twentieth our size and maybe a tenth as active. The amount in the bowl must reflect this size and activity level difference.

Start out by feeding the stated directions on the container for one day. Give one half of this in the morning and the other half in the evening. Then watch the cat and after a week make an assessment.

To summarize what we have covered, our cat should be on the hungry side. She should eat everything in about five minutes. We should be able to feel her ribs and hip bones with a light covering of fat on them. When we stand above and look down on our cat, her ribs should be wider than the abdominal area. Her skin should be loose and her hair glossy and thick. She should be active and her temperament happy and inquisitive.

In order to have such a cat

- we have done our homework with regard to purchasing and offering nutritious food
- the amount given is just enough to maintain condition and activity level
- we include between meal snacks in the whole picture, (give that much less in the evening if giving snacks)
- we don't give in to fussy eaters

The amount we feed our cat depends upon

- his or her individual requirements, and
- the nutrient value of the cat food.

Cats eat to satisfy their need for energy.

From the direction on the container we can calculate the amount of cat food that we should give per day. Use the maintenance level that the company suggests for our cat. This is the best place to start; later on we may have to make changes.

The correct amount will be that which is necessary to maintain

- desired body weight,
- desired body condition, and
- desired activity level.

EXCERCISE

> Activity and exercise gives our cat
> greater flexibility, strength,
> stamina and vitality;
> her body systems all work better
> and
> she is happier with better spirit.

All breeds and ages of cats benefit from exercise, both physical and mental. This is not a nutritional topic but is such an important part of the health and well being of our cats that some points must be mentioned.

Let's begin with a few words about mental or brain activities. Our cats need mind stimulation just as we do; hide and seek games, playing and jumping activities that they would perform if hunting, keep them fit and healthy.

Physical and mental activity has been part of the cat's survival since the beginning of time. As a hunter she had to think and move faster and quicker than her prey if she was to eat. Domestication brought a greater dependence upon us for her food, such that she may not have to use her head or body very much. This lack of exercise slows down all her body systems and shortens her life. We have seen with ourselves how modern means of transportation and work saving devices have affected our bodies. Our cats today are no different.

Exercise retains muscle tone, maintains strong bones and keeps the joints flexible. Physical activity maintains a strong cardiovascular system which in turn supplies all the other systems with oxygen and nutrients.

Exercise builds stamina and endurance and also keeps an old cat younger. If the cat's body is in tone and all systems are active, illness and disease can be prevented. Time for convalescing is shortened.

Excellent medicine for behavior problems is exercise. A tired cat is not bored. Instead she is happy and less likely to take out her frustrations on the curtains or furniture.

Scratching posts, catnip toys, retrieving and a light spot from a flashlight in a dark room all can offer exercise for a shut-in cat. Walks with a body harness - as opposed to a neck collar and leash - work well.

I don't believe that there is any argument against the benefits of some sort of physical activity for the maintenance of health and well being.

A few precautions are in order. Start out slowly, build up endurance and don't over do it. Assume our cat is in good health and if in doubt ask our veterinarian. Early morning or later in the evening are good times for exercise.

Any type of activity will be beneficial. The exercise should be done on a regular basis and geared to the type, condition and age of the cat. Cats that are overweight and in poor condition should be started slowly in combination with a diet program.

Exercising on an empty stomach is best. Do not worry about her immediate energy requirements during exercise as this will be delivered from her glucose and glycogen store. Her blood, muscle and liver are all ready to supply the energy and any undigested food in her stomach would just cause her trouble.

Allow some time after vigorous activity before feeding.

Basic common sense and discretion should be used when we ask our cats to do physical activities; however, some sort of exercise is beneficial, healthy and normal.

SUMMARY

When we purchase commercial cat foods, it would be reasonable to conclude that we are buying based on cost and palatability. If the price is reasonable and our cat likes it, we buy it. Barring any obvious problem such as loose stools or other major upset, we are happy. From a nutritional standpoint, we now know that this is not enough. When we were children candy tasted good, but we wouldn't have done very well if that was all we ate. Cats must have a balanced diet containing all the required nutrients in forms that are acceptable.

All cat foods are not the same. Just like many other things that we buy, there is a big difference between brands. We also must not fall into the trap (that advertising promotes) that more is better. We may be led to believe that more protein or more fiber, for example, is best. Our cat tells us what is best. We must observe the signs.

Manufactured cat food is a mixture of food and other ingredients combined to provide the cat with all her needs. By using the NRC recommendations for the amounts of each nutrient, manufacturers formulate a recipe of ingredients, then add preservatives, antioxidants and flavors or flavor enhancers. Depending on ingredient sources and costs, including processing and packaging, the final product is made and priced accordingly. If the ingredients are all present in the minimum amounts and in the correct proportion, the product is sold as complete and balanced.

Oftentimes the manufacturers will put in more than the minimum amounts of nutrients to be on the safe side. Ingredients vary in their nutrient content. The volume of food a cat can eat in a day is important in the selection of the ingredients. All of the required nutrients must be present in the daily portion for the diet to be complete and balanced.

We must be confident in the product. By reading the label and examining the food, we go ahead and feed according to the directions. Since every cat is an individual with varying needs, we continue to observe and make changes, if necessary, either to the amount, the brand or we may supplement with other foods.

Possible Problems with Commercial Cat Foods

- convenience leads to overfeeding and obesity
- lack of nutrients can lead to poor growth and health
- continual use of one brand can lead to deficiencies
- cost is a prime concern not quality of nutrient
- inadequate or incomplete knowledge of feline nutrition on the part of the manufacturer
- NRC minimum may not be adequate for all cats
- uniform standards are quite basic
- amounts of vitamins or minerals may not be listed
- nutritional claims are not backed up with feeding trails
- manufacturers do not perform adequate feed trials
- processing and storage leads to losses of nutrients
- the food may be manufactured for the average cat
- long term effects of additives may not be fully known
- do they have a "use before" date like people food?
- ingredients may or may not be "Government Inspected"
- actual ingredients are not listed so we really do not know what we are buying.
- by-product labeling is all encompassing covering a large range of possible ingredients
- uniformity suffers between batches, ingredients may change
- there are no standards for moisture content
- fats must be processed or treated for storage and shipping
- ingredients may have been contaminated before or after processing.
- the amount suggested to feed is only a guideline.
- quality control is up to each individual manufacturer
- there may be errors in feed formulations
- the prime purpose is to sell more cat food.

PART THREE Getting Started

Our own Thing

we can do "our own thing"
with a little knowledge
    a little extra planning
    a little preparation
we can present our pets with meals that are
    cheaper
free of additives and preservatives
    as fresh
    as nutritious
    as tasty
and with as much variety
    as the foods we serve our family.

"Every single cat carries with it an ancient inheritance of amazing sensory capacities, wonderful vocal utterances and body language, skillful hunting actions, elaborate territorial and status displays, strangely complex sexual behavior and devoted parental care. It is an animal full of surprises."

Desmond Morris

Part Three will look more like the "cookbooks" that we are familiar with. Ingredients are listed that we can use in recipes for our cats. The ingredients are all familiar. The format, measuring and equipment are the same as we would find in a cookbook for us.

Before we go any further, we must outline the basic feline differences as they apply to the ingredients and recipes we use.

BASIC FELINE DIFFERENCES

The first thing we must realize about our cat is her size. She is much smaller than we are. Her stomach is small. When empty her stomach is the size of a fifty cent piece. When full, a mouse will fill it. In other words, two to three heaping tablespoons of food will fill her stomach. These are facts we must consider.

Other than size, when preparing recipes for our cat we have to consider the other basic differences between us. For us colour and appearance of food are important. Colour and appearance are not important to our cat; smell and texture are. We enjoy the aromas of food cooking but not nearly as much as a cat with her very sensitive nose.

The sense of smell is very acute in the cat. Scientists have concluded the cat has such a keen sense of smell because she has a larger area in her nose with more olfactory cells for this purpose. These are the specialized cells that smell.

The cat also has a very well developed organ for smell called the vomero-nasal or Jacobson's organ located on the roof of her mouth. This organ is a very important taste-smell organ. It is important not only for smelling and identifying food, but is also used to identify territories. We may have seen our cat with her mouth partly open, her tongue wagging and a look of concentration in her eyes. What she is probably doing is using this organ to help her identify some smell or taste.

For the cat as hunter, the sense of smell is a very valuable asset to her survival. This acute sense is not only used to smell and identify food but also to recognize friends or enemies. Smell is also important in mating and identifying young.

Scientists also tell us that the sense of smell is used by the cat to identify foods she eats based on experiences from the past. Smells and experiences, rather than taste, are important because the number of taste buds present in the cat is quite low.

Taste is believed to be of less importance because there is such a small number of taste buds in the cat's mouth compared to the number of olfactory or smell cells. Let's look at other species and their total number of taste buds: human 9,000 cells, kitten 475, dog 1,700, pig and goat 15,000, chicken 24 ... (taken from Dukes' Physiology of Domestic Animals).

Taste buds are on the tip, sides and toward the back of the tongue. The middle of the tongue is covered with sharp rasp-like projections that are used for licking off bones and grooming. Kittens also have these projections along the outside edges which help them coil their tongue around their mother's nipple when nursing.

We are able to differentiate sweet, sour, bitter and salty. From observations of cats, they appear to be able to taste sour best, than bitter, salt and last is their ability to taste sweet. Rather than the specific tastes, we observe the cat's responses to various foods. We classify them as pleasant, unpleasant and indifferent. Anyone who has a cat has seen these and know they can vary.

Why will our cat refuse to eat one day and not the next? Perhaps she is ill, in heat or full. Remember our cat is not very big and her stomach is quite small and a mouse size portion of food can fill her up. Sometimes hot humid weather, a noisy place or some other disturbance in her environment can turn her off.

Cats use their noses and smell to identify their food. If the nose should be plugged, for example, her appetite will be poor. Cleaning the nose can help.

Cats are creatures of habit and can, if allowed, develop a strong preference for one food only. They love the organ meats such as liver or kidney and if we should continually offer these, because they like it and turn their noses up at other foods, the habit could become detrimental. While these foods provide many nutrients, a continual diet would hurt as some nutrients are lacking.

Each species of animal has a taste for those foods that are suitable for it. The cat, being a carnivore, has tastes developed for the prey that it has hunted for millions of years. Taste can also vary between individuals depending on past experiences.

If the cat, as a carnivore, can smell very well, not taste too well and sweet, sour and salt are not important, we should feed accordingly. Her carnivous diet for millions of years was flesh, fat, bones, stomach and intestinal contents combined with hair and feathers. This then is what we should duplicate.

The cat also is a solitary hunter. Other hunters, such as wild dogs, are pack hunters that depend on each other to work together. Because cats do not hunt together, socializing and being friendly with other cats, or people is not important. This helps explain their independent nature, not coming when called or not being as friendly to everyone the way our dog is.

Fat is tasty for the cat, as it is for us, because many flavours are fat soluble or have fat type molecules. Sugar is not important to the cat but some cats, as we know, can develop a taste if trained.

Salt is of less importance to the diet of the cat in that she does not perspire or sweat, like we do, to remove heat. When we perspire to keep cool, we lose salt. Cats do perspire some through the pads of their feet. Since the cat can conserve salt better than we can, especially when the weather is warm, salt is not an important ingredient. Cats, we know, tend to sleep and are quite inactive during the hottest part of the day and become active during the cooler evenings and mornings, part of their ancestral desert nature, thereby conserving water and salt. In the wild, the cat gets her salt requirements from her flesh diet. Many of our foods today have salt in them so the addition of salt to a cat diet is unnecessary.

Spices and pepper are of no use in a cat's dish and if anything may be harmful to the lining of her stomach and intestine. Spicy left-overs should be avoided in a cat's menu.

The bones that the wild cats consume provide them with calcium and phosphorus minerals and the hair and feathers supply the fibre or roughage. The hair and feathers also, plus their own hair that they may have consumed during grooming, protect their insides from fragments of bones. These sharp pieces could do damage if it weren't for the protection that this material provides. By forming a ball around a bone fragment, the lining of the stomach and intestines are protected.

Because we don't feed bones, hair and feathers to our modern cat, we have to replace what they would miss. The minerals we have to replace with bonemeal, for example, and the roughage we can make up with fiber foods such as cereals and grains.

Cats like their food fresh. Being hunters eating fresh kill that is warm and clean, as opposed to dogs that also eat carrion, as specialized scavengers, the cat's natural defenses against bad bacteria are not as good. Therefore, we have to be more careful when feeding meats, for example, that they are free of contamination by heating to kill any disease causing bacteria - the good bacteria are also killed. We do not leave food out for this reason. We also warm up the food to near body temperature to approximate what they have eaten naturally for many years.

Therefore what is important and what is unimportant to a cat?

Important	**Unimportant**
smell	sight
cleanliness	color
texture	spices
fat	sugar
freshness	salt
minerals	bone
roughage	hair

EVALUATING TABLE SCRAPS

"The table scraps from the human food industry may not be as good as the table scraps from our own table."

Bruce Cauble, D.V.M.

Table scraps? What do we think of when we hear the words table scraps? I believe the food that is left over from our dining table that our family has not eaten is what we are referring to. We also have the "table scraps" of the food industry that are not used for people food but are processed, packaged and end up as pet food. Either the scraps from our table or the scraps (by-products) from the food processing industry are edible foods that can be eaten by our pets.

The advantage of using our table scraps as opposed to those of the food industry is that we know the ingredients. Also our scraps have not been processed, are from fresh sources and are free of preservatives and additives. Many people believe that our table scraps are better than the by-product table scraps of the human food industry.

When feeding home left-overs there are some precautions:
- Milk and milk products may not be tolerated by the adult cat.
- Fat is very tasty but also very powerful with calories.
- Canned fish, like Tuna, can lead to steatitis.
- Too much liver can lead to an excess of Vitamin A.
- We should cook egg whites as raw egg whites bind biotin.
- Cooked vegetables are fine but raw should be mashed or aged.
- We should avoid raw fish (fine bones and thiaminase).
- Onions can affect the red blood cells resulting in anemia.
- Over-cooking leads to vitamin losses.
- Cooked bones become brittle; raw bones are better.
- We should avoid small bones, the bigger the better.
- We should shun spicy chili, pepperoni or luncheon meats.
- We should discard spicy and salty left overs.

Can Do's with table scraps

- Cook extra so that we have left-overs.
- Left-overs can be stored for several days and used a little at a time for flavour enhancing.
- Pressure cooking bones softens and exposes the marrow
- Utilize left-overs in recipes.
- Keep trimmings from meat, fish, select vegetables and fruit as they can be used later in a recipe.
- Remember that spinach and rhubarb (oxalic acid) bind calcium.
- Feeding left-overs, up to twenty-five per cent of the diet with a quality commercial cat food will not affect the balance of the other nutrients within the commercial food.

Have a Left-Overs Container

A left-overs container or a "kitty bag" (Doggie bag) is a good idea. I use a plastic container with a tight cover that I set in the fridge. Cats prefer their food fresh and warm so I warm it up after taking it out of the fridge. The container is easily washed and I store those left-overs that I consider good. I do not save spicy or salty foods. Fat, meat trimmings, fish trimmings (no bones), dairy products (if tolerated by our cat) will go into this container. If it is meat, fat, fish oils, or dairy products, I will add some of this directly to the commercial dry cat food that I normally feed or use in a recipe.

The amount of dry food will be less in volume depending upon the quality and the amount of left-overs. If the left-overs are vegetable and fruit trimmings, I puree this in the blender and let sit in the container for a day or two (duplicating what happens in the prey's stomach). I then feed this later in the same way I would the fat, meat or fish trimmings or use in a recipe. Again I watch the amount. Too much can result in stomach upset and diarrhea.

Remember the cat's small stomach, short digestive system and her difficulty digesting vegetables and fruits. Sweet foods, cookies and cakes do not go in the cat dish. Understand, evaluate the left-overs from our knowledge of nutrients and foods and feed accordingly.

Learn to identify the nutrients in the scraps.

If primarily
> fat - add protein, carbohydrates,
> protein - add fat and carbohydrate,
> carbohydrate - add fat and protein.

Table scraps have been labeled as causing obesity in our pets. This may be in some cases, but I believe pet obesity today is due to lack of exercise and overfeeding. Our modern cats do not get the exercise that pets did several years ago. This is especially a concern with urban, shut-in cats. Commercial cat foods of good quality are so readily available and convenient that, I believe, we overfeed. Years ago the cat got to hunt and may have had some table left-overs, a homemade recipe if there was not enough left from the table, and that was it. I think we see more obese cats today because of the big boom and availability of commercial cat food and lack of exercise.

If we are feeding a good quality brand of commercial cat food adding no more than twenty-five per cent or one-quarter table scraps, we will not disrupt the balance of nutrients that the manufacturers have put into their product.

Raw ground beef that's red on the outside and brown on the inside is fine. The natural brown meat turns red when exposed to oxygen, not affecting the quality or safety. Spoiled beef is grey and has an off smell and feels slimy. Cats like their food "fresh killed", so to speak, as opposed to dogs that often prefer theirs aged after being buried in the back yard.

Most of our cats today do not have the good fortune to go out and hunt for their fresh food daily as their wild ancestral cousins did. Instead they are given foods that have been processed and chemically preserved or are from fresh foods that we have purchased.

The so called fresh foods that we purchase from our grocery stores, including the meats, eggs, dairy products, fruits and vegetables, have all been exposed to many things between the time of butchering or gathering until they are eaten. This is different from the "fresh kill" situation of the wild cat. Because these foods are all vulnerable to spoilage from just being exposed to the air and contamination from bacteria, some precautions must be taken. The handling of the food is done with care and regard for contamination, and it is generally kept cool under refrigeration to prevent the ever present bacteria from growing to large enough numbers to be harmful.

When this occurs, food poisoning can result. Food poisoning is a general term used when a particular food has been "infected" with harmful organisms that produce a variety of symptoms in the cat that consumes them. Symptoms such as stomach cramps, vomiting or diarrhea can develop as the cat's gastrointestinal tract is affected. Healthy individuals may be able to overcome this; however the young, old or chronically ill may not.

Food may be contaminated by

- bacteria, mold or fungi,
- a naturally occurring toxin in the food or
- a toxic chemical present by accident or design.

Bacteria, as an example, can cause poisoning either by their actual presence in large numbers or by the toxins that they may produce. Both situations can be harmful. Food can be contaminated at any time between the butchering or gathering stage and the time that it is actually consumed.

Once contaminated, if adequate precautions are not taken, such as refrigeration or air tight packaging, the bacteria or other organisms are allowed to multiply or to produce their toxic by-products.

To be sure that the foods are free of bacteria, we heat or cook foods. The toxins and some spores made by some organisms may not be destroyed by these processes, however. The danger zone is between 40^0 F (5^0 C) and 140^0 F (60^0 C) Below or above these temperatures, the organisms are dormant or cannot grow, multiply or produce toxins.

Food safety, therefore, becomes a matter of keeping hot foods hot and cold foods cold until they are eaten. Adequate care is essential with regard to handling, packaging and storing so that first the food is not allowed to be contaminated and secondly the organisms are not allowed to grow to large enough numbers to be harmful.

Other poisons include those that may naturally occur when a food spoils or when a harmful chemical accidentally contaminates a food. Some chemicals are purposely put into foods as additives for various reasons. Additives to give flavor, preserve, provide color or that are put in food for esthetic reasons may become poisonous over an extended period of consumption if the cat's body cannot eliminate them and they become residues. More on this in the section on allergies and intolerances.

In summary, foods become poisonous for our cats in several ways. Organisms such as bacteria or molds, toxins or chemicals all have the potential to become harmful. Careful regard to purchasing foods that have been adequately packaged, refrigerated or cooked before being given to our cat will prevent the main sources of food poisoning. Reading the labels of commercial preparations and watching for additives as well as changing brands and giving variety will help to avoid a chronic build up of a particular additive or additives.

EQUIPMENT

Basic kitchen equipment will not vary from what we have in the kitchen now. If we are going to do a lot of cooking for our cat or if we have many to feed we may want to have larger pots and storage facilities.

A list of commonly used kitchen equipment:

- sauce pan
- frying pan
- cake pans
- small loaf pans
- ice cube trays
- small pie pans
- cookie sheets
- small casserole dish
- mixing bowls
- measuring cup
- measuring spoons
- metal spoon
- wooden spoon
- paring knife
- meat, bone saw
- food grinder, blender
- biscuit cutter
- rolling pin
- cutting board
- dropper bottle, tsp. size from baby supply
- 1 to 3 cc. syringe, from the vet
- screw top storage jars
- refrigerator containers
- baby food containers
- plastic food wrap

INGREDIENTS

Before we get started listing each ingredient, some general comments are appropriate. Meat, eggs, milk, fish, liver, vegetables, fruits and cereals will be listed but each has its limitations. Excesses of any one ingredient can be detrimental in that usually some required nutrients are missing or too much of another is present. As we know, our cat can easily train us to give it one particular food by refusing others. This can lead to trouble.

Meats are good sources of protein and energy for our cat; however, they are low in some minerals and vitamins, in particular, calcium, phosphorus, sodium, iron, copper, iodine and vitamins A, D and E. Meats are the muscle tissues and we know that the wild and ancestral cats ate more of their prey than just the muscles. The limitations of meat is a consideration when feeding our cat by providing other foods so that the missing nutrients are supplied.

Eggs are also a good source of protein as well as fats and vitamins and are easily digested. If only raw whites are fed, a substance called avidin will destroy the B vitamin biotin. However, if the whites are cooked, destroying avidin or if the whole egg with the yolks is fed, this is not a concern as there is enough biotin in the yolks to compensate. Feeding eggs may improve the hair coat. This is probably due to the fat content in the yolks, especially linoleic acid.

Milk, cheeses, yogurt and ice cream are excellent sources of calcium, phosphorus, protein and fats; however, milk and ice cream may not be tolerated by the adult cat due to the lactose or milk sugar present. Kittens do not have this problem.

Fish is also a good source of protein. With fish we must watch for bones. Fish, especially carp and herring, should be cooked to eliminate the enzyme thiaminase which destroys the B vitamin thiamine. Raw salmon and trout may contain a parasite that can cause a disease called salmon poisoning that can lead to death, so they should be cooked as well. It is best to cook all fish.

Liver and the other organs are also very good ingredients to use. Liver is most nutritious when fed raw as it is filled with protein, fat, carbohydrate, vitamins and minerals and cooking may destroy some of these nutrients. Again, a little is good; a lot is bad. A diet of only organs can lead to trouble; for example, too much liver can lead to too much vitamin A.

Vegetables may be used in moderation when mashed, ground or cooked so that they can be digested by our carnivorous cat. This is the same for fruit. These ingredients are not the cat's natural food; however, a little, if eaten occasionally, can give our cat a change and she may receive benefit from them.

The cereal grains need the same considerations. When used in moderation, processed and in combination with animal proteins and fats, cereals can supply some energy. The prime benefit; however, is as fiber to replace the hair and feathers our cat would get from prey if it had the opportunity to hunt.

Sweets, spices, chocolate, onions and other condiments that we see in recipes for us should not be fed to our cat, even though she may like them. These ingredients have little nutritional value for the cat and can be harmful. Chocolate can be poisonous to cats and dogs and onions can affect the red blood cells which can lead to anemia and death.

The ingredients listed on the following pages are those that we can use. Always think about the limitations discussed, using moderation and variety, so that problems from deficiencies or excesses do not arise.

Ingredients

The ingredients are listed with a view to their importance in a cat's diet and our awareness of their nutrient content. The predominant nutrients are listed with the greatest first. Letters A, B, B_{12}, C, D, E, refer to the vitamins.

Alfalfa sprouts	protein, fiber, C and minerals
Baby foods	lamb, beef, pork
Bacon	fat, protein, sodium
Beef	protein, fat, B_{12}, niacin, thiamin, riboflavin, iron
Bologna	fat, protein, sodium, B_{12}, minerals
Bones	minerals: calcium and phosphorus (ham bones, steak bones, knuckles) Bonedust bone, meat, fat, marrow, and blood
from butcher	minerals, fat, protein
Bone meal* (ground bones)	calcium, phosphorus, fluorine and other trace minerals
Bouillon cubes	sodium, carbohydrate
Brain	protein, fat, phosphorus, iron
Bran	high in thiamine and fiber (Bran is the outer coat of the seed of cereal grains like wheat, rye, corn or rice,)
Breads	carbohydrate, (often fortified with vitamins & minerals, not necessary to toast, starches cooked already)
Bread crumbs	carbohydrate, fiber, sodium, B, iron
Brewers yeast	vitamin B complex, protein (12 amino acids) minerals, carbohydrate and fat
Brisket	fat, protein, B_{12}, B, zinc, iron
Bulgar	carbohydrate, protein, B, minerals
Butter	fat, A, D, E, sodium
Buttermilk	protein, riboflavin, B_{12}, calcium, sodium

Calcium and phosphorus sources are meat and bone meal, bone meal, dicalcium phosphate, calcium carbonate and limestone.

Cereals	Brand name breakfast cereals:
All Bran ®	fiber, A, B, C, D, iron, minerals
Corn Flakes ®	carbohydrate, A, B, C, D, iron, sodium
Mueslix ®	fiber, carbohydrate, A, E, B, B_{12}, iron
Granola	carbohydrate, protein, fat, E, B, minerals
Oatmeal cooked	carbohydrate, protein, fat, fiber, B
Rice Krispies ®	carbohydrate, A, B, C, D, iron

Cheese	protein, fat, calcium, B_{12}, zinc
Chicken	protein, fat, E, B, B_{12}, minerals
Chicken liver	A, B_{12}, protein, C, B, E, iron, fat, zinc
Corn	(see vegetables)
Cornmeal	fiber, carbohydrate, B, sodium, iron
Corn oil	fat, E
Corn syrup	carbohydrate, iron
Cottage cheese	protein, fat, iron, B_{12}, B, calcium
Crackers	carbohydrate, fat
Cream	fat, carbohydrate,
Dandelion greens	carbohydrate, protein, sodium
Duck	protein, fat, E, B_{12}, B, iron, zinc
Eggs *	protein, fat, D, E, B, B_{12}, iron
	(avidin in raw whites binds biotin)
Eggnog	fat, protein, A, D, riboflavin, B_{12}, calcium
Epsom salts	magnesium sulfate (magnesium source)
Fish **	rich in fluorine, iodine & zinc
(see seafood)	(cook to destroy thiaminase and worms)
Fish liver oil	only concentrated natural food sources of
cod liver oil	vitamin D and true vitamin A, also small amounts of phosphorus, iodine & sulfur (use natural oils - not flavored oils)

Cook eggs or pour boiling water over the outside to destroy food poisoning bacteria that may be present such as Salmonella.

**Fish containing a lot of fat are salmon, tuna, mackerel, herring and white fish. Founder is a lean fish.*

Flour	carbohydrate, protein, vitamins, minerals
Wholewheat	carbohydrate, protein, fiber, B, iron
Soy flour	protein, fat, fiber, thiamine, riboflavin, high in iron, calcium, potassium
Corn flour	carbohydrate, fiber, thiamine, iron
Buckwheat flour	carbohydrate, protein, fiber, thiamine, B_6 high in iron, potassium
All purpose	carbohydrate, protein, fiber, B, iron
Frankfurters	fat, protein, sodium
French toast	protein, fat, sodium, B_{12}, B, iron, minerals
Fruit	(raw, cooked, stewed or dried)
Apples	fiber, C, E, B, potassium
Apricots (dried)	A, E, potassium
Bananas	fiber, C, E, B6, potassium
Berries	fiber, carbohydrate, C, E, B, potassium
Dates (dried)	fiber, carbohydrate, B, potassium, iron
Grapefruit	carbohydrate, C, E, B, potassium
Oranges	carbohydrate, C, E, B, potassium, calcium
Pears	carbohydrate, fiber, C, E, potassium
Prunes (dried)	fiber, carbohydrate, A, B, potassium, iron
Raisins	carbohydrate, fiber, E, B, potassium, iron
Garlic	carbohydrate, potassium, calcium (appetizer, digestive stimulant, use powder, oil or cloves, not garlic salt - too much salt)
Grains (see flour)	energy, carbohydrate, protein, vitamins not more than 30% of Dry Matter of cat diet, always, processed, cooked to break down starches
Granola	(see cereals)
Greens	calcium, vitamins & minerals (chopped, beet, dandelion greens, Swiss chard, kale, parsley, spinach, collards)

Ham (smoked)	protein, fat, C, D, B, B_{12}, sodium, minerals
Hamburger	protein, fat, carbohydrate, B_{12}, B, E, iron
Honey	carbohydrate, riboflavin, iron, potassium
Hot Dog	fat, sodium, protein, C, B_{12}, B, minerals
Kidney	protein, B_{12}, B, A, iron, zinc, fat
Lamb	protein, fat, B_{12}, B, E, minerals
Lard pork	fat, E
Lentils	protein, C, E, B, iron, potassium
Lettuce	fiber, A, C, E, folate, potassium
Liver beef	protein, fat, A, B_{12}, B, C, D, E, iron, zinc "miracle food, unidentified liver fractions, natures mystery food ..... Dr. Collins

"If there is one single food that every dog should have in its diet, that food would have to be liver". "It contains more nutrients in one package than any other natural food available to man or beast"
                                                Dr. Collins, Dog Nutrition.

This holds true for cats as well. Carnivores go for the liver and kidneys of their prey first and the flesh or muscle meat last.

Macaroni	carbohydrate, protein, E, B, iron
Meat	protein and fat

Meat, or animal flesh, is easily and almost completely digested, all of the protein, and ninety-five percent of the fat. Raw meat requires about two hours for digestion whereas cooked to well-done may take four hours. Grade or colour does not affect the nutrient value.

Milk	carbohydrate, protein, fat, vitamins & minerals
skim, whole	Adults may have hard time digesting lactose.
condensed	Most store-purchased is fortified with vitamins
Muffin Bran	fat, carbohydrate, fiber, sodium, B, iron
Nuts	fat, protein, vitamin E and some B's

Oats	carbohydrate, protein, B, magnesium, iron
Oils	fat, essential fatty acids, E
Peanut Butter	fat, protein, E, niacin,
Parsley	C, folate, iron, potassium, calcium
Pasta	carbohydrate, protein, E, B, iron
Popcorn	carbohydrate
Pork	protein, fat, B, B_{12}, iron, zinc
Potatoes	(see vegetables)
Potato Pancakes	fat, carbohydrate, B, E, sodium
Rabbit	protein, B_{12}, B, iron, minerals
Rice (brown)	carbohydrate, fiber, E, minerals
Salt	sodium (Sea Salt, sodium chloride plus iodine)
Sausage	fat, protein, sodium, B_{12}, B, minerals
Sea Food	
Fish Sticks	protein, fat, E, B, B_{12}, potassium
Cod fried	protein, fat, E, B, B_{12}, potassium, sodium
Oysters Eastern	:B_{12} & zinc, iron, A, D, C, E, B
Salmon (canned)	protein, fat, high in D, B, E, calcium, iron
Shrimp (canned)	protein, D, E, B, B_{12}
Tuna (canned)	protein, fat, iron, sodium
Seeds Sunflower	fat, high E, B
Soups	dehydrated high in sodium
Beef/Barley	protein, fat, carbohydrate, A, B_{12}, sodium
Clam Chowder	protein, fat, carbohydrate,
Chicken Noodle	protein, A, B, sodium, iron
Chicken Rice	protein, fat, A, B, sodium, iron
Consomme	protein, potassium, sodium, iron
Minestrone	protein, carbohydrate, fat, A, B, sodium
Tomato	carbohydrate, A, C, B, sodium, potassium, iron
Steak (round)	protein, fat, B_{12}, B, iron, zinc, potassium
Swiss cheese	protein, fat, calcium, B_{12}, D, zinc
Tofu	protein, fat, E, B, magnesium, iron, calcium
Tomato Paste	carbohydrate, A, C, B, sodium, potassium, iron
Tongue	protein, fat, B_{12}, B, iron, zinc

Tripe	protein, fat (Tripe is the muscular lining of the four stomachs of cattle and sheep)
Turkey	protein, fat, B_{12}, B, E, zinc, iron, potassium
Turkey roll	protein, fat, sodium, B, minerals
Veal	protein, fat, B_{12}, zinc, iron, potassium
Vegetables (cooked)	given occasionally in small amounts
Asparagus	protein, carbohydrate, C, E, B, minerals
Baked Beans	protein, carbohydrate, fiber, A, B, minerals
Beans (green)	fiber, carbohydrate, C, B, potassium, iron
Lima Beans	fiber, protein, high E, B, minerals
Beets	fiber, E, C, B, potassium, iron
Broccoli	fiber, protein, C, A, E, B, calcium, magnesium
Brussel sprouts	fiber, carbohydrate, protein, C, E, B, iron
Cabbage	fiber, C, E, B, minerals
Carrots	carbohydrate, C, E, B, minerals
Cauliflower	fiber, C, B, minerals
Celery	fiber, C, B, potassium
Corn	carbohydrate. fiber, protein, C, E, B
Mushrooms (raw)	fiber, C, E, B, potassium, iron
Parsnips	fiber, carbohydrate, C, E, B, minerals
Peas	fiber, carbohydrate, protein, C, B, potassium
Potatoes	carbohydrate, protein, C, niacin, potassium
Spinach	fiber, carbohydrate, protein, A, C, E, B, iron
Turnips	fiber, carbohydrate, A, C, E, B, potassium
Zucchini	fiber, A, C, B, potassium
Vegetable oil	fat, E
Venison	protein, vitamins and minerals
Waffles	fat, carbohydrate, D, E, B_{12}, B, sodium
Wheat germ oil (extract of the wheat germ)	fat, all vitamin E s, B, A and fatty acids
Yogurt	protein, fat, B_{12}, riboflavin, calcium
Yeast dry	protein, B especially: thiamine & riboflavin, calcium, iron
Water	distilled, filtered or spring

HEALTH FOOD STORE INGREDIENTS

Ingredients that can be picked up at a Health Food Store should receive the same consideration discussed before for other ingredients. Stick to the basic raw ingredient and read books which discuss the use of herbs and other products made especially for the cat.

alfalfa powder	protein, vitamins, minerals
baby foods	meat, vegetables, fruits
bone meal	calcium and phosphorus
bran	fiber, thiamine
Brewers yeast	B vitamins
Cod-liver oil	vitamins A and D
dessicated liver powder	vitamins, protein
dicalcium phosphate	calcium and phosphorus
dried fish	protein, fat soluble vitamins
dried sea weed	minerals, vitamins
dried spinach	iron, vitamins, protein
glandular organ powder	protein, vitamins
Infant liquid vitamins	vitamins
kelp powder	minerals (iodine)
"Lite salt"	regular salt & potassium chloride
vitamin B complex	B vitamins
vitamin C	powder or tablets (ascorbic acid, sodium or potassium ascorbate)
vitamin D	tablets
vitamin E	capsules
wheat germ	vitamin E
yeast	B vitamins

Other items available

blackberry leaves	for pregnant queens
charcoal tablets	for flatulence, foul smelling stools
catnip (*Nepeta cataria*)	stimulant, toys
kaopectate, unflavored	for diarrhea
raspberry leaves	for pregnant queens

Remember what we have said with regard to many of these ingredients in the first part of the book. If our cat has been diagnosed to have a particular deficiency consider that the cat's body is a complete organism that is in balance and to feed one particular nutrient, especially to excess can disrupt this balance. All systems work in harmony for the good of the whole cat so that experimentation should be done with caution and close observation.

A few words about catnip.

Catnip *Nepeta cataria* is a plant of the mint family hepetalactone (also Valerian *Valeriana officinalia*) which contain unsaturated lactones that gives some cats about a ten minute "trip". Kittens will avoid for the first several months then will avoid or like. We do not think it is harmful.

We may have heard or read about chelated minerals and wondered about such mineral supplements.

Chelated minerals are minerals in which the mineral or ion is bonded, usually to an amino acid or other acid which shields the mineral from external influences. This can affect how the mineral is absorbed through the intestine or if the mineral can be attracted to another mineral. For example, calcium binds zinc; however, chelated zinc is not affected by calcium so that this zinc may be absorbed whereas before it may not be.

Whether giving chelated minerals is of benefit to the cat will depend on whether the cat needs that mineral, what other minerals are present in the diet and what the mineral is chelated with. This may actually be harmful if the cat should receive more than is required. As this is a very involved process, it is better to ensure that the diet has the right amounts of all the nutrients, including minerals, rather than perhaps too much of one or another mineral.

NUTRIENT COMPARISONS OF INGREDIENTS

The classes of ingredients are listed for some of the basic nutrients. The food on the top of the list contains the highest amount, then the next highest and so on.

PROTEIN

Beef & Game
venison
rabbit
round roast (lean)
steak (lean)
chili with beans
kidney
tongue

Pork, Veal & Lamb
leg of lamb
calf liver
ham
lamb chops
veal cutlets
pork butt
ham (canned)

Poultry
turkey (diced)
chicken (diced)
chicken breast
goose
chicken liver
pheasant
duck

Dairy & Eggs
quiche
omelette
cottage cheese
yogurt
goat milk
cow milk

Cooked Grains
oat bran
millet
rice bran
bulgur
rice
corn

Cooked Vegetables
beans (all)
tofu
peas
lentils
spinach
potatoes

FAT

Meat
brisket
corn beef
meat loaf
ground lamb
duck
tongue

Dairy & Eggs
quiche
omelette
goat milk
cheddar cheese
whole milk
egg

Butter & Oils
corn oil
olive oil
vegetable oil
pork lard
margarine
butter

CARBOHYDRATE

Cooked Grains
millet
oat bran
rice
bulgur
corn grits

Cooked Vegetables
sweet potatoes
beans
corn
potatoes
carrots

Cereals
Raisin Bran ®
Rice Krispies ®
Cream of Wheat ®
oatmeal
Corn Flakes ®

FIBER

Cooked vegetables
beans (all)
peas
parsnips
corn
broccoli

Fruit
berries
dried prunes
raisins
apples
oranges

Cereals
All Bran ®
Mueslix ®
Bran Flakes ®
oat bran (cooked)
oatmeal (cooked)

VITAMINS

Vitamin A
cod liver oil
beef liver
chicken liver
Eel
Halibut
egg yolk

Vitamin D
cod liver oil
salmon
sardines in oil
milk (fortified)
chicken liver
Swiss cheese

Vitamin E
wheat germ oil
sunflower seeds
vegetable oil
corn oil
shrimp
egg yolk

MINERALS

Calcium
bonemeal
yogurt
milk
sardines
salmon
Fava beans

Zinc
Oysters Eastern
beef shank
liver
beef ground
lamb
pork

Sodium
salt
smoked ham
soups (dried)
bouillon cube
luncheon meats
wieners

UNDERSTANDING THE MEASUREMENTS

Measurements for the cat recipes are the same as those in any cookbook. You will note in some recipes that when the measurements are converted to metric, ounces may be converted to mL when it really should be to gm. As cooks, this eliminates the need for us to weigh an ingredient and use a volume measurement like a tsp. or tbsp. Strictly speaking, mL are used for volume measurements of liquids; powders and solids are measured and weighed in grams. For example 8 oz. may be converted as 250 mL.

From my experiences with animal health students and animal owners there sometimes is confusion with regards to the various metric measurements; therefore, I have included this outline.

METRIC (milli = 1/1000th., centi = 1/100th. & kilo = 1000)

WEIGHT	milligrams		grams		kilograms
	1 mg.	=	.001 gm.	=	.000001 kg.
	1000 mg.	=	1 gm.	=	.001 kg.
	1000000 mg.	=	1000 gm.	=	1 kg.

LIQUID	milliliters		liters
	1000 mL	=	1 L
	1 mL	=	.001 L

LENGTH

millimeters		centimeters		meters		kilometers
1000 mm.	=	100 cm.	=	1 m.	=	.001 km.
10 mm.	=	1 cm.	=	.01 m.	=	.00001 km.
1 mm.	=	.1 cm.	=	.001 m.	=	.000001 km.

VOLUME a cubic centimeter (cc) = a cube: 1 cm/ 1 cm/ 1 cm
The standard used is water;

weight		**liquid**		**volume**
1 gram	=	1 milliliter	=	1 cubic centimeter of water
(1 gm	=	1 mL	=	1 cc. of water)

All ingredients other than water will either weigh more or less for the same volume. Non liquids like powders and solids will also vary. For example, oils are lighter than water; that is why they float to the top. 1 mL of oil = 1 cc. but will weigh less than 1 gm. Mercury, a very heavy liquid, the volume of 1 mL = 1 cc but weighs much more than 1 gm.

PART FOUR Recipes

When feeding our cat we have probably observed some of her basic feeding habits. These we take into consideration when we are developing and testing recipes. All cats are not the same however. A cat that has been given a variety of foods right from the start as a kitten will seem to eat anything, whereas a cat that has eaten only one particular brand of food may take a long time to adjust to new and different foods. We can either mix a little of the familiar food with the new until the cat adjusts or only offer the new. This adjustment may take several days. Remember a cat in the wild may not eat every day but go without for days, so skipping a few days is natural and often healthy. As predators in the wild, prey may not have been plentiful so that cats would be on a feast and famine cycle. After a successful hunt they would feast for several days then go without for days. Many of our domesticated cats could, in fact, go for some time without food which would not only trim them down but they would become more active and healthy. Our cat will tell us what is best by her body condition and activity level. Variety is best when feeding cats so that bad habits are prevented.

Here are a few guidelines to consider when feeding our cats dishes that we have prepared.

- cats eat small portions often.
- texture is important especially if the cat is on dry cat food; we may have to offer the same texture
- fat tastes good especially animal fat and fish oils
- liver and fish taste good
- cats may be reluctant to change to something new and different; be patient and give them time
- a well-fed cat can go without eating for a week or more
- she must have water available everyday
- cats are carnivores; cereals, fruits and vegetables are not a big part of their natural diet.

Cats eat food that smells right and has a familiar texture. They eat to fill their basic requirement for energy. Appetite governs the basic urge to fulfill these needs. This primitive instinct (hunger) to ingest food is the way cats will seek out the nutrients they require. With our knowledge of nutrition we give them the nutrients in various combinations or recipes so that they can live long and healthy lives. As stated earlier this is solely our responsibility as many of our cats cannot go out and "hunt" for those nutrients that may be lacking.

Recipes in this section were developed and tested using nutritionally sound ingredients. Many of the recipes are modifications of recipes for us. There are no reasons that we cannot make up recipes for our cat if we take into consideration the basic differences between our cat and us. We must also learn the nutrient contents of the ingredients that we are to use and how they can best fill our cat's requirements.

The recipes are designed for an average cat on a maintenance level of nutritional requirements. That is to say, a cat that is fully grown, in good body condition, with moderate exercise and under no stress - not a growing kitten or a nursing queen. A kitten or queen has different special needs. These are dealt with later.

Before we get to the Special Recipes for those cats with additional nutritional requirements we will outline four areas that I have called Traditional, Natural, Price Conscious and Gourmet. Again these are for the "average" cat.

Traditional refers to how we may be feeding our cat today. We buy what we believe to be a good commercial cat food and we might add left-overs or throw something else in. We might even have a recipe or two that we use. We may have doubts about this method but up until now our cat has been doing well and enjoys the change. In this section I have followed this same "traditional" approach with guidelines where necessary.

Natural, Health Conscious or Organic recipes are for those of us who would like to feed our cat ourselves. We want to use foods that are either fresh or not processed trying to get away from the commercially prepared cat foods. Here we discuss this approach and offer recipes that we might try.

The Price Conscious, economy and bulk section is presented for the cat feeder who may want to economize for whatever reason. We may have more than one cat and would still like to supply all the required nutrients but ease up on the grocery budget.

Gourmet is where we have some fun. We indulge in some fancy recipes for those special occasions: birthdays, Thanksgiving, Christmas or just letting our hair down and enjoying. Why shouldn't our cats have these same opportunities as well? With these recipes we are not as concerned with cost, calories or nutrients but good taste. The recipes are not meant to become a daily routine but rather a one time culinary gift for our best friend to enjoy.

The four areas: traditional, natural, price conscious and gourmet are just simple classifications that may help us understand the different recipes.

To repeat: the type of cat we are feeding is the cat on a maintenance level of nutrition, the typical house cat that most of us have, a cat that is reasonably active, in fair body condition and leading a normally stress-free life, "our pet".

Again, remember variety is best so that our cat does not get "hooked" on one particular food but rather a variety. This training is best started early with the kitten. Don't fall into the trap of our cat training us to give her only one specific brand of say liver or tuna to the exclusion of all others.

Just a few words on feeding cooked vs. raw food. The cat's body is perfectly designed to digest animal protein and fat raw, something she has done for millions of years. However, in our modern day culture we cook, especially meats. There are reasons for this, the first being the possibility that these foods are not clean or rather free of bacterial contamination and second the possible presence of parasites.

Cats in the wild and their ancestral cousins hunted prey and ate them fresh killed. No time was allowed for much bacterial contamination, bacterial growth or spoilage. This is not the situation today. The foods that our cats are offered today may have many opportunities for contamination between the time of butchering and when the food will be consumed so we have to cook or heat these foods to destroy potential disease-causing bacteria, bacterial toxins or parasites. Modern agricultural methods have come a long way in supplying safe food but all is not perfect.

Cats can be infected and become carriers of a parasite called *Toxoplasma gondi*. This protozoan parasite is not only potentially harmful to cats but also to humans. The greatest at risk are the fetuses of women and persons with compromised immune systems.

This is a topic that should be discussed with your veterinarian.

Cooking, however, not only destroys the bad bacteria and parasites but this process also destroys the good bacteria and alters or destroys some of the other nutrients. For example, cooking removes water soluble vitamins and can alter some of the proteins as well. Some pediatric hospitals for human babies are not microwaving baby foods today because we really don't know what microwaves do to the proteins in the foods.

Cooking, microwaves and other processing procedures used on foods today have the potential of altering the composition of nutrients that are present in their natural state. We still have much to learn in this area when it comes to discussing the pros and cons of cooked vs raw.

Cooking or some kind of processing is required for the cereals, vegetables and fruits, as we have said before. These foods are not naturally eaten raw but only after they have been semi-processed by the digestive system of the prey. From observations of wild cats we see that they do not eat much of this type of material but rather prefer the other parts of the prey. Dogs, on the other hand, do eat and enjoy these contents.

The cat's digestive system is designed to eat raw animal proteins and fats and some semi-digested vegetable matter.

The question arises: what do we feed, raw or cooked? The answer becomes one of a balance between the nutritional benefits for our cat consuming raw foods and the harmful potential of being infected with disease-causing bacteria, bacterial toxins or parasites.

A few quidelines may help:

- Routinely have our cat examined for worms and deworm, especially if the cat has access to the outdoors.
- Cook meat products if the possibility of contamination is present, ie. left in room air, refrozen or poorly packaged. When in doubt cook.
- Pregnant women must be particularly cautious around cats. This situation should be discussed with her doctor and the cat's veterinarian.
- Cereals, vegetables and fruits are better digested if they have been processed, mashed, pureed, or cooked. And these foods should be only a minor part of the diet.
- The fresher the better.

SUMMARY

Before we start to cook for our cat a review of some of the basic nutrition principles are in order.
- The food must be nutritionally adequate.
- The food must supply sufficient calories or energy.
- The nutrients within the foods must be usable, that is edible, digestible and metabolizable.
- The food must be accepted or palatable, which involves texture, fat content and moisture content.
- The ingredients used must remain relatively constant.

Nutritionally adequate means that the foods contain enough good quality animal protein and fat as well as the vitamins and minerals. The protein must be of sufficient biological value with at least two gms / Kgm of body weight supplied per day. And thirty per cent of the cat's daily calories should come from protein. The protein must be of animal source so that the amino acid taurine is supplied as this is only present in animal tissue.

Fats, preferably animal fats, should be of high quality and supply fifty per cent of the cat's daily requirements for calories. That leaves twenty per cent of the daily caloric requirements to be filled in with carbohydrates.

Remember, the cat is a carnivore that is very well adapted to live and strive on animal protein and fat with little or no carbohydrate. As we have said before, protein is required on a regular basis in that extra protein is not stored but is converted to body fat to be used later as energy.

Vitamins and minerals must also be present in usable forms with amounts sufficient to supply the cat's daily needs. A prime example is vitamin A. The cat can only use vitamin A as the fat soluble, animal or fish source vitamin A and not as the precursor beta carotene which is water soluble and present in plant material.

TRADITIONAL RECIPES

The traditional Cat owner feeds a commercial cat food, either from a bag, box or can and may or may not add table scraps with the odd treat now and then.

Tradition today involves purchasing either a bag, box or a number of cans from the supermarket, pet food store or vet clinic and taking this home and giving it to our cat. From experience we know what she likes. We may or may not give left-overs, or a little piece of food while preparing dinner. We may feed once, twice a day, or we may just fill up the cat dish and refill it when it's empty. Our cat may have a preference for one brand in particular; maybe this is too expensive, so we have convinced her that a dry food in a bag is also tasty, good for her and cheaper for us.

Perhaps our cat is a little overweight and our veterinarian has suggested that she should lose a few pounds. "Since she has been spayed and will not be as active, she will not need as much."

We say "Gee we don't feed much now, just some cat food that we picked up at the supermarket and now and then some left-overs." The good doctor then suggests that our pet go on a reducing diet and may suggest a special diet that we should feed and nothing else. This is fine, but it seems that we are spending more money now on cat food then we had before and really have not noticed any weight loss.

We may have just bought a kitten or someone has given us one and now we have to feed it. The kitten is still growing and we want to do everything right. Or we have a female and have had her bred and we are concerned that she have the adequate nutrients during her pregnancy and nursing stage. What do we do? For these special individuals refer to the Special Recipes section starting on page 219.

We may have heard that we should only feed commercial food and nothing else because they are advertised to be 'complete and balanced' and we may also have heard that some people don't feed any of this kind of food but only feed home prepared foods because their cat has problems with the commercial foods.

"And their cats look so good."

Again we may have heard that we should be supplementing the cheaper store-bought food because it does not have enough of the right things for our cat or that the good commercial food is so expensive.

"It seems a shame to throw out trimmings and left-overs. Why can't I give it to my cat?" After all, "When I was a child our cats at home got table scraps and what they hunted".

These may be situations that we have encountered. We may have dealt with them in the traditional manner, bought some prepared food, given some table scraps or a bit of meat or fish once in a while and "My cat is doing fine". Maybe we didn't understand completely what we were doing and still have some concerns.

There are good commercially prepared pet foods on the market today. There are also poor ones. As we look at all the brands and the great variations in prices we are baffled. Some companies spend many dollars on nutritional research, manufacturing techniques and on flavour and storage chemistry. Others may not. It is up to us to become knowledgeable consumers so that we can buy and feed those products that are the best for our cat. Our cat will tell us what is best for it.

Refer to Part Two for more details on commercial cat foods. Especially read the summary and problems we may encounter with commercial cat foods on page 150.

The following recipes will utilize commercial cat food, fresh ingredients and table scraps. Again refer to "Evaluating Table Scraps" on page 156 for precautions. Rather than discarding left-overs we can use them for their nutrients and flavours.

We may not have the time to prepare the complete meal so we use a good quality cat food that we have bought. Some of us just may not like to cook. Remember cooking can be an art and a very satisfying accomplishment when we see an individual really enjoying a preparation we have made.

Maybe our objective is to "stretch out" the commercial cat food while adding some fresh home ingredients. We always pay attention to the amount that we give, by mentally calculating the kind and amounts of left-overs we are giving and then reducing the amount of commercial cat food accordingly. If the table scraps contain a lot of fat, and our cat is overweight, remember fat has over 2.2 times the amount of calories of other foods so cut back on the other. In other words we are always watching the amount of calories we give. On the other hand, fat is an important nutrient.

Most cat nutritionists, cat food manufacturers and cat feeders agree that we can replace twenty-five per cent of a good quality commercial cat food with other foods and not disturb the balance appreciably. With poor quality food the percentage is much more.

You will see that many of the recipes call for B complex and C vitamins. These vitamins are water soluble and are easily lost when foods are heated and stored for any length of time. Since B's and C are water soluble, the dangers due to slight overdosing are not a big concern, in that extra is eliminated by the cat. However, with the fat soluble vitamins A, D, E and K and the minerals, we must be careful and not give too much as these are stored and problems can arise, as we have discussed earlier in previous chapters.

HEARTY BREAKFAST

This breakfast will last all day.

Bacon, slice	1	1
or Bacon drippings	1/4 cup	50 mL
Egg	1	1
Dry cat food	1 cup	250 mL

Chop the bacon into 1/2 inch pieces and fry in a pan. Put the egg into boiling water for about a minute. This kills any bacteria that may be present on the egg as well as partially cooking the white. Take the egg out of the water with a table spoon and hold under cold running water. Crack the egg in half with a table knife and scoop out the contents onto the dry food. Add the bacon pieces with the drippings to the dry food and stir. Put into the cat's dish. Serves an average size cat a hearty breakfast that will last all day.

This is an excellent way to start the day, with protein, energy and vitamins. The bacon and egg supply quality, concentrated protein and animal fat, two important ingredients to start off the day. The egg is also abundant in vitamins and minerals which after all is the complete and balanced diet for a chick embryo. For cats that are well nourished with the right nutrients, feeding them raw egg whites is not a concern as they will get adequate biotin from other sources. Poorly nourished cats, such as those on poor quality commercial diets containing a lot of cereal products as opposed to animal products, should be fed cooked eggs whites in that the avidin present will bind the B vitamin biotin.

Saving the drippings from bacon, roasts or other meat dishes to be used later is a good way to enhance the fat content of dry cat food. Dry cat foods often are low in this valuable and tasty nutrient. Offering fresh, unpreserved animal fats in this manner ensures that our cat receives the important fatty acids that are so important for healthy skin and nervous tissue. Adding a teaspoon of warmed drippings to the dry food also improves the taste or palatability.

LEFT-OVER OMELET

A good way to use left-over beef, chicken, turkey or pork.

Left-over meat	**4-6 oz**	**125-170 gm**
Melted butter or Vegetable oil	**2 tbsp.**	**30 mL**
Dry cat food	**2 cups**	**500 mL**

Chop the meat scraps into small bite-size pieces. Warm a small skillet with butter or oil. Mix in dry cat food (rice, mashed potatoes or other carbohydrate left-overs can be used here as well). Beat eggs gently and pour over the meat and dry food and continue frying. Cool and cut into pieces.

This will feed an average size cat two days or two cats for one day.

RESTAURANT, KITTY BAG, LEFT-OVERS

We often have the opportunity to take "Kitty Bag" left-overs home with us after eating out. This has become socially acceptable as frugality is "in". Most restaurants will "bag" the left-overs.

Typical foods we can consider to take home for our cat include
- fish, watch for bones and spicy sauces.
- trimmed fat from beef, pork or lamb.
- fat and skin from chicken, turkey or goose
- meat, left-over hamburgers and hot dogs
- potatoes, rice, pasta and French fries
- vegetables and fruits
- breads, buns, cheese cake
- pizza: cheese, meats, vegetables and anchovies

Leave:
- sweets, chocolate, ice cream, desserts, cakes, cookies
- chili - high in spices
- onions - detrimental to the cat's red blood cells
- any foods salted or laden with spicy sauces

When we get home, refrigerate the kitty bag and plan the next days menu around the left-overs. Identify what we have brought home with regards to the main nutrient present. Fat and skin is fat with spices; rice, pasta, vegetables and breads are carbohydrate; meats and cheese are protein and fat. French fries are carbohydrate, fat and salt.

Bones can be given to cats with certain exceptions. Cats will take their time and do enjoy and get nourishment from chewing and eating bones. After all they have been eating them for millions of years. They obviously ate raw bones. Cooked bones such as chicken or turkey bones become brittle and may break off into sharp fragments while some bones such as from sweet and sour ribs are softened by cooking and can be enjoyed and nutritious for cats. Cats are very careful when they eat bones and they have the natural protection of swallowed hair that wraps around undigested bone fragments in their stomachs and intestines protecting the intestinal walls from possible puncture. Avoid fine fish bones. If in doubt avoid bones and purchase and feed bonemeal in which the bones have been ground into a meal. Cats not only obtain calcium and phosphorus from eating bones; they also get nutrients from the marrow, especially fat.

BUDGET STRETCHER

Stretches the budget and uses left-overs

Left-over: rice, mashed potatoes or pasta	1 cup	250 mL
Canned cat food	1, 4 oz can	113 gm

Empty the contents of the canned cat food into a medium size bowl and stir in the left-over rice, mashed potatoes or pasta. Mix well and then serve one-half and save the rest for another day in the refrigerator. Canned cat food is predominately water which will be absorbed by the left-overs giving them a familiar flavour as well as providing carbohydrates or energy.

PRINCESS'S PASTA PIE

A pasta treat that is wholesome and nutritious.

Macaroni or pasta, cooked	4 1/3 cups	1 L
Beef, pork, chicken or lamb meat & drippings	2 cups	500 mL
(or Canned cat food)	2, 4 oz cans	
Liver pate	2 tbsp.	30 mL
Catnip	1/4 tsp.	1 mL

Put the cooked macaroni or pasta into a casserole dish. Add the meat and drippings (or contents of the canned food) and mix. Bake at 350° F (180° C) for about 20 - 30 minutes. Cool and spread pate over the top and garnish with catnip.

Slice and serve warm. Will feed an average size cat four days.

PANTHER PIZZA

Panther's very own pizza

Frozen pizza dough	1	1
Tomato paste	1/3 cup	75 mL
Water	1/3 cup	75 mL
Vegetable oil	1 tbsp.	15 mL
Catnip	1 tsp.	5 ml

Toppings: pieces of left-over meats, a small can of favorite cat food, fish (watch for bones) cheeses, garlic cloves, cooked vegetables.

Mix up the 4 ingredients and spread over the defrosted pizza dough. Cut up the toppings into small pieces and spread. Bake at 400° F (200° C) for 20 - 25 minutes.

Cool, slice and serve according to size of cat.

SAUCES

These "sauces" can be made beforehand and poured onto commercial cat food or vegetable or cereal type table scraps.

VITAMIN & MINERAL GRAVY

A powerful gravy topping

Gravy, left-over	2 cups	500 mL
Cod Liver oil (unflavoured)	4 tbsp.	60 mL
Bone dust or		
Bone meal (minerals)	1 tbsp.	15 mL
Vitamin C powder		
(or 500 mg crushed tablet)	1 tbsp.	15 mL
Brewers yeast (B complex)	1 tbsp.	15 mL
Wheat germ oil (vitamin E)	1 tbsp.	15 mL

Mix into a 2 1/2 cup container with a cover. Add as topping to dry cat food or left-overs for flavour, vitamins and minerals. Amount will vary with the size of the cat. 1 tablespoon for an average size kitten, up to 3 tablespoons for a large cat. Refrigerate the rest.

SOUR CREAM SAUCE

Sour cream	2 cup	500 mL
Cod Liver oil - unflavoured		
(vitamins A & D)	4 tbsp.	60 mL
Vitamin C powder		
(or 500 mg crushed tablet)	1 tbsp.	15 mL
Brewers yeast (B complex)	1 tbsp.	15 mL
Wheat germ oil (vitamin E)	1 tbsp.	15 mL

Mix and use as toppings for dry cat food, table scraps, or homemade cat biscuits. The "red" and "white wine" recipes on page 215 can be used over dry cat food and other recipes in this same manner.

Traditional recipes use commercial cat foods and left-overs to advantage. By using our imagination to provide variety, we can do many things to the regular, traditional cat food.

NATURAL, HEALTH-CONSCIOUS, ORGANIC RECIPES

> *"Consumers today are looking for natural products free of preservatives and made with natural food ingredients for themselves."*
>
> Debra Lynn Dadd, Editor, *The Earthwise Consumer*

What does *natural or organic* mean? Natural and organic can mean different things to different people. Do they mean that the foods are free of
- artificial colours, flavours and preservatives?
- meat by-products and meat from animals fed heavy grain rations?
- synthetic vitamins and minerals?
- grains grown with pesticides and synthetic fertilizers?

If this is what some of us believe natural and organic foods are, then we must question many of the products that use the term *natural* today because the label often doesn't support this view.

Natural is a term that is used more and more today in response to a public demand for foods that are like those our ancestors ate.

Many of us, including pet owners, are becoming more and more concerned with the foods we, our families and our pets eat. This leads to questions about preservatives, pesticides, herbicides, additives and residues in our foods. Prepared foods that have been processed and altered to prevent spoilage and maintain shelf-life fill our shelves. We buy fresh items that we can eat to complement the commercially prepared foods. If we would like to do the same for our pets, it requires some effort and some basic knowledge, but the task is not impossible.

Cats can be fussy so we may have to experiment a lot.

We are starting to see the pet food industry responding to the "additive free" requests by the buying public with new products appearing on the market. Fresh frozen is another form that is becoming available in some stores.

Terms like *natural, organic,* and *additive-free* have to be and will be defined in specific terms so we all know what is meant by their use in advertising and labeling.

The Association of American Feed Control Officials (AAFCO) defines the term natural as
> *"of or pertaining to a product wholly comprised of ingredients completely devoid of artificial or man-made substances, including, but not necessarily limited to, synthetic flavors, colors, preservatives, vitamins, minerals, or other additives, whether added directly to the product or incidentally as a component of another ingredient".*

We may have seen these terms such as *natural* used loosely on labels today; however, in the future as labeling laws catch up they will be defined and meaningful.

If we want to feed our cat *naturally* with natural and organic foods, we must first understand what is natural for the cat.

Being a hunter, survival for the ancestral cat was based on what she could catch. This not only required mental effort but physical exertion as well. Hunting provided a mental challenge and also much physical exercise. Mental and physical fitness was imperative if she was to survive. She also had a choice. This way of life and particular diet is what she is suited for.

As we have said earlier the cats of these early days ate the complete prey be it a mouse, bird or other creature, almost everything was eaten.

Observing the wild cousins of our domestic cat today we note that they go for the internal organs: liver, pancreas, kidney etc first. We also observe that they consume the muscle, bones and even some of the hair and feathers. Cats are less interested in the intestinal contents than are members of the dog family. The semi-digested plant material, if the prey should be a herbivore, is left, again reminding us that the cat is indeed a carnivore. It is interesting that they eat the meat or "steak" last and tend to eat the organs first.

Our cat and the wild felines have adapted to their environment over millions of years. On the other hand, the cat is also able to change and adapt to different environments and diets; however, these changes cannot be great and take a lot of time. Cats are more carnivorous than dogs, for example. Dogs can survive as an omnivore to a certain extent. Omnivores receive nutrition from animal and plant sources and we know that wild dogs do consume partially processed plant material when they eat of the stomach and intestinal contents of their prey. The wild cat doesn't seem to relish these parts of the carcass and tends to leave them for scavenging type animals and birds instead. The cat is built and adapted to a more strict carnivore diet.

We also can easily see that the cats ate their prey raw rather than cooked. This is natural. Many years ago Dr. Francis M. Pottenger, while working at his father's sanatorium for the treatment of human tuberculosis patients in Monrovia, California, conducted what became known as the Pottenger Cat Study. This study, over a ten year period, on 900 cats looked at the differences in cats fed raw vs cooked meat. This series of controlled experiments showed some startling differences between cats fed raw meat and those fed cooked meat.

The diet of all the cats consisted of meat, bones, organs such as liver, heart, brains, kidneys and pancreas, raw milk and cod liver oil. One group was given raw meat and the other cooked meat; everything else was the same.

The raw meat group, over the ten year study were healthy, of uniform size, skeletal development and fur. Each litter averaged five kittens, miscarriages were rare and causes of death were usually due to old age.

In contrast the cooked meat group had no end of problems. Litter mates varied in size and skeletal structure. Vision problems, infections, arthritis, heart problems, inflammation of joints and nervous tissues, skin problems, allergies and intestinal parasites were common. Common causes of death in adults were pneumonia and lung abscesses while pneumonia and diarrhea were the common causes of death in kittens. Reproductive and behavior problems were also common in the cooked meat group.

This study conducted on 900 cats over a ten year period on the effects of cooked meat fed to cats may help to explain some of the health problems we encounter in our modern cats today. Today our commercially-prepared cat foods are not only cooked - to remove contamination from harmful bacteria - but also use cereals and vegetable products in their formulations primarily for a source of energy and fiber. These ingredients are not only cheaper but require less attention to preserving and maintaining shelf life. Animal products: proteins and fats are much more expensive and must be processed to remove possible contaminants, then preserved to maintain shelf life. Canned foods need only be processed with heat as the air-tight can then maintains the shelf life without the need for preservatives.

So why is cat food cooked today? Raw is obviously natural as the cats of old and in the wild didn't cook their food before they ate it. However, their food was cleaner in that it was killed relatively recently and not exposed to too many other things by the time it was eaten. Foods today have great opportunity for contamination from many sources before our cat gets to eat them so cooking is important to kill harmful bacteria and parasites that may cause disease.

However, Pottenger's study showed that cats fed raw meat were healthier and more resistant to diseases and parasites. So in other words, if the cat is on a totally natural diet it is better able to resist infection from disease causing organisms. Once we alter the natural diet, problems arise which lead to other solutions which in turn lead to other problems. For example a diet high in meat, which is low in calcium, must be supplemented with ingredients such as bone meal to balance the diet. The ancestral cats ate bones.

Some sort of processing is required for the vegetable and cereal ingredients much like the digestion undergone in the stomach and intestines of the captured prey. Cooking or some sort of processing of plant products makes digestion easier because some breakdown has been started. Cooking, as we have said before, does remove and change some nutrients. We must then replace these lost nutrients after cooking. An example is the water soluble B vitamins.

Just a few words about a feline vegetarian diet. This type of diet is impossible in my opinion without the aid of animal source supplements for the cat. A vegetarian diet is not natural. Two very important nutrients, Vitamin A and the amino acid, Taurine, are only present in animals or fish as both of these are not present in plants. Cats, for millions of years, ate and thrived on animal proteins and animal fats with very few carbohydrates or direct plant source foods in their diet. Their bodies, especially their digestive systems, are adapted and specially suited for this type of diet. Therefore, to totally eliminate all animal products and only feed plant products or vegetables is unnatural and in my opinion, inhumane.

Vegetables, fruits, and cereals are hard for her to utilize. Balancing the diet for all necessary nutrients becomes quite difficult considering her shorter digestive system and lack of room for prolonged bacterial digestion. Herbivores - plant eaters - are built differently so that they can eat these foods.

Lastly, cats aren't particularly fond of these foods, obviously not part of their heritage, and getting them to eat strictly plant food in large enough quantities to get all of their requirements becomes a challenge and a great burden on their nature. This is where additives such as flavours, either natural or synthetic come into play. A total vegetarian diet is unnatural and stressful on their system and must be supplemented with animal products.

If we are to feed our cat in a natural and organic manner we take all these considerations into our plans.

- The cat is naturally a carnivore.
- Some essential nutrients must come from animal sources.
- If commercially-prepared cat food is not canned or frozen, it must be preserved with preservatives.
- AAFCO has a definition for natural when referring to commercial cat food.
- Wild cats eat the internal organs of their prey.
- The complete prey is eaten with less preference for the stomach and intestinal contents.
- Cereals, vegetables and fruits can provide some energy and fiber but require some processing.
- A totally vegetarian diet is impossible for the cat.
- Raw is natural and best nutritionally - however, because "fresh kill" is not always possible, cooking is necessary to remove potentially harmful bacteria and parasites.
- Certified organically grown foods more closely resemble the foods that the ancestral cats had available.

Preparing a complete diet at home can be relatively easy when balancing for proteins, fats, carbohydrate and fiber. Vitamin and mineral formulating is a little more involved. To be sure that we have adequate vitamins and minerals, we can use a prepared supplement or make one ourselves from ingredients that we assemble.

As we have discussed in other parts of the book, understanding what nutrients are present in the foods that we offer our cat and which ones are not or are lost due to cooking is a concern. Those lost nutrients, in particular vitamins, must be replaced for the diet to be complete and balanced.

I believe with some basic knowledge of feline nutrition and a little common sense we can offer healthy and enjoyable meals for our four-legged friends. We can then watch the compliments as our friends display their enjoyment as they purr, lick and groom themselves after a good meal.

Here are some recipes for vitamin-mineral supplements that can be given to ensure that our cat is receiving the requirements. The natural way a cat received its vitamins and minerals was through the food that she ate. For many of our cats today a totally natural diet of fresh mice etc is impossible, so we must do the best we can with what we have. In this situation it then becomes important to consider supplementing with specific foods and recipes to insure that our cat receives all of her required nutrients.

Cats can be finicky and refuse to eat some recipes or mixtures of various foods. They tend to like their food plain, something they can recognize. By mixing several ingredients together, we may turn them off when we place it into their dish. They recognize the smells but somehow they're different so the automatic, natural response is to refuse it all or pick out what is recognizable. If our cat is this way we may have to feed each ingredient separately. For example, cod liver oil may be licked up by itself but when mixed in with other ingredients may be refused. This then requires patience and trail and error to see what our cat will eat. Often it just may take time. Or the other alternative is to give each separately. Also we know that each cat is an individual with her own tastes, what one will eat, another within the same household may not.

VITAMIN & MINERAL FOODS

Cod Liver Oil (pure unflavoured)　　1 tsp / week - adult
　　vitamins A and D　　　　　　　　　1/2 tsp / week - kitten

Raw fish eyes, a rich source of vitamin A, were eaten by indigenous peoples for eye problems. Liver of any kind and fish liver oils are rich in vitamin A and D.

Liver (fresh - raw, or lightly heated)　1 tbsp / day - all ages
　　vitamins A, D, E & K and minerals
Wheat germ oil (cold pressed)　　　1 tsp / 3 days - adult
　　vitamin E　　　　　　　　　　　　1 tsp / 5 days - kitten
Brewer's yeast (flakes)　　　　　　1 tsp / day - all ages
　　vitamin B complex
Sunflower seeds (ground fine)　　　1/2 tsp / day - all ages
vitamins E and B's

The natural source for vitamin C is the raw adrenal gland, if you can get it. It is the small gland just next to the kidneys. Indigenous peoples ate these raw.

Sodium ascorbate (powder)　　　　1/8 tsp / day - all ages
　　vitamin C
Ascorbic acid (powder)　　　　　　1/8 tsp / day - all ages
　　vitamin C

Kelp (powder or liquid)　　　　　　1/4 tsp / day - all ages
　　iodine + minerals　　　　　　　　1 drop / day - all ages

Bone meal or bone dust (Cooked　　1/4 tsp / day - all ages
　　if not fresh)
　　calcium and phosphorus

　　High meat diets give 1/4 tsp / day to all ages.

Oysters (Eastern)　　　　　　　　　1 / week - all ages
　　zinc

DRY VITAMIN & MINERAL SUPPLEMENT

If our cat will eat a mixture of these so much the better and more convenient for us.

Brewer's yeast (B vitamins)	1 cup	250 mL
Bone meal or bone dust (Ca, & P)	1 cup	250 mL
Sunflower seeds, ground fine (E & B)	1 cup	250 mL
Sodium ascorbate (C)	1/4 cup	60 mL
Kelp (I)	1/4 cup	60mL
Catnip (flavour)	2 tbsp.	30 mL

Mix all of these ingredients together and store in an air-tight container in the refrigerator. Give 1/2 tsp. for kittens, 1 tsp for adults and 1 1/2 tsp for queens with kittens. Cut the recipe in half for one kitten so that the preparation stays fresher.

LIQUID VITAMIN & MINERAL SUPPLEMENT

Cod liver oil (vitamins A and D)	1/2 cup	125 mL
Wheat germ oil (vitamin E)	1/4 cup	60 mL
Garlic oil (flavour, Ca. & potassium)	1 tbsp.	15 mL

Mix together in a suitable, air tight, amber container and store in the dark. Give 1/4 tsp. for kittens, 1/2 - 1 tsp. for medium-size cats and up to 1 tbsp. for large, active and pregnant cats once a day with regular meal.

The Dry Supplement, you will note, contains the water soluble B vitamins and C whereas the Liquid Supplement contains the fat soluble vitamins A, D and E - therefore in oil and liquid. Alternate the dry and the liquid so that all the vitamins are offered. Remember we can over do it with some vitamins especially A and D and also the minerals calcium and phosphorus. Refer to the sections on pages 59, 62, and 80 to 84 for precautions. Learn the nutrient contents of foods and use accordingly.

A Few Points When Feeding a Cat Naturally

- use fresh and frozen ingredients vs canned
- use powders vs salts, example garlic powder vs garlic salt
- buy salt-free butter
- make home made meat stocks vs bullion cubes (high salt)
- make home made soups vs prepared soups (additives and salt)
- use animal origin products vs plant sources: butter vs margarine
- bone meal or bone dust vs rock mineral
- raw vegetables can inhibit protein digestion
- cereals are better for fiber than vegetables and fruit
- cats can only digest about 30 - 50 % of most vegetables due to their short intestines
- vegetable nutrients are hard for the cat to digest and utilize
- pectin and fiber help for diarrhea and constipation
- egg has a Biological Value of, 100, rice 75
- organ meats are the wild cats first choice of the carcass
- cooking meats provides some breakdown of proteins
- cats like fresh foods
- cats like their food warm - body temperature
- fish was not a big food source for the ancestral cat
- milk and some milk products have indigestible lactose
- cooking, heat, exposure to light and air can decrease or destroy some vitamins, especially water soluble vitamins

YOGURT

"the milk of eternal life" Emperor Frances I of France

Yogurt is cultured milk that has been eaten for over 4000 years and is much easier to digest than milk. Yogurt has been heralded with many health benefits over the years. It is a good protein source for cats as well as being low in calories.

KITTY CRUNCHIES

Using ingredients from the kitchen we have a recipe that duplicates the texture of dry foods that our cat may be accustomed to.

Hamburger	1 lb.	500 gm
Flaked White Tuna	1 can	1 can
Wholewheat flour	5 cups	1250 mL
Wheat germ	1 cup	250 mL
Powdered milk	1 cup	250 mL
Cornmeal	1 cup	250 mL
Eggs	2	2
Bone meal	2 tbsp.	30 mL
Kelp	3 tbsp.	45 mL
Butter melted	4 tbsp.	60 mL
Cod liver oil	4 tbsp.	60 mL
Catnip	2 tbsp.	30 mL
Water	4 cups	1 L
Brewers yeast	1/2 cup	125 mL

Mix ingredients to make a firm dough. Spread flat on a cookie sheet about 1/4 to 1/2 an inch thick. Bake in a moderate oven until golden brown for 1/2 to 3/4 of an hour. Cool and break into small pieces with a rolling pin and store in an air tight container in the refrigerator.

Feed 1/2 cup in the morning and 1/2 cup in the evening for one adult cat.

Texture is one way that cats learn to recognize food. If our cat has been on a dry cat food, then duplicating that texture may make a new food more palatable. Cooking some foods or recipes to give them a crispy texture may be required, until our cat has become accustomed to the new recipe.

CHICKEN LIVER DELIGHT

A nutritious meal filled with vitamins and minerals.

Chicken livers, cut into small pieces	8 - 10	8-10
Rice	1 1/2 cup	375 mL
Butter	1/4 cup	50 mL
Cheese, grated Parmesan	1/2 cup	125 mL

Cook rice as per direction on the box or your own method. In a frying pan, melt the butter and cook the liver pieces for about 5 minutes stirring occasionally. When rice is cooked, stir in livers and sprinkle with garlic powder and cheese. Will serve a 10 lb (4.5 kg) cat one week.

SAMBO'S SHRIMP SALAD

A tasty seafood salad, offering protein and vitamins A,D & B.

Shrimp (frozen or canned)	2 - 4 oz	55-125 g
Cooked rice	1 1/2 cups	375 mL
Butter	1/2 cup	125 mL

Melt butter. Add shrimp to rice and stir. Blend in butter. Sprinkle (1/4 tsp.) sodium ascorbate power, cool and serve. Serves a 10 lb (4.5 kg) cat 4 times.

SARDINE SALAD

A fishy salad that no cat can resist.

Sardines, can	1	1
Cooked rice	2 cups	500 mL
Cod Liver Oil	2 tbsp.	30 mL

Cook rice as directed. Mash up the sardines and oil and add to the hot rice. Serves a 10 lb (4.5 kg) cat 3 times.

CREAM & VEGETABLE SOUP

Can be served hot on cold days and cool on hot days

Soup stock, chicken, or meat	5 cups	1 L
Carrots, scraped and finely chopped	2	2
Eggs	4	4
Cream	1 cup	250 mL
Flour	2 tbsp.	30 mL
Butter	2 tbsp.	15 mL

In a large saucepan melt the butter and add flour making a smooth paste. Add stock slowly avoiding lumps. Stir in carrots, bring to a boil stirring constantly. Reduce heat, cover and simmer until carrots are tender. Beat the eggs and cream in a small bowl and add to the soup. Cook another 5 minutes, stirring, do not let boil. Cool and serve. Serve warm or cool.

LINUS'S LAMB WITH RICE

Lamb and rice have become popular in commercial cat foods.

Lamb, stewing or shoulder chops	2 lbs.	1 kg
Cooked rice	4 1/2 cups	1 L
Water	2 cups	500 mL
Butter	1 tbsp.	15 mL
Flour	2 tbsp.	30 mL
Kelp	1 tsp.	5 mL
Bone dust or bone meal	1 tsp.	5 mL
Vitamin C (sodium ascorbate)	1/2 tsp.	2 mL

Mix flour, kelp and bone meal. Cut lamb in small pieces and roll in flour mixture. Melt butter in frying pan, add meat and brown slightly. Add water, lamb and the rest of the flour mix to a casserole dish and bake at 350° F (180° C) for about 45 minutes. Mix and serve with the rice. Should feed a cat a week or more. Sprinkle the vitamin C (little less than 1/4 tsp.) each serving.

FELIX'S FISH WITH MILK SAUCE

Thyme has lately been acclaimed to contain antioxidants.

Fish (fillets)	1 lb	1/2 kg
Boiling milk	1/2 cup	125 mL
Butter	1 tbsp.	15 mL
Flour	1 tbsp.	15 mL
Thyme	1/4 tsp.	1 mL

Cut the fish into bite size pieces and place in boiling milk. Simmer until well cooked. Make a sauce with the milk and other ingredients. Will feed three 10 lb (4.5 kg) cats.

You may note that I have deliberately used butter in the recipes as opposed to margarine. Margarine was an invention developed during World War One due to a shortage of butter. It is made from the crushed seeds of either soybeans, cottonseeds, canola or corn that are flushed with a petroleum solvent that is then evaporated off and the oil extracted with lye. This vegetable oil is then heated to drain off volatile components. The liquid oil is then hydrogenated which involves heating the oil with hydrogen at high temperatures and pressures to give the margarine its thickness or smooth texture. This process changes the fat structure from what the organic chemist calls the natural cis form to the trans form. These trans fatty acids are not discriminated against but are incorporated directly in the cellular structures of the cat. As we have said before fats are important in all cell structures, especially the delicate membranes around nerves. This unnatural trans form of fats is now being questioned by scientists and consumers alike as to what the long term effects of eating hydrogenated oils might be.

> *"If adult human beings wish to impose upon themselves an inappropriate and inefficient diet, that is their own business, but if they impose such a diet on their pet cats, they should be prosecuted for cruelty to animals."*
>
> Desmond Morris

PRICE CONSCIOUS RECIPES

We could call this section 'bulk or economic recipes'. These are recipes and ideas aimed at feeding one cat for a long time or for feeding a group of cats. The goal is to feed our cats the best possible foods we can and save money at the same time.

One trap we should not fall into, because it looks like we could save money, is to feed dog food. This might look cheaper but dog food is entirely different and should not be fed to cats even if they should show an interest.

Some of the differences are
- cats require four times as much protein and in particular the amino acids arginine and taurine (animal source)
- cats require more fat, in particular the fatty acid arachindonic acid (animal source)
- cats require twice as many B complex vitamins
- cats can readily absorb iron from meat
- cats cannot convert the amino acid tryptophan to the B vitamin niacin
- cats cannot convert Beta carotene to vitamin A
- cats have no taste response to sugar or sweetening

Dog food is formulated to meet the requirements of dogs and because cats have different requirements, feeding cats dog food would quickly have them in trouble.

Depending on circumstances such as availability of ingredients, help and time available, bulk feeding on our own may not be that economical. Storage also becomes a problem with bulk purchases. However, with a steady supply of ingredients at a reasonable cost with adequate and efficient means for preparation, bulk home feeding can be economical.

Buying ingredients, cooking, and storing for bulk recipes will take time and effort; however, money can be saved.

Purchasing in large quantities from butcher shops, fish shops, grocery stores and other food processors that may be in our neighbourhood can save us money. As with all buying, buy wisely and consider quality, freshness and storage methods.

Some Tips on Stretching Out Our Cat Food Budget.

- Ask neighbours and friends to save table-scraps. (Give them a covered container and guidelines on what to save and what not to save)
- Buy large volumes with friends and split (co-op style)
    - egg powder, milk powder for kittens
    - whole wheat flour, rolled oats, rice and corn flour
    - brewers yeast, cod liver oil, wheat germ oil
    - Ascorbic acid or sodium ascorbate (vitamin C)
    - Alfalfa powder, bone meal, kelp powder and catnip
- Ask grocers and butchers for
    - bulk discounts on organ meats: liver, kidney, heart, sweet bread, pancreas, brain and tripe.
    - fat trim, bone dust, large bones for soups
    - discoloured and freezer burnt meats and fish
    - out of date dairy products and eggs
    - off colour bulk items, cereals, pasta and flours
    - meat and fish trim

When offered out of date foods be sure that the packaging and containers are not damaged and they have been stored properly.

Stay away from sugar, (cakes, cookies) salt (chips, tacos) and damaged canned goods (Botulism). Avoid restaurant scraps which may contain spices and hydrogenated fats.

A few things to remember:

- an all meat diet can lead to calcium deficiency
- heart is cheap but also requires calcium supplements
- Red Tuna can lead to vitamin E deficiency
- beware of freshness and the opportunity for contamination. If in doubt cook well.
- ask to have meat and fish scraps frozen immediately

FELINE FEAST

We all can make recipes similar to this one.

Chicken fat, skin (from 1 chicken)	1 cup	250 mL
Kidney, beef (sliced into small chunks)	1	1
Water	6 cups	1 1/2 L
Oatmeal	4 1/2 cups	1 L
Kelp powder	2 tbsp.	30 mL
Cod Liver oil	2 tbsp.	30 mL
Bone meal	1 tsp.	4 mL

Put the first 3 into a large pot and simmer on low heat covered. After about 20 minutes add 1 cup of the oatmeal. Let simmer for 5 minutes then stir and add another cup of oatmeal. Continue to add more oatmeal and stir until all the oatmeal is added. Stir in the last three. Let cool, spoon out an amount reasonable for your cats and put the rest into an ice cream pail and save.

Nutritionally we have provided fat (chicken fat), protein (kidney), carbohydrate and fiber (oatmeal), vitamins and minerals (kelp, cod liver oil and bone meal).

BIG FAMILY DISH

A bulk recipe for a big eater or a group, look out stand back.

Rice (cooked)	4 cups	1 L
Oatmeal	2 cups	500 mL
Pork sausages (cut in small pieces)	1 lb	1/2 kg
Cod Liver oil	2 tbsp.	30 mL
Brewers yeast	2 tbsp	30 mL
Sour Cream	1 cup	250 mL

Place the cooked rice on the bottom of a medium roaster. Sprinkle the oatmeal evenly on top of the rice. Spread the sausage pieces evenly on top. Cover and bake in 300° F (150° C) for about 30 minutes. Cool, sprinkle cod liver oil and brewers yeast, and top with sour cream. Serve portions depending upon the size of the cats.

SIR VIVER SALAD

A cool salad for those hot days of summer.

Macaroni (or pasta noodles)	2 cups	500 mL
Regular ground beef or pork	1 lb	1/2 kg
Water	2 cups	500 mL
Garlic cloves, finely chopped	1	1

Cook macaroni or pasta according to directions. Fry ground beef or pork. Drain macaroni and mix in meat including fat and chopped garlic. Cool and serve. 1 cup will serve a 10 lb (4.5 kg) cat her morning or evening meal. Vitamin and mineral mix can be sprinkle on top.

BARNABY'S BISCUITS

Treat biscuits or "bones"

Whole wheat flour	5 1/2 cups	1.25 L
Cracked wheat flour	3 cups	750 mL
Cornmeal	1 cup	250 mL
Milk powder	1/2 cup	125 mL
Yeast, envelope	1	1
Water, warm	1/4 cup	50 mL
Chicken or Beef broth	3 cups	750 mL
Egg, slightly beaten	1	1
Bone meal or Bone dust	4 tbsp.	60 mL
Catnip powder	1 tbsp.	15 mL

Mix the first 4 ingredients in a large bowl. Dissolve yeast in the water and add to the mixture. Add broth and form dough. Roll out about 1/4 in. (.5 cm) thick cut into "bones", makes 30 large bones. Brush with egg glaze and bake at 300º F (150º C) for 45 min. Turn off oven and leave in oven overnight to harden.

ECONO MIX

This mix can be made in large quantities and stored in the refrigerator and used either with left-overs or other recipes. Since this is predominately carbohydrate mixing with fat, protein, vitamins and minerals complete the meal.

Rice white or brown	2 cups	500 mL
Cereal grain		
(oats, barley or wheat)	1 cup	250 mL
Water or broth	3 cups	750 mL

In a large pot mix the three and bring to a boil. Simmer for about 15 minutes. If using brown rice use 3 times the time. Cool and refrigerate for later use. Depending upon the number of cats mix this base with the drippings from a roast and some protein such as cottage cheese, eggs, or meat or fish scraps and a vitamin-mineral supplement for a complete meal.

SOUP A LA SAMBO

Use our imagination and what we have available to make a soup that can be fed by itself or poured over dry cat food.

Raw soup bones	2 - 3	2 - 3
Water	2 qts.	2 L
Carrots, medium sized	2	2
Garlic powder or catnip	1/2 tsp.	2 mL

Put the bones and water into a large pot and bring to a boil. Reduce heat and simmer for 1 1/2 to 2 hours. Puree the carrots and add to the soup. Cook for another 30 minutes. Sprinkle in the garlic or catnip stirring as you add it. Remove the bones, cool and give to your cats, preferably outside to save the carpet. Feed the soup warm by itself or pour onto dry cat food or left-over rice, potatoes or other foods. Save the rest for later use. Many variations can be developed from this basic recipe using ingredients we have on hand.

Remember to heat up cold food right out of the refrigerator to "blood heat" temperature. This is just a term that is sometimes used which means body temperature. We wouldn't think of feeding a young baby of our family milk straight out of the fridge. without warming it up first. Warming up the food for the cats does several things:

- it is more "natural" for the carnivorous cat to eat warm food.
- by warming food the aromas produced stimulate appetite
- warm food should be easier to digest as chemical reactions of enzymes etc. require heat

On hot days we may want to give cool foods and the sudden lump of cold within the very core of the cat right next to the vital organs may be harmful.

BEAR'S BREAKFAST

Pan fry this breakfast that will last all day.

Bacon, slices	3	3
Eggs	2	2
Porridge (oatmeal)	1 cup	250 mL
Milk	1/4 cup	50 mL
B complex 50mg tablet (crushed)	1	1
Vitamin C 250mg tablet (crushed)	1	1

Chop the bacon into 1/2 inch (cm) pieces and fry lightly in a pan. Add the porridge and continue until brown. Beat the eggs and milk in a small dish. Add the milk and well beaten eggs to the frying pan stirring the while as the eggs cook. Cool and sprinkle on the crushed vitamin tablets.

This is a powerful way to start the day with protein, energy and vitamins. This will feed four cats all day.

KITTY SQUARES

We eat squares; here's some for our cats.

Commercial Cat Chow	4 1/2 cups	1 L
Flour	1 cup	250 mL
Water	1 1/2 cups	374 mL
Eggs	2	2
Cooking oil	3 tbsp.	45 mL
Liver pate	3 tbsp.	45 mL

Mix flour, water, eggs and oil in a mixing bowl. Add cat chow and mix well. Put into an oiled 8x8 inch baking pan. Bake at 350^0 F (180^0 C) for about 45 minutes. Cool and spread liver pate on top as "icing". Cut into squares and enjoy.

Dry cat food can be put in a blender to make a meal of varying consistency depending on how long and how fast we run the blender. Add liquid if the nuggets are very hard.

Cooking is an art as well as a science. Trying a favorite recipe for our cat with a few modifications for the reasons we have discussed can be done by all of us. Commercial cat food can be used as an ingredient as we have done in several recipes utilizing the texture and nutrient content accordingly. We may be surprised when we heat some cat foods especially the poorer quality ones for the unusual aromas that develop. Make your own judgments.

All cats are different and all have their own tastes and preferences. Cooking for them becomes, just as cooking for our family, a trial and error procedure to find what they like and what they do not. Some recipes might end up in the dog's dish as dogs are less fussy. Once we know what our cats like and what is nutritious for them, cooking their favorite recipes is something that they can hardly wait for.

JOAN HARPER'S KITTY CRUNCHIES

Adapted, with permission, from Joan Harper's *Feed The Kitty Naturally*

Ingredient	US	Metric
Chicken necks or gizzards (ground)	1 lb	500 g
Mackerel, canned, including liquid	16 oz	455 mL
Soy flour, full fat	2 cups	500 mL
Wheat germ	1 cup	250 mL
Skim milk, powdered	1 cup	250 mL
Cornmeal	1 cup	250 mL
Whole wheat flour	2 cups	500 mL
Rye flour (or wheat four)	1 cup	250 mL
Bonemeal, only with gizzards	3 tbsp.	45 mL
or Bone dust, only with gizzards	1 2/3 cup	420 mL
Iodized salt	1 tbsp.	15 mL
or Kelp	3 tbsp.	45 mL
Vegetable oil/meat drippings or butter	4 tbsp.	60 mL
Cod Liver Oil	1 tbsp.	15 mL
Alfalfa powder	1/4 cup	50 mL
Nutritional yeast	1/2 cup	125 mL
Garlic cloves, minced	3	3
Water	4 cups	1 L
Vitamin E	400 i.u.	

If using necks use a meat grinder or have your butcher grind them. Mix all ingredients except the yeast into a firm dough. Roll it out on a cookie sheet about 1/4 to 1/2 inch thick. Bake at 350 degrees for 30 to 45 minutes. Cool and break into bite size chunks. Sprinkle with yeast and store in air tight containers. Two or three days' worth will keep a few days without refrigeration. Refrigerate or freeze the rest.

Tip: If this treat is still not tempting enough for the finicky cat, try pouring a little bacon fat or gravy over it. If you use this as a mainstay diet, supplement it with some raw vegetables, cottage cheese or yogurt.

GOURMET RECIPES

"It was so good, I don't feel an ounce of guilt".

Here we are going to be a little decadent and enjoy ourselves. Some recipes we have thrown all caution to the wind. Fancy dishes can still be nutritious. Birthdays, parties, Thanksgiving or Christmas. Over indulging? Yes, but who cares.

Every Gourmet meal starts off with a salad, soup, main course, dessert and of course a wine either, red or white. This meal may stretch out over a week or two because each one of these dishes is a daily meal in itself.

CLEOPATRA SALAD

A seafood salad with greens, vitamins and minerals.

Shrimp, small or broken	2 - 4 oz	55 - 125 g
Lettuce or wheat grass, finely chopped	1/2 cup	125 mL
Tomato juice	1/2 cup	125 mL
Cod Liver Oil	1 tbsp.	15 mL

Mix the shrimp, greens and tomato juice well and top with the cod liver oil, " salad oil " and serve.

CASPER'S CLAM CHOWDER

A gourmet meal must start with a small bowl of Clam Chowder.

Clams, canned	1	1
Water	3 cups	750 mL
Flour	3 tbsp	45 mL

Heat the clams in the water for about 5 minutes and sift in the flour and stir until blended. Serve. Save the rest and serve another day warmed as all soups should be served.

OSCAR'S DEEP FRIED OYSTERS

Truly a feline delicacy.

Oysters, canned	4 oz	125 g
Egg	1	1
Bread crumbs	1/2 cup	125 mL

Drain the oil from the oysters and beat oil with the egg. Add the oysters to the beaten egg and gently stir. Roll the oysters in the bread crumbs. Let dry on a rack for 30 minutes. Fry for about 2 minutes in deep fat at 190° C (375° F) or in a skillet with a 1 tbsp. of butter. Serve one at a time as an appetizer. Refrigerate the rest to serve another day gently warmed in the microwave.

HANNIBAL'S HAM & PEA SOUP

A filling soup that lasts all day.

Ham bone	1	1
Ham, chopped	1 cup	250 mL
Split peas	1/2 cup	125 mL
Water	10 cups	2.75 L
Garlic cloves (crushed)	3	3
Butter	2 tbsp.	30 mL

In a large pot simmer the ham bone and water for about 1 hour. Remove the bone (give to your dog, preferably outside) In a saucepan melt butter, add crushed garlic, split peas and cook for about 5 minutes. Add this to the liquid from the ham bone and let simmer for about 2 hours. Let cool for 15 minutes then puree the mixture in a blender. Add the pieces of chopped ham. Serve warm, portion depending upon the size of the cat. Save the rest to serve by itself or in combination with dry cat food, as a topping. Can also be used with leftovers.

CHOU CHOU'S DELIGHT

Excellent on cold winter days

Chicken cooked, shredded	2 oz	55 g
Pearl barley	1/2 cup	125 mL
Chicken stock	5 cups	1.25 L
Yogurt plain	2 cups	500 mL
Butter	2 tbsp.	30 mL
Bone dust or bone meal	2 tbsp.	30 mL
Brewers yeast	2 tbsp.	30 mL
Vitamin C (500 mg crushed tablet)	1	1
Cod Liver Oil	2 tbsp.	30 mL

Melt butter in a large saucepan, add chicken stock and bring to a boil. Reduce heat, add barley and simmer for 50 minutes. Add shredded chicken and simmer another 10 minutes. Beat yogurt and add to the soup. Add last three ingredients at this time. Serves a 10 lb (4.5 kg) cat four times.

DEEP FRIED CHICKEN GIZZARDS OR LIVERS

A tasty, nutritious feline delicacy.

Chicken gizzards or livers	1 lb	500 g
Whole wheat flour	1 1/3 cup	325 mL
Butter, melted	1 tbsp.	15 mL
Egg yolks, beaten	2	2
Egg whites, stiffly beaten	2	2

In a medium size bowl mix the flour, butter and egg yolks. Rest with cover in the refrigerator for 3 to 12 hours. Cut the gizzards or livers into teaspoon size pieces. Just before use add egg whites and organ pieces to batter. Fry in deep fat, heated to 365° F (185° C) until reasonably brown. Cool and give as treats, save the rest to be warmed and enjoyed later.

CHRISTMAS CASSEROLE

A Christmas treat using turkey left-overs.

Cream of chicken soup	10 oz	284 mL
Water	1/4 cup	50 mL
Chow mein noodles	1 cup	250 mL
Turkey (chopped)	1 cup	250 mL
Garlic powder or catnip	1/4 tsp.	1 mL

Place soup, water, noodles, and turkey into a 1 1/2 - quart casserole. Stir and bake for 45 minutes in a 375° F (190° C) oven. Cool and serve two heaping tablespoons per meal. Serves a 10 lb (4.5 Kg) cat six to seven days. Add vitamin and mineral treats as listed on page 196.

THANKSGIVING FEAST

This is a delicious turkey variation.

Turkey (chopped)	1 cup	250 mL
Rice or mashed potatoes	1 cup	250 mL
Butter	2 tbsp.	30 mL
Vitamin C, 250 mg crushed tablet	1	1

Warm the turkey with the butter in a medium sized pan. Mix in the rice or potatoes and continue frying for a minute stirring continuously. Cool, stir in the vitamin C and serve.

Vitamin C is susceptible to loss by heat or exposure to air so we always add it last to keep its potency.

Left-over turkey skin and fat can be saved and used later. Small pieces of skin can be fed as treats and the fat can be used in recipes as a substitute for butter or as a topping for commercial dry cat food. One half to one teaspoon at a time.

GOURMET DRINKS

A Gourmet meal must have wine, red or white.

RED "WINE" FELINE STYLE

After roasting beef, lamb, or pork remove the roast and quarter fill the roaster with water. Warm for several minutes and add a sprinkle of garlic powder or catnip, whatever is your cat's preference. Stir and scrape the roaster bottom to lift off any meat. Pour into a container to be used as a cold or warm drink.

WHITE "WINE"

Do the same as above with a chicken or turkey roaster to make a white "wine". These can be used by themselves as a drink or added to dry cat food or another recipe.

COUGAR-AID

A drink that will quench the thirst on a hot day or after vigorous exercise. Also a good drink for a nursing Queen

Water	9 cups	2 L
Lite salt (potassium chloride)	2 tbsp.	30 mL
Vitamin C		
(powder or crushed tablet)	500 mg	500 mg
Vitamin B complex (50 mg	3	3
crushed tablet)		

Crush the tablets well and dissolve in the water. Serve cold.

PUSS'S POPSICLES

Something to lick on those hot days of summer.

Using any of the top three recipes pour the liquid into ice cube containers or popsicle molds and freeze. Once frozen remove from container and store in a plastic bag for later use. Can be put into empty food dish for a cool refreshment.

CHUMLEY'S MEAT LOAF

A nutritious, " stick to your ribs," meat loaf.

Beef or Pork regular ground	1 1/2 lbs.	700 g
Egg beaten	1	1
Water	3/4 cup	175 mL
Rolled oats	1 cup	250 mL
Brewers yeast	1 tbsp.	15 mL
Bone meal	1 tsp.	5 mL
Kelp	1 tsp.	5 mL
Grated Cheddar cheese	1/2 cup	125 mL
Garlic powder or catnip	1/2 tsp.	2 mL

Put first 7 ingredients into large bowl. Mix together well. Pack into a loaf pan 9 x 5 x 3 inches (23 x 12 x 7 cm). Bake uncovered in 350° F (180° C) oven for 1 hour. Spread grated cheese over meat and return to oven to melt. Garnish with garlic powder or catnip. Cool, serves 15 - 18 lb (7 - 8 kg) cat a week.

SYLVESTER'S SALMON PATTIES

Better than fresh canary (Tweety Bird).

Salmon, fresh, smoked or canned	4 oz	125 g
Crackers	15 to 20	
or bread crumbs	1 1/2 cups	375 mL
Egg	1	1
Water	2 tbsp.	30 mL

Break up the crackers with a rolling pin, not too fine. Beat the egg and water. Stir in the crackers or bread crumbs. Add the salmon, mix well. Form small patties, about large egg size and flatten. Fry lightly in a buttered skillet. One will last a medium size cat one half a day. Refrigerate the rest and serve warm.

SARDINES ON TOAST

A treat that can last all day.

Sardines, canned	3.75 oz	106 g
Bread, toasted	2 slices	

Toast the bread. Spread sardines, let liquid from the sardines soak into the bread for a minute and serve. One half slice will get her purring and grooming with satisfaction.

BIRTHDAY PARTY CAKE

Be sure to sing Happy Birthday before serving this cake.

Cake flour	1 cup	250 mL
Baking powder	1 1/2 tsp.	7 mL
Garlic powder	1/4 tsp.	1 mL
Shortening, softened	1/4 cup	50 mL
Sugar (required in a cake recipe)	1/2 cup	125 mL
Egg	1	1
Milk	1/2 cup	125 mL
Liver pate (for "icing)	3 tbsp.	45 mL
Catnip	1 tsp.	5 mL

Sift flour and measure. Resift with baking and garlic powder. In a mixing bowl beat shortening until creamy. Add sugar gradually, beating well. Add egg and beat until the creamed mixture is light and fluffy. Add milk alternating with the flour mixture to the shortening mixture 1/3 at a time; ending with the flour. Stir after each addition until the mixture is smooth. Place in a 8 X 8 in. (20 X 20 cm) pan or 6 greased muffin tins. Bake at 350° F (180° C) for about 25 to 30 minutes. Cool and "ice" with liver pate and garnish with catnip. Cut into 6 equal parts.

Candles are optional.

Our cat can overindulge with extra calories now and then; however, there are a few definite "no-no's". Our cat is our best friend and we definitely don't want to hurt her.

Foods to avoid and why

- "junk-foods" chips, tacos, cheezies etc.
  high in sodium, the cat does not need salt
- spicy foods: can cause stomach irritations and upsets.
- candy and sweets: high in refined sugar, empty calories
- ice cream: lactose may be upsetting causing diarrhea
- rhubarb: calcium binding and the leaves are poisonous
- Licorice: is potassium binding
- Chocolate

We know that dogs are very sensitive to theobromine, a compound in chocolate, which can cause vomiting, diarrhea, seizures and death. Four oz. of baking chocolate can poison a thirty pound dog. I don't know if the same is true for cats but I wouldn't take the chance.

Here are a few things to avoid and be aware of. Basically what a cat likes are the flavours in fats. Overindulgence of fat can be upsetting and remember fat has over twice the calories of other foods and may diminish appetite for other nutrients. Always remember that our cat is a lot smaller than we are, a 7 or 11 lb cat could be 1/15 th. to 1/25 th. our size. We are 15 to 25 times bigger!

Cats like most kinds of fish and liver; these foods are gourmet to them, but too much of a good thing can lead to trouble. Variety is best.

In this section we are having a little fun with our feline friends by giving them a taste of the good life. They have a chance to indulge in some feline culinary delights and in turn give us a warm feeling because we are pleasing our dear friends.

SPECIAL INDIVIDUALS

In this section of Recipes we shall discuss the feeding of cats with special requirements. Until now we have presented recipes for cats requiring the maintenance levels of nutrients. The following are for special case individuals.

Separately we shall cover the feeding of the
- Overweight Cat
- Underweight Cat
- Sick and Convalescing
- Queen, mother
- Kitten
- Sick Kitten care
- Orphan Kitten
- Neutered Individual
- Seniors

Adjustments are made for these individuals as their requirement levels for the various nutrients are different from those of the average cat on a maintenance diet. Each special situation will be covered from a nutritional stand point followed by some recipes.

Some of these special case cats are under a common term we call stress. It is appropriate to discuss stress at this time. Stress is involved in such things as illness, surgery, queening, nursing, growing or geriatric. Other things like travel, fear and lack of accustomed affection are also stressful. Important is how the cat responds to stress and how we can help.

What is stress? Stress is a physical or psychological demand that is put upon our cat. What happens? The internal systems go on the alert, nerves tingle and hormones pump into the blood stream causing heartbeat and breathing rates to increase and muscles to tense. If the stressful situation should continue for any length of the time the results can be overwhelming. The cat must be able to cope.

As the cat's body reacts extra energy and protein are needed to repair damaged cells, produce antibodies and make new red blood cells. Extra vitamins and minerals also become important to furnish the added requirements to cope with the stress.

A certain amount of stress is healthy; it keeps the cat alert and responsive, all part of survival. However, problems start when the stress becomes continuous. Constant demands, pressures and uncertainties draw on reserves of nutrients and body cells. If the stress is more than the cat can handle, changes become apparent. Increased susceptibility to disease, premature aging and behavioral changes can result. If our cat is suffering from too much stress, whatever the source, he or she will be depressed, inactive and unresponsive, the typical "burn out" syndrome.

The amount of stress our cat can tolerate will depend upon his or her general health, nutrition, breed personality, and owner support and caring. Some breeds and certain individuals thrive on action and are capable of coping with more stress.

Quality protein, fat, vitamins and minerals become important in the diet. Fat for concentrated fuel and the amino acids of protein for tissue maintenance are important. Animal proteins and fats serve best here in a balance with all the other nutrients.

We have to help our cat to manage stress by identifying it and giving him or her assistance to deal with it. We can start by reducing the stressful environment and giving as much comfort as possible. Regular feeding of a nutritious diet, with fresh water and a quiet place to rest is half the battle. Attention and affection can help lessen their burden. When in doubt we can think like a cat and image ourselves in the situation.

Routine vaccinations and treatment for internal and external parasites become part of the health regime.

OVERWEIGHT AND OBESITY

"An overindulged cat may become soft and sluggish, factors that shorten its life and expose it to illness."
Norman H. Johson, D.V.M.

"Our foods are being devitalized by over processing, and this is the cause of much over-eating in the body's attempt to acquire the needed nutrients for good health."
Renee S. Torit

Obesity is the increase in body weight beyond the limitations of skeletal and physical requirements. This increase is due to an excessive accumulation of body fat. The mass of fat is more than twenty per cent of the total body mass. Or in other words if our cat is fifteen per cent heavier than other cats for his or her age then it is overweight and should lose some weight. We should be able to feel our cat's ribs with a light covering of body fat and not with a lot of loose abdominal fat around the lower abdomen.

The first signs are a less active cat with an unkempt coat. As our cat becomes overweight her activity level decreases and she develops a dull, listless personality. Playing and exploring activities decrease. Grooming becomes a chore for the obese cat in that this daily routine - usually 15 - 30 times a day - becomes an effort and due to fat deposits many parts cannot be reached to be properly groomed. This lack of grooming leads to unkempt hair, mats and an unhappy cat.

Obesity is the number one disease problem in our pets today. There are more fat cats - that is the four-legged ones - today then ever before and the numbers are increasing every day. The primary problem is too many calories and not enough activity. Overweight cats go on to have other problems caused by carrying this excess "baggage". There is no question a lean cat is far healthier and will live longer. Body fat, however, does reduce the risk of osteoporosis and increases a cat's tolerance to cold weather.

Problems arise from Obesity:

- less active and playful
- life expectancy is greatly shortened
- more veterinary medical costs
- greater susceptibility to disease and injury
- increased anesthetic and surgical risk
- longer time needed to recover after surgery or illness
- poor wound healing
- lower fertility, difficult queening and poor lactation
- contributes to nutritional deficiencies
- increased pressure on internal organs
- constipation
- increased blood pressure
- contributing factor to heart, lung and skeletal problems
- shortness of breath and greater risk of heat stroke
- increased risk of diabetes, liver and kidney problems
- decreased ability to exercise and play
- decreased grooming, unkempt hair and mats

Causes of Obesity:

- consuming more calories than required due to
  - poor quality cat food loaded with empty calories
  - convenience of high quality commercial cat food
  - table scraps high in fat
  - being fed by the neighbours
  - fed snacks between meals
  - receiving food instead of love and attention
  - we give in to begging
  - boredom
- neutering, decreases hormones and resulting activity
- pregnancy, consuming more in preparation for lactation
- lack of exercise
- advancing age with less activity
- congestive heart failure, hypothyroidism, diabetes mellitus
- breed and individual differences; the Domestic Short Hair seems more prone to becoming overweight

Cats require energy for the basic body functions and activities. Any extra is saved as body fat for the day when they may be short of energy. In the wild, where hunting and scavenging are the means of getting food, saving for the days when food may be in short supply is important. Feast and famine. Our domestic cat today gets to feast everyday but continues to prepare for famine. We must reduce the feast and add a little famine.

How can we tell if our cat is overweight? We can assess our cat by weighing and comparing to other cats or we can do a physical examination. Ribs should not be visible but be easily felt. We should feel a light cover of fat under the skin. The stomach should be tucked up not loose and flabby. All of our domestic cats of all breeds, crosses or pedigrees have the same requirements and the same internal structures with very few exceptions. Unlike dogs that come in many shapes and sizes, our domesticated cats are relatively all the same with very few differences between breeds.

Prevention is the best medicine. However, if our cat is a little "fat" what should we do? First we must determine the cause. If we have eliminated any medical problem and too many calories is the cause, reducing the number of calories is the treatment.

Our objective is to promote a loss of body fat while conserving lean muscle tissue. When we put our cat on a reducing diet we must remember this. We want the cat to lose body fat but not affect the other tissues like muscles and bones. There are commercially-prepared reducing diets on the market today that are primarily low calorie and high fiber. Indigestible fiber levels of fifteen to twenty-five per cent give the cat of feeling of satisfaction - from the bulk nature of the fiber - because she has something in her stomach. Fiber does not supply any calories or nutrients. The fat content is less than nine per cent as well. Protein, vitamins and minerals are kept at the regular amounts so that muscle and bone tissue is not affected by the diet. The goal is to reduce the number of calories without affecting intake.

I believe another, natural, way to lose weight is to provide high quality ingredients that supply top quality proteins and fats with the correct amounts of vitamins and minerals but less volume. The quality diet will provide everything just less of it.

How to Lose weight?

- make a commitment and set a weight goal
- monitor weight loss and body condition regularly
- feed less and more often, 20 to 30% less
- leave food out for only 15 to 20 minutes
- don't forget protein, vitamins and minerals
- create good eating habits, regular and on time
- avoid high empty calorie foods such as sweets
- give love and attention instead of snacks
- give attention to behavioral changes
- have only one person in charge of feeding
- increase exercise and play
- try to eliminate boredom with toys or other pets
- if a house pet keep the house cooler
- if two or more cats separate at feeding
- commercial reducing diets require the same commitments
- be firm and don't give in

A cat can go for many days without eating. Fasting in the wild was common so don't think that our cat has to eat every day. Going without food for several days wouldn't hurt. Be sure that water is available at all times.

Remember this is all in the cat's best interest. Obesity is detrimental to the cat's health and life expectancy. Dieting need not be severe. What is required is an awareness of the problem and the benefits of the final results.

The wonderful thing about losing weight is that the cat's activity level increases and she becomes more playful and active. This activity even uses up more calories so that weight loss is then more effective and efficient. The cat is happier.

Our cat starts to feel better and starts to look better as her muscles are toning up. Her hair coat gets a shine of inner health as she takes an interest in herself and is able to groom herself. She once again becomes the athlete that she was meant to be, the slick and shining desert hunter of her ancestral heritage. We in turn enjoy her more and like to show her off.

Overweight and Obesity: (Warrants repeating)

- most important problem of our pets today
- have medical conditions attended to
- obesity shortens life span and increases medical problems
- obesity is carried from kittenhood to adulthood
- reducing requires commitment and firmness
- feed less of regular food or try reducing preparations
- utilize indigestible fiber to decrease hunger
- increasing fiber content may hinder absorption of nutrients
- body fat as well as muscle may be lost when reducing
- exercise, burning more calories, is part of the program
- prevention by providing only enough calories to maintain a normal body weight

I have found a good way to trim a cat down is to offer high quality bits of food often during the day. High quality animal proteins and fats are not only natural but these foods are satisfying so that the cat will go away contented. This takes time and effort on our part in that someone has to be around all day to feed the cat.

Small portions and feeding often are the keys. A teaspoon of food every three or four hours or more is sufficient. The small portions allow the stomach to shrink so that hungry is easily satisfied and fat foods give the cat a feeling of well being and fullness.

A teaspoon of these foods given often will trim down a cat:

yogurt	roast turkey	roast chicken	fish
cottage cheese	roast beef	roast duck	cooked egg
sour cream	roast pork	hamburger	kidney
sardines	roast lamb	liver	kippers

LOW FAT HIGH FIBER

If our cat will eat vegetables this is a recipe that may work. Balanced for protein, vitamins and mineral. Low in calories and high in fiber. Here we use bulk to give a feeling of fullness.

Beef lean ground	4 oz	125 g
Cottage Cheese dry	1/2 cup	125 mL
Carrots cooked	2 cups	500 mL
Green Beans cooked	2 cups	500 mL
Bone meal	1 tsp.	5 mL
Garlic powder or cat nip	1/2 tsp.	2 mL

Cook beef drain fat. Mix in other ingredients. Sprinkle with garlic or catnip. Feeds a 15 lb (7 kg) cat three days

Utilizes vegetables to provide fiber and bulk. Low fat dairy products supply protein, vitamins and minerals while reducing calories.

BEEF TONGUE

Tasty low calorie, high fiber reducing recipe.

Beef Tongue diced	1 lb	500 g
Carrots sliced	2	2
Celery stalks, with leaves chopped	2	2
Tomato juice, low sodium	1 cup	250 mL
Water	1 cup	250 mL
Bone meal	1 tsp.	5 mL
catnip	1 tsp.	5 mL
Corn starch	2 tsp.	10 mL
Parsley chopped	3 tsp.	15 mL

Mix first six ingredients in a blender and simmer for 1 hour. Mix corn starch with 2 tbsp. water and add slowly to tongue mixture. Stir and cook until thickened. Add parsley and cool. Feeds 15 - 18 lb (7 - 8 kg) cat 4 days.

UNDERWEIGHT

Some cats by nature and /or breed are "hard keepers". Get a professional opinion on the cat's condition as health and well being are what is important, not external appearances. Fit cats are not fat. Be sure that no medical problem is evident.

Underweight is usually the result of an inadequate amount of nutrients or energy consumed for the nature and situation that the cat is in. A growing kitten, a lactating queen or an active outside tom use and require more nutrients.

Three things may be the problem. Not enough food is provided or the cat does not consume enough or the cat cannot physically consume enough to meet all its requirements. The last would apply to a queen heavy with kittens.

Barring any medical condition or parasite load and if we believe that our cat should have a little more "fat on her bones", then a diet with an increase in caloric intake or an examination of the feeding routine may be appropriate.

A few hints for these individuals:

- develop a feeding routine, feed at the same time every day
- if limited feeding try free choice
- develop an exercise and play schedule to improve appetite.
- all cats are individuals, some may need company or activity going on for them to eat.
- or feed in a quiet place were the cat is not disturbed
- try wholesome meal snacks
- change the diet, try fresh food such as raw meat or liver
- warm and/or moisten the meal
- top dress with table scraps, especially fat drippings
- try a kitten type of cat food which has more protein and fat in the ingredients.
- always have water available

Refer to the gourmet section, page 211 for high calorie recipes.

SICK AND CONVALESCING

There is a harmony that exists in the cat's body with the many complex interactions of all body functions playing all in tune to the same symphony. When the cat is sick for whatever reason the harmony is "out of tune" and healing is the body's way of getting back in tune.

Feeding the sick during illness or while convalescing after surgery deserves special attention. By nature a cat will lose its appetite and not eat when it is sick or distressed. This is nature's way of trying to "heal thyself". By not eating, the cat is giving its digestive system a rest so that all the body systems can concentrate on getting better. Loss of appetite is a good indicator of a digestive problem or poor health and a return to eating is a sign that things are improving.

With diminished appetite and a reduction in food intake there may be a decrease in the intake of protein, the essential nutrient for the repair and building of tissues. Other nutrients such as energy, vitamins and minerals may also be reduced.

Some conditions such as a sore throat or a plugged nose may also add to what appears to be a lack of appetite. Offering warm, moist, soft food and cleaning the nostrils may help.

The primary aim in feeding the sick is to give easily digested highly concentrated, nutrient-rich foods, especially protein. Since the amount of food ingested will be small we should ensure that what is eaten will be useful. Protein is given so that the cat will recover.

Oral medications, such as antibiotics, given during illness often disrupt the digestive system resulting in abdominal discomfort and diarrhea with loss of nutrients and fluids. This places more importance on replacing those nutrients and watching for dehydration. Water should always be available.

MOM'S CHICKEN SOUP

Good for us and good for cats

Chicken noodle soup package	1	1
Water half as much called for		
Butter melted	1 tbsp.	15 mL
Brewers yeast	1 tsp.	5 mL
Vitamins infant liquid	6 drops	.5 mL
Vitamin C tablet crushed, or powder	250 mg	250 mg
Garlic powder	1 tsp.	5 mL

Heat the soup mix as directed on the package with only 1/2 the amount of water. When ready add the other ingredients. Cool and serve warm.

HOSPITAL GRUEL

Easily digested, high protein, and fortified.

Canned meat baby food	2 cans	
Cottage cheese creamed	1 1/2 cup	375 mL
Egg	1	1
Brewer's yeast	2 tbsp.	30 mL
Butter melted	2 tbsp.	30 mL
Bone meal	1 tsp.	5 mL
Vitamin C (tablet crushed) or powder	250 mg	250 mg
Vitamins infant liquid (or 1 adult multi-vitamin tablet crushed)	10 drops	

Mix all ingredients and warm to slightly cook the egg. Cool and serve warm. Will feed a 10 lb (4.5 kg) cat three days.

Experiment, try combinations or single foods like raw beef heart, liver, kidney, lean fish, chicken giblets, liver pate or baby foods. High quality animal proteins and fats that are warmed to body temperature stimulate the natural appetite for nourishment.

LIVER MUFFINS

Good every day supplement or meal for convalescing cats with poor appetites, or cats with skin problems. Liver contains a high concentration of vitamins and minerals.

Chicken livers	1 lb.	.5 kg
Butter (melted)	1/2 cup	125 mL
Bran	4 cups	1 L
Bone meal	1/2 tsp.	2 mL

Melt the butter. Blend the livers in a blender until quite liquid. Add all other ingredients and blend again. Put into ice cube tray or into muffin tin with cups. Use ice cube trays or egg cartoons. Freeze. Can remove from trays and store in large plastic bag frozen. Feed warmed one per day.

GET BETTER SOON

Highly nutritious and tasty

Yogurt plain (not low fat)	1 cup	500 g
Honey warmed or liquid	3 tbsp.	45 mL
Vitamin C tablet crushed	250 mg	250 mg
B complex adult tablet crushed	1	1

Add honey to yogurt and warm in Microwave or on stove. Mix in vitamins and serve warm.

To feed the sick and convalescing cat use ingredients that are highly palatable, easily digested and rich in nutrients. Serving the food warm makes it easier for the cat to smell the aromas and improves her appetite. Foods rich in protein and fat supply nutrients for building, repair of tissues and concentrated energy. The aim is to feed several small, meat-based meals in a quiet environment. Remembering that the cat is a solitary carnivore used to a high protein animal based diet.

MOTHERS

A queen well-nourished during gestation and properly fed during lactation will be able to provide for her kittens for the first three weeks of their lives. Queens bred at optimal weight should return to optimal weight by weaning.

When the queen has been properly nourished, breeding and conception conditions are optimal. Poor nutrition may result in low conception rates, fetal abnormalities, hair loss and mammary gland changes affecting the quality and quantity of milk. Poor quality feeding to a pregnant mother can cause loss of body weight. Uncontrolled diarrhea from poorly digested low quality food may occur. Weak and dead kittens, no milk, or little milk and anemia may also develop. Feeding a diet that is balanced for her condition in sufficient quantity that she can digest starts early in her reproductive career and doesn't end until the kittens are weaned. Her ration should have at least 1600 digestible calories per pound of food at this time.

The standard commercial maintenance diets for adult cats do not have the required amounts for protein, energy, vitamins and minerals so just giving more of this type of ration is not enough. A kitten growing formula is more appropriate for the gestation/lactation requirements. A gestation/lactation formula cat food having: 29% protein or more, 17% fat or more, less than 5% fiber, calcium 1 - 1.8%, and phosphorus .8 - 1.6 % on a dry matter basis is essential. These are the same requirements for the growing kitten so the whole family can eventually eat together. This level is particularly important during the last three to four weeks before queening and the first three weeks of lactation. Find a good quality cat food that meets these requirements, balanced with vitamins and minerals and additional supplementation is not necessary. Feeding a poor quality cat food and supplementing in hopes of improving the formulation will only make matters worse.

Excessive supplementing with few exceptions will induce problems. Excess calcium and phosphorus, for example, may lead to tissue calcification and abnormalities in the kittens. In turn a diet with a lot of meat and no bones can lead to calcium deficiency.

Gestation is about sixty-three days. In other words around nine weeks after breeding the kittens should be born.

Approximately a third of the fetal growth happens in the first five weeks of gestation and no change in the mother's weight will be evident. The rest of the growth occurs in the last four weeks with her weight increasing by fifteen to twenty-five per cent. This being the case she can be fed the same amount as she normally would have but gradually increased by fifteen to twenty-five per cent by the time she queens. As she is gaining weight she should be fed at least four times a day or free choice. She is physically limited in how much she can consume at one time because of the presence of the enlarging kittens in her abdomen. We also can moisten her food at this time to increase her water intake. Always have free access to good water.

Queening Tips

- use a large sturdy queening box with a cover about two times her length
- have the box prepared several weeks before so that she can become accustomed to it
- use towels or carpeting that can be washed for flooring
- cleanliness is very important
- cats being nocturnal usually queen at night
- labour is normally several hours with 10 to 60 minute rests in between kittens
- do not interfere unless necessary
- kittens are born blind, deaf and completely defenseless

- once a kitten is born the queen will continue to lick the newborn until she hears it squeak. If the kitten is not alive or the queen is deaf she may actually devour the kitten to remove all evidence of the birth.
- if she has not removed the placenta from the kitten soon after birth we must, allowing them to breath
- be sure all afterbirth, placenta, has been expelled
- a reddish-brown discharge usually means all afterbirths have been expelled
- any other colour, brown or greenish, up to 48 hours later may mean that afterbirth, uterine infection or another kitten is retained and veterinary attention is required.
- be aware of eclampsia or milk fever, a condition seen soon after queening in which the queen will appear weak and listless. She needs immediate veterinary attention
- hair loss in a nursing queen indicates a poor diet. Low protein is the culprit so feed good quality protein and the hair will grow back.

Once the kittens are born and nursing begins we must increase the amount fed. The queen must be given enough energy so that she can produce sufficient milk to meet the needs of the nursing kittens. With big litters the queen must produce a lot of milk if the kittens are to survive and grow. If the intake is not adequate she will take more from her own body stores and milk production levels may drop. The first week she should be fed at least one and a half times the amount she would get before breeding, twice as much for the second week and three times as much in the third week.

These amounts are a guideline and will depend upon the size of the litter. Weighing the kittens regularly can help to monitor their progress. Feed the queen or supplement accordingly. Free choice feeding or meal feeding at least four to five times a day ensures that she gets all she wants and also encourages the kittens to start eating solid food.

Caloric density, the concentration of calories, must be high in the diet for the nursing queen in that she has to eat, digest, absorb, and use large amounts of nutrients to produce large quantities of milk. As her stomach and digestive system is only so big, the concentration of energy in the diet must be high. This is why the protein and fat content of gestation/lactation is so high. To increase this density we might give additional fat, one tablespoon (15mL) of fat/cup of dry food. Butter, lard, tallow, bacon fat are all suitable. Doing this will bring up the caloric density by twenty-five to thirty per cent. Greater than this may cause her to cut back on total intake jeopardizing her intake of other nutrients such as protein, vitamins and minerals. Supplementing the queen with the water soluble B complex vitamins and vitamin C can be done with little danger; however, the fat soluble vitamins A and D can be overdone. Vitamin E excess is not believed to be as critical.

We can start decreasing the mother's food after three weeks as the kittens are beginning to eat solid food. Continue to decrease up to six weeks when they will be weaned. This gradual decrease of food intake has her producing less milk as the kittens are becoming less and less dependent on her. During full lactation she should be up to three times the amount she would get before she was bred. On the day of weaning the following procedure will help her "dry-up".
- 1st. day no food and all the water she would like
- 2nd. day 1/4 of her regular maintenance amount
- 3rd. day 1/2 of her regular amount
- 4th. day 3/4 of her regular amount
- 5th. day feed her her normal pre-pregnancy amount

Start changing over to an adult maintenance food and off the gestation/lactation ration unless she is down in condition. This changeover is done over several days by mixing the two foods together so as not to upset her.

(Some breeders will also limit water intake to two small drinks a day at this time. Limiting water should be done with care so she does not become too dehydrated.)

SUMMARY

- the better condition the mother is in the better chance the kittens have
- provide a quality diet, balanced for gestation/lactation
- high caloric density is essential
- caution adding minerals especially calcium and phosphorus
- queening is a natural phenomenon that has been done for millions of years
- intervene only if the queen is unable or unwilling to do her job
- first milk or colostrum is imperative for every kitten soon after birth, rich in nutrients and antibodies
- fifty per cent of early kitten loss is due to chilling; a warm and moist environment is essential
- the queen will lick and handle the kittens to remove gas and stimulate the excretion functions
- monitor the weight of the kittens regularly, preferably daily, for signs of poor growth; half an ounce per day is good by a week of age.
- supplement kittens if necessary
- increase the amount fed and frequency, or allow free choice
- handle the kittens daily for about fifteen minutes each
- kittens start to hear during the first week and their eyes start to open during the second week
- start kittens on solid food after the second or third week
- start preparing for weaning after the third week
- weaning begins after the fourth week of age; kittens have their milk teeth by now
- kittens will weigh about a pound by now, four times their birth weight
- around week five they will discover the litter pan and know what to do. They do not need to be trained.
- make weaning a smooth transition for mother and kittens
- always transport in a carrier or suitable box
- enjoy and take satisfaction in a job well done.

KITTENS

Growing kittens are very vulnerable to an inadequate diet. Kittens will have completed their physical growth by the time they are nine months old, which is 1/20 th. of the time required by humans. If the kittens have been properly fed during their youth there is little, under normal circumstances, that can harm them later as adults.

The demands for growth are great and if they are not met a cat will not reach its genetic potential. If this potential growth is not reached it can never be regained. Contrary to this a cat cannot be fed so much that it will exceed its genetic potential. The growth of the kitten starts with the queen at conception. Her proper nourishment begins the process that continues on until weaning. Proper nutrition is essential. Early neutering will produce larger cats as removal of the sex hormones allows the growth plates in the cats' bones to close later allowing for greater growth of the bones, especially the long bones of the limbs and spinal processes.

As soon as possible after the birth the kittens will start nursing. This first milk, colostrum, is important as it provides passive immunity which will protect the kittens against infectious disease until they produce their own active immunity. Colostrum is rich in antibodies that the mother's immune system has made from her various vaccinations and exposures to disease organisms during her life. In cats very few of these antibodies are passed through the placenta making the first suck of colostrum very important.

Initially the kittens will only eat and sleep. Their eyes and ears open around the second week of age. During this time they should be gaining weight and have normal stools. If the queen is short of milk, for whatever reason, refer to the section on orphan kittens (241) for supplementing.

As well as supplemental feeding the queen should have a medical examination by a veterinarian to diagnose and treat any medical problem that may be the cause of poor milk production. Barring this she may not be getting adequate nourishment herself. Refer to the section on nursing queens for guidelines.

Kittens that are hungry will cry and be restless, whereas well-fed kittens will be contented and gain weight. A kitten should gain about 1 - 2 grams/day/lb of the expected adult weight for the breed. A kitten who will weigh 10 lb as an adult should gain 10 to 15 grams per day for the first five to six months. Or a kitten weighing about 4 oz when born should be about a pound at four weeks. That is growth of 1/2 oz per day.

Weighing the kittens will give a good indication if the queen is feeding them adequately and they are growing to their potential. Kittens will lose ten per cent of their weight in the first twenty-four to forty-eight hours after birth and from then on should gain everyday. If this general goal is not being met, supplemental feeding is in order. Some breeders alternate bottle feeding half the litter every day so that all kittens get a chance to nurse. The rapid rate of growth is continued for six to nine months.

Overfeeding on the other hand can be detrimental. "Roly-poly" little "butter balls" will have problems later on. Overfeeding, supplying a greater intake of calories to protein, can result in disproportionate growth for the kitten. Their body systems grow from protein, building nervous, skeletal, and muscular tissue. Carbohydrate or fat calories are used for energy and extra is saved as body fat. The result is fat, plump kittens that are not developing the muscles and bones as they should. Overfeeding calories develops many more fat cells that will predispose to obesity in adulthood. This extra weight also puts added stress on the soft growing bones and joints. It has been shown that it is better to slightly under feed, in that growth will be even for all systems and the cats will live longer with fewer problems.

The best opinions of the day advise that a controlled intake of quality kitten food fed two to three times a day, as opposed to free choice, is best for growth and the prevention of obesity and skeletal problems.

Kitten nutrition is critical for adequate protein, vitamins and minerals as well as the correct balance of energy.

When purchasing a commercially prepared catfood for the kittens look for a high quality growth kitten food. The label should show at least 45 % protein, 30 % fat, less than 3 % fiber, 1.0 - 1.8 calcium, 0.8 - 1.6 phosphorus and 80% digestible. If the company has done feeding trials so much the better. These high quality foods are balanced and, when fed in the correct amounts, will supply all the nutritional requirements for all breeds of cats. Additional supplementation, especially the minerals calcium and phosphorus, have been shown in many studies to be detrimental. Many cat foods contain more than the NRC recommendations for calcium and phosphorus so we do not have to worry or supply extra. If we still are unsure consult with our veterinarian, cat nutritionist or contact the quality cat food manufacturers for more information.

If we are to prepare our own home-formulated recipes for growing kittens, be aware that this is a critical period in their lives and slight miscalculations can be disastrous. Much time and money has been spent in research on this topic so we should take full advantage of it. Replacing no more than twenty per cent of the diet with home recipes will not disrupt the balance seriously.

Feeding solid food by three weeks of age or soon after the kittens' eyes are open will start the weaning process which is planned for around six weeks. Start by moistening the kitten food. The queen can be taken away several hours before so that the kittens will be hungry and mother will not be tempted to eat it herself. From three to six weeks, feed the kittens at least four times a day or free choice and slowly decrease the amount of food given to the mother. This gets the kittens eating their new food and reduces the queen's milk production. During this time we are taking the queen away for longer periods of time, which she probably appreciates. We are preparing for the day when the queen will not be returned and weaning is complete. On the day of weaning leave the kittens in familiar surroundings and remove the queen.

SUMMARY

- kitten nutrition is critical to their entire life
- proper nutrition starts with the queen
- colostrum is paramount
- monitor weight gains and stools
- help the queen if necessary
- overfeeding is more detrimental than underfeeding
- purchase high quality kitten food
- use caution when supplementing
- start planning for weaning early
- stay on kitten food until nine months of age

KITTY TREATS

Liver, natures "miracle food," makes tasty treats for kittens.

Chicken livers (cut into thirds)	1 lb	500 g
Whole wheat flour	1 cup	250 g
Butter (melted)	1 tbsp	15 mL
Egg yolks (beaten)	2	2
Egg whites (stiffly beaten)	2	2

In medium size bowl mix flour, melted butter and beaten egg yolks. Cover and refrigerate for 3 to 12 hours. Just before use add stiffly beaten egg whites. Dip livers into batter and fry in deep fat heated to 365° F (185° C) until reasonably brown. Cool and give to kittens individually as treats. Use high Biological Value animal protein ingredients. Chicken and pork fat is more easily digested. Infant human vitamin preparations work well.

SICK KITTEN CARE

Signs of a Sick Kitten
- rejection, the queen shows no interest
- kitten stops nursing
- cries, healthy kittens sleep peacefully
- weak and limp
- dehydrated, eyes sunken, skin stays up when pinched
- pale gums, anemic
- dark tinted skin, dark blotches
- bloated
- diarrhea

These are all signs of a sick kitten that requires attention.

About 1/4 of all kittens born alive die within the first week of life and another 1/10th in the second week. Causes include starvation and cold. This is a very critical time.

Be sure that the queening box is large enough for the whole family. And make sure that the kittens start nursing soon after being born. The first suck of colostrum is very important in that this milk is rich in nutrients and antibodies. If the queen is short of milk or the kittens orphaned refer to the section on queens and orphan kittens (page 231 and 241).

Warm temperatures, as high as 85^0 - 90^0 F (30^0 -32^0 C) are necessary during the first week. If the kittens become chilled their body functions slow down and the queen may reject them. Warming them up slowly and getting them to nurse must be done. Starvation (hypoglycemia) and dehydration happen very rapidly with the new born so get veterinary attention quickly if the situation cannot be corrected at home. The veterinarian will administer glucose and electrolytes and also oxygen if required.

Good management and awareness will help prevent the problems.

ORPHANS

Queen's milk is about 7 % protein, cow's milk about 3.8 %

An orphan is a kitten that does not have access to the natural milk of the mother. This can be the result of the death of the queen or her inability to allow nursing. This inability could be because of surgery such as a caesarean section, mammary gland infection, (mastitis) or from uterine infection (metritis). Whatever the situation kittens must be fed and raised as orphans.

If we are to take on this task we must be prepared. The task is very demanding, time consuming and requires strict attention to detail and keen observation. It is not difficult but can be frustrating. Some basic guidelines will help our success.

Our goal is to have a steady weight gain from day one with normal stools, no diarrhea or constipation. These are the best indicators of good health and a proper diet.

Environment: all kittens need a very warm, moist environment.
- $86°$ F ($30°$ C) for the first five days of life
- gradually reduced to $80°$ F ($27°$ C) for the second and third weeks
- then $75°$ F ($23°$ C) for the fourth to sixth weeks
- to $70°$ F ($21°$ C) by the eighth week
- do not overheat, kittens will pant if too hot

Additional heat can be provided either by a covered heating pad or a heat lamp. A thermometer should be hung and monitored and the kittens must be able to move away from the heat source if they desire to cool off or move around. If the relative humidity is low, pans of water or a humidifier should be near by; kittens are very susceptible to dehydration. The place of rearing should be clean, warm and free of drafts and noise. A box divided into compartments or individual boxes are fine. The kittens should be separated for the first two to three weeks of life. Separation allows for better monitoring of stool consistency and prevents the kittens from sucking their siblings tails, genitals and ears etc.

Weight: the kittens should be weighed every day and be gaining about one half of an oz. per day or:
- 1 - 2 grams/day for every pound of desired adult weight (a 10 lb adult; the kitten should gain 10 - 20 gm per day until five months of age)
- birth weight should double in the first eight to ten days
- Most cats by three months are half grown
- rapid growth continues until six - nine months

A gram scale works well to keep a record of the daily weights.

Milk: If at all possible try to have the kittens suck the first milk or colostrum from the queen. Colostrum is rich in maternal antibodies, the very important substances that will protect the kittens from infectious diseases, until they are able to produce their own.

Queen's milk is higher in protein and fat content than cow or goat's milk. There are very good commercial preparations available today for orphans. Several recipes are included for home preparation.

Feeding: The amount and frequency is really determined by the condition and weight gain of the kittens. Satisfied kittens are gaining weight, plump, quiet and spend most of their time sleeping. Kittens that are restless and cry and fuss will not gain.

Kitten's weight	How much to feed	How often
less 4 oz	about 1 tsp	every 2 hrs/2 weeks
4 to 8 oz	2 to 4 tbsp/day	every 3 hrs/third week
8 to 24 oz	6 to 10 tbsp/day	every 4 hrs/fourth - fifth wk

Method: Nipples and bottles are the best. It is difficult to guage the amount fed using eye droppers and feeding too fast, too much or getting some into the lungs can result. Make the hole in the nipple large enough so that milk will drip out when the bottle is inverted. If too large the kitten may choke and if too small the kitten may become discouraged. Always warm the milk to body temperature and tip the bottle up so no air will be swallowed. Kittens must be burped after each feeding, done by sitting the kitten upright and bouncing gently while massaging the abdomen. All feeding equipment should be washed in hot soapy water and rinsed thoroughly in hot water after each use.

We must replace the licking and grooming normally done by the queen. It is especially important to gently rub the anus and genitals with a cotton ball moistened in baby oil to stimulate urination and defecation. Whimpering indicates a need to eliminate so continue the massaging. Wiping the eyes daily with baby oil until open is also a good idea.

Weaning: We can start the weaning process at four weeks by putting a shallow dish of soft gruel in with the kittens. A good quality kitten food, wet but not soupy, starts the kittens on solid food. Some breeders start this after the eyes are open as the curious kitten will investigate. Gradually reduce the amount of water used as hard food is good exercise for the young jaws and teeth. We can use the milk formula to wet the solid food. All the time we are gradually decreasing the amount of bottle feedings so that by six weeks the kittens are off milk and on to solid food. Fresh, clean water should always be available.

At four weeks when we start with the solid food we may leave it with the kittens or we can feed four or five times a day. A litter box with commercial litter or sand should be available so that the kittens can defecate and urinate.

The meat, lamb, chicken, and beef baby foods are a good start for kittens on to solid food also yogurt, cottage cheese, liver pate and mashed salmon or white tuna. Watch for bones.

SUMMARY

- orphans require a lot of attention
- warmth is a must
- weigh regularly to monitor gains
- keep environment clean, warm and humid
- first milk or colostrum is essential
- milk replacer should be the same as natural milk
- develop a feeding routine and do not overfeed
- watch for diarrhea and dehydration
- correct size nibble holes and burping are essential
- massaging replaces mother's licking
- start on solid foods early
- plan for weaning after 3 weeks
- a ticking clock can simulate a mother's heartbeat and adds comfort to a lonely orphan

MILK REPLACEMENT RECIPES

Milk, cow or goat (3 1/2 % fat)	1 cup	250 mL
Egg yolk	1 lg.	1 lg.
Infant vitamins (human)	2 drops	2 drops
Corn oil	1 tsp	5 mL
Cod liver oil	2 drops	2 drops

(refer to Appendix to compare cow and goat milk nutrients)
Mix and refrigerate. Warm to body temperature before feeding. Feed as much as the kitten will eat or until their tummies are full and they are content.

Whole cow's milk	3 1/2 cups	800 mL
Cream 12%	1 cup	250 mL
Egg yolk	1 lg.	1 lg.
Bone meal (steamed)	1 tsp.	6 g
Vitamin A	2000 IU	2000 IU
Vitamin D	500 IU	500 IU
Citric acid	1 tsp.	6 g

Mix, refrigerate and warm to body temperature. Vitamins can be obtained from your veterinarian.

NEUTERED INDIVIDUALS

Spaying a female cat or neutering a male should not increase the cat's weight. The cat's activity level may be lessened due to the removal of the reproductive organs and their subsequent hormones. However, the decrease in activity may be due to obesity and a lack of exercise. Neutered individuals have the same nutrient requirements as intact cats with the exception of fewer calories. The same guidelines for feeding apply. Monitor the cat's condition, weight regularly and feed accordingly.

Osteoporosis may be a concern that we can discuss with our cat's veterinarian as the cat gets older. Thinning of the bones may develop in later life in spayed females much the same as with menopausal women. Here the best prevention is a well balanced diet throughout life including adequate calcium and phosphorus with vitamin D and regular exercise. High meat diets are low in calcium and high fiber diets tend to bind calcium so foods high in this mineral should be included in the diet. Foods like yogurt and cheeses increase the absorption of calcium. If in doubt talk to you veterinarian.

COMING HOME FROM SURGERY

Spaying is abdominal surgery so a concentrated nutritious diet given in small amounts is appropriate.

Farina (Cream of Wheat ®) cooked to make 2 cups	1/2 cup	125 mL
Liver	1 lb	500 g
Butter	1 tbsp.	15 ml
B complex tablet (crushed)	1	1
Vitamin C tablet (crushed)	250 mg	250 mg

Cook farina according to directions. Chop the liver into cubes and lightly fry in butter. Mix into the cream of wheat with vitamins. Serve warm in eight equal portions to a 10 lb (4.5 kg) cat.

SENIORS

Older cats have special needs compared to younger cats. Seniors need more attention paid to coat condition and dental health as well as protection from extremes of heat, cold and dehydration.

Not all cats age at the same rate; each one will vary depending on its breed, environment, diet, general health and activity level throughout its life. Cats are considered old, or 'geriatric', around ten to fourteen years of age.

Growing old is unavoidable and with age certain changes occur within the cat's body. Cats age faster than we do but with good nutrition throughout their lives, this process need not be dramatic. Some chronic diseases may start to show their signs as the years go by, so more attention has to be paid to the cat's general condition, so that abnormalities can be detected early and corrected. Regular check-ups should be part of a senior cat's itinerary.

Exercise is still an important part of an older cat's life style. Reasonable physical activity maintains muscle tone, promotes circulation, improves elimination, reduces the threat of obesity and promotes mental health and well-being. This can be play indoors as well as outdoors or routine walks with body harness and leash.

Changes due to aging are inevitable. Being aware of the changes, we can help to slow down the process and maintain our pet's health and well-being in her later years. As cats age they become quite sensitive to deficiencies or excesses of nutrients, so we must be sure to supply all of the required nutrients and not to overdo others. If obesity is a concern, energy or calories have to be reduced but not at the expense of the other nutrients such as the vitamins and minerals. As well, supplementing with too much of the minerals or the fat soluble vitamins A, D and K can be detrimental.

Weight loss in the older cat may be due to a medical problem such as gum disease or some other medical condition which should be attended to. As our cat gets older, many body activities slow down or decrease which can lead to potential problems.

With aging there is:

Decreased	**Potential Problems**
temperature regulation	less tolerant to cold or heat
sensitivity to thirst	dehydration
sense of smell and taste	loss of appetite and weight
immune response	greater susceptibility to illness
restful sleep	irritability
activity and metabolism	obesity
tooth and gum health	reduced food intake
digestive function	constipation and flatulence
skin elasticity	susceptibility to skin disease
kidney function	nutrient deficiencies
hormone production	diabetes, cysts and tumors
cardiovascular function	heart, blood and vessel problems
lung function	bronchitis and emphysema
muscle and bone mass	loss of tone and bone fractures

Temperature regulation, or thermoregulation, the ability to respond to extremes of cold and heat, is reduced in the older cat. Being left outside in cold and wet weather should be avoided. For hot weather we should provide shade, water and reduce the amount of food fed per meal and increase the number of meals. Eating food, especially proteins, increases the cat's body temperature due to the metabolism of these foods, a process called specific dynamic action. We know how we warm up after a big meal, which is similar. So for older cats smaller meals fed more often, especially in hot weather or in very warm homes.

Be aware of the other changes listed. By giving special attention we can keep our older cat in good health for many more years. Warming and moistening the food may help appetite and water intake. Feeding more often with smaller portions or feeding free choice with dry food always available, if obesity is not a problem, may also work. These are all little things that help the seniors.

The digestive system does not seem to wear out as compared to the other parts of the cat; however, obesity, weight loss, constipation and recovering from illness takes more time and treatment than for younger cats. An older cat in sound health has little need for a special diet as digestive efficiency has not shown to decrease with age.

Overfeeding contributing to obesity is the quickest way to shorten the life span of our cat. As our cat gets older her daily activity slows down so we must reduce the number of calories that we feed. Just feeding less and increasing her exercise may not be the correct thing to do because we may be reducing some very important nutrients (see section on obesity).

A quick review of the basic nutrients with a few comments applicable to the senior are in order at this time.

Protein must be of good quality for the older cat so that there is adequate and easy digestion, absorption and utilization of all the amino acids. Those with high Biological Value are animal protein sources. Excesses, however, can be a problem if there is some existing liver and kidney damage in the older cat.

Good quality dietary fat, as with protein, is essential. The fatty acids are important especially for a healthy skin; poultry and pork fat are better than beef tallow. As with protein the animal fats are better for the older carnivore. Butter, animal fats and fish oils are natural sources as opposed to vegetable oils and margarine. These heavily processed oils and hydrogenated margarines are not natural fats for the cat.

Carbohydrates, although not an essential nutrient for the cat, have the same consideration for the aged cat. Raw carbohydrates are poorly digested and must be properly cooked and should only be a minor part of the diet.

Fiber levels and quality are critical in the older cat. Less is known about the role of fiber in the cat's diet than for us; however, the vegetable fiber that is present in the cereals used in dry cat food plays a useful role in the consistency of the stools and bowel movements. If constipation or diarrhea are problems, have the cat examined by the veterinarian, who will advise on diagnosis and treatment.

Greater vitamin amounts are required in the older cat such as vitamins A, B complex, C and E. Even though the food is advertised to be complete and balanced, supplementing may be beneficial because the older cat may be eating less food in general and requiring more vitamins. Again, avoid excess supplementation as the older cat may not be as able to tolerate the excess as might a younger cat. Refer to the section on vitamins at the beginning of the book for more details.

Minerals needs are much the same. There is no evidence that we know of at this time to suggest we should increase minerals over the maintenance level. However, there is reason to lower phosphorus, to reduce osteodystrophy - bone density reduction - and calcium deposits in the kidneys for the older cat. There is also a concern that zinc absorption may decrease with age just as with low protein and high fiber diets. Poor hair growth and skin problems may be corrected with zinc. Ask advice from your veterinarian as to amounts of zinc. Older cats should not get excess amounts of sodium (salt) as this promotes retention of fluids, hypertension, cardiovascular and kidney problems. Remember the cat doesn't lose salt the way we do and salt is not important to taste as it may be for many of us.

EBENEEZER'S SPECIAL

A simple senior's recipe prepared from ingredients on hand.

Cooked rice or pasta	2 cups	500 mL
Flaked chicken, can	6.5 oz	184 gm
Egg	1	1
Cottage Cheese	1/2 cup	125 mL
Butter	2 tbsp.	30 mL
Kelp	1 tbsp.	15 mL
Brewer's Yeast	2 tbsp.	30 mL
Bone Meal	1 tbsp.	15 mL
Garlic Powder	1/2 tsp.	3 mL

Mix ingredients and warm in microwave. Will feed a 10 lb (4.5 kg) cat four to five days.

OCTAVIUS CASSEROLE

A gourmet meal fit for a King or Queen.

Cooked Turkey or Chicken	1 cup	250 mL
Bacon Fat or Butter	2 tbsp.	30 mL
Lasagne noodles	8	8
Egg	1	1
Wheat germ oil	1 tbsp.	15 mL
Bone meal	1 tsp.	5 mL
Garlic powder	1/4 tsp.	1 mL

Cook noodles as directed on the package. Drain. Line bottom of 8 X 8 inch (20 x 20 cm) pan. In medium sized bowl mix chopped turkey or chicken with bacon fat, egg, wheat germ oil and bone meal. Spoon over noodles and spread. Cover with layer of noodles and sprinkle with garlic powder. Bake 30 minutes in 350° F(180° C) oven. Let stand for 15 minutes before cutting. Will serve a 10 lb (4.5 kg) cat four or five days.

HOBART'S HAMBURGER HASH

A tasty hamburger and ground vegetable meal.

Ground Beef	1 lb.	500 g
Peas, frozen or fresh	1/2 cup	125 mL
Carrots, sliced	1/2 cup	125 mL
Butter	1 tbsp.	15 mL
Water	1/2 cup	125 mL
Catnip or garlic powder	1/4 tsp.	3 mL

Blend peas, carrots and water in blender. Brown ground beef with butter in frying pan. Mix in mashed vegetables and a 1/4 cup of Geriatric Vitamin Mix (see below). Cool and serve. Serves a 10 lb (4.5 kg) cat four or five days.

GERIATRIC VITAMIN MIX

Adapted, with permission, from Joan Harper's; The Healthy Cat and Dog Cookbook.

Bran	1 cup	250 mL
Wheat germ	1 cup	250 mL
(leave out unless refrigerating the complete mix)		
Brewers yeast	1 cup	250 mL
Lecithin	1/2 cup	125 mL
Bone meal	1/2 cup	125 mL
Kelp	1/3 cup	75 mL
Alfalfa	1/3 cup	75 mL
Magnesium oxide	4 tsp.	20 mL

Mix together and store in at least a 5 cup container. Add 1/4 cup for an average size dog's dinner. For a cat, use one tablespoonful.

The main consideration for the senior cat is not to overfeed but to keep our older cats trim, active and happy well on into their golden years.

NEEDS FOR SPECIAL BREEDS

Some breeds of cats can be prone to certain specific health problems as well as special dietary needs. This can be over and above any temperamental differences.

Man has selected and bred cats with particular characteristics which then resulted in these particular cats being classified as a breed. All of our domesticated cats are within the same species. Some breeds have existed for a long time as man started to make selections and bred individuals with similar traits and culled those with undesirable traits so that a pure line of cats would develop.

The definition then of a breed, when referring to Genetics, is a relatively homogenous, or similar, group of animals within a species, developed and maintained by man. This is to imply that individual cats within a certain breed will have the same characteristics such as coat colour, adult size and temperament. As well when males and females of the same breed are bred, the offspring or kittens will be uniform and have the identical characteristics of the parents. This is also referred to as being pure.

As the breeds developed and cats were selected and bred for whatever characteristics the breeders had in mind, be it coat colour, length of hair or temperament, some peculiar health and nutritional aspects also became apparent, aspects specific to an individual breed.

If you should have a specific breed of cat and would like to read more, Dr. Jane R. Bicks book *The Revolution In Cat Nutrition* has an excellent chapter, "Special Needs of Special Breeds", explaining some of the breed differences she has found. She writes about thirty-seven breeds in her book outlining some nutritional and health peculiarities.

PART FIVE Nutritionally Related Problems

"The road to better health will not be found through more drugs, doctors and hospitals. Instead, it will be discovered through better nutrition and changes in lifestyle."

William Crook, MD

"St. Thomas, the great doctor and theologian, warns about the proper use of animals, lest they appear at the final Judgement against us: and God himself will take vengeance on all who misuse his creatures..."

Rt. Rev. Msgr. LeRoy McWilliams

Certain conditions and diseases of cats have a specific food related aspect. Some may require the elimination of a particular food or group of foods while others may need the addition of a supplement. Disease prevention and diagnosis go hand in hand with our pet's diet and veterinarian. Treatment of these conditions involves some dietary management and this is the part we will cover, things we can do at home.

I believe that the two most prevalent health problems seen in our pet population today are obesity and skin conditions. I also believe that the majority of our cats' problems are related to diet, either feeding too much or not enough of the required nutrients. However, it may not be that simple. When we combine a poor diet with a lack of exercise, an ever increasing exposure to chemical pollutants, a large gamut of medications and an ever changing environment, we have a very complex set of circumstances. This makes the diagnosis and treatment of our cats' problems quite complex. Everything must be considered.

To understand and treat health problems we have to start with the "Big Picture" and examine all aspects. Our primary focus is on the digestive system, from one end to the other. Some other conditions that have a relationship with diet are also discussed. The approach will be an explanation of the condition followed by a discussion of dietary management.

All of these conditions or problems have many factors involved that may complicate the diagnosis but let us try to understand the situation and how we can correct and prevent the problems for the general well-being of our cat.

The main topics that will be covered in this section:

- Appetite
- Digestive System Problems
  - Mouth and Dental problems
  - Halitosis, bad Breath
  - Stomach Problems
  - Liver
  - Pancreas
  - Intestines
  - Vomiting
  - Diarrhea
  - Constipation
  - Flatulence
- Food Allergy and Intolerance
- Behavior Problems
- Skin Conditions
- Skeletal, Bone problems
- FUS - Bladder and Kidneys
- Heart Problems

Digestive disorders in the cat may show a combination of signs or symptoms or possibly just one. We, as the ones living with the cat and seeing it every day, are in the best position to observe any changes in attitude or physical nature of our cat. Our cat may just not be herself of late.

Digestive system disorders may have symptoms such as

- drooling as a sign of nausea
- vomiting, more than on the odd occasion
- diarrhea, possibly with blood
- severe constipation or diarrhea
- a bloated stomach from an accumulation of gas
- presence of undigested food in the stool
- a strong or unusual odour to the feces and/or urine
- a rise in body temperature - fever
- presence of worms in the feces
- passage of hair balls - either vomited or in the feces
- foreign bodies in feces or vomit - sticks, plastic, stones
- listlessness and exhaustion
- a generally depressed and poor looking cat

All of these signs may indicate a problem with the digestive system. The cause, treatment and prevention may be medical and require a diagnosis made by a veterinarian with specific medication or it may be just a food problem. Either condition, however, will require nutrition management, involving foods.

The digestive system deals with food for the cat on a daily basis so treatment and prevention of disorders require a basic knowledge of nutrition and what our cat can or cannot tolerate. Often when a cat is sick the diet has to be questioned and examined if a diagnosis is to be made. Once made, treatment and prevention require the use of or elimination of certain foods. Nutrition must always be considered.

It is with regard to these areas of the cat's body and a few others, not part of the digestive system, that this section deals with. Skin conditions and the urinary condition known as FUS or Feline Urological Syndrome are conditions of the cat directly related to the diet or nutrition.

One hopes not too many factors are overlooked by simplification. With this type of an overview, we can start to appreciate how foods play a very important role in the health of our cat. Proper nutrition is an all-encompassing term that can mean many things. By understanding what problems can arise from improper nutrition, we can be on our way to feeding our cat properly to keep her in a state of good health and well-being.

Nutritional management of diseases involves the treatment and prevention of deficiencies using nutrients either to diagnose, treat or to prevent a problem. We might eliminate certain foods to try to detect an allergy, for example, or we may feed another food to correct a suspected deficiency. Or we may just feed a well-balanced diet with all the required nutrients on a continuous basis to prevent any unforeseen problems from arising. Or our cat's veterinarian may prescribe a special diet or supplement. Whatever the reason, we are using foods to either correct a problem or to maintain our cat in a state of good health.

"Let food be your medicine and medicine be your food"

Hippocrates

APPETITE

The desire to eat and drink is obviously an important part of nutrition and health. This desire, or appetite to eat, is basic to life. If our cat does not want to eat those foods that it normally would, something must be wrong. What does appetite do, what can change it and how can our cat get it back?

Appetite influences the anticipation of food as well as how much and how fast our cat will eat.

Factors that can modify appetite

- how recently the cat has eaten
- type of food dish
- type of detergent used
- off or unusual smell or taste
- fasting or food deprivation
- anticipation of being fed
- past experiences with a particular food
- general health
- end of the rapid growth stage
- puberty, interest in other things
- general nutritional state
- a plugged nose
- sore mouth, teeth, gums and/or throat
- tonsillitis
- parasites
- upset stomach
- pain from injury or surgery
- drugs or medications
- anxiety and depression
- spoiled, used to being catered to

All of these by themselves or in combination can alter the cat's appetite. If our cat does not want to eat, we become concerned and if it should continue the cause may be serious.

To remedy the loss of appetite, start with determining the cause and correcting it. If the neighbours or someone else in the house is feeding the cat, this may be the problem. If this is the case the cat will appear full and contented. When a cat has not eaten for a while she will appear gaunt with stomach tucked in and when we lift her up the abdomen will feel empty.

A change in food or a dislike for the new diet could be the reason the cat is not eating. We can stimulate appetite often by just warming the food so that some aroma is given off. If changing brands of cat food, do it over several days by mixing some of the previous with some of the new and gradually making the change. Tasty ingredients like liver, chicken, fish, meat drippings and cat nip may create some interest.

Cats, by their nature, can be very particular about what they eat, a survival habit that is instinctive. Cats of old and those in the wild eat fresh killed prey guaranteeing them fresh and healthy food. Even then they are still cautious. Spoiled or unfamiliar foods may signal danger so the best prevention is to avoid it completely.

If we find that our cat is not eating for whatever reason and want to entice her to eat, we have to question what we are feeding and take into consideration the cat's ancestral habits.

Fresh animal organs and fats such as liver, kidney, pancreas, or ground meat may have to be tried. Warm the food to body temperature, again to simulate the natural situation.

If the cat is not feeling well, the natural instinct is to fast. This gives the digestive system a rest but it also focuses the cat's energy on the body's defense systems such as the immune system. All energy is directed to getting better. Remember a cat can fast for a week or longer without difficulty. Fasting is a normal and natural phenomenon for carnivores. Water must always be available.

DIGESTIVE SYSTEM PROBLEMS

Mouth & Dental Problems

The mouth, teeth, tongue and throat can be affected by nutritional factors. Pain or disease in this area will also affect appetite and prevent the cat from eating and getting all nutrients. Drooling, head shaking, swelling on the side of the face and pawing at the face are all signs of a tooth problem.

A sore mouth and gums can be from a deficiency of riboflavin, vitamin B_2 and the other B vitamins. A sore throat from tonsillitis can also reduce appetite. The most common mouth conditions, however, have to do with the teeth and gums.

Dental problems in our modern cat stem from breeding and diet. We have selected some breeds of cats with short jaws, where the teeth may be crowded. Some cats also are more prone to overlapping and retention of "baby teeth" that can lead to gum disease and sore mouths.

Dr. Weston Price, a dentist and researcher, in his book *Nutritional and Physical Degeneration*, writes of the dental problems of children including decay, crowded and crooked teeth and general health problems as being related to our modern diet. Anthropologists had always observed excellent teeth in primitive cultures so Dr. Price set out to study primitive peoples around the world with regard to their teeth and their past and present diets. With extensive travel and studies of indigenous groups of people and their ancestors' skulls in museums, he came to the conclusion that the modern dental and health problems were directly related to the modern refined diets. Those peoples that continued to eat their local foods included animals and fish, with some parts raw, continued to have good dental health. As with generations of their forebearers before them, their teeth were free of decay and the dental arches full with no crowding of teeth.

If we can compare Dr. Price's work in man to our cats today, I believe we are seeing the same situation. We have been feeding refined diets for about forty to fifty years which includes many generations of cats. This may explain some of the problems we are seeing in our present day cats including teeth and gum problems. Many of our cats today do not have access to the natural prey for their supply of nutrients as well as the physical action required in tearing and chewing this food.

The 90's cat receives soft, easy-to-chew refined foods containing a lot of carbohydrate as opposed to the foods that the wild cats eat. The latter chew on bones, gristle and eat a raw, high protein and high fat diet.

A common problem today is periodontal disease. In this disease material such as food, bacteria and mineral deposits build up around the teeth causing the gums to recede. Inflammation and pockets develop making matters worse. Bacterial growth can continue affecting not only the cat's mouth but other parts of her body. Bad breath, bleeding gums, loose teeth, painful chewing, excessive salivation, lack of appetite and weight loss can all result.

Sound nutrition including fresh foods with no refined carbohydrates (including refined sugar) plus enough of the vitamins and minerals help to prevent these problems. Vitamins A, C, D and B complex as well as the minerals calcium, phosphorus and zinc will improve these situations. Brushing and/or cleaning cats' teeth seems to be in vogue now but we must not forget to deal with the causes.

A diet of fresh foods consisting predominately of animal proteins and fats will go a long way to improving and maintaining a cat's mouth in a state of good health. Slightly cooked and raw foods are also something to think about if we are to have a cat with a healthy mouth and in turn a healthy body.

Halitosis, bad breath

Foul breath can be a problem especially in older cats and is a sign of poor health that should be looked into. Common causes

- eating something smelly
- tooth and gum disease
- mouth, throat or lung infection
- food allergy or intolerance
- low stomach acid with an increase in bacterial activity
- underlying illness such as diabetes or kidney disease
- certain medications and foods

Have the cat looked at by our veterinarian to determine the cause and start appropriate treatment. Again good nutrition with all required nutrients including the vitamins and minerals can help to prevent halitosis.

Stomach Problems

The stomach is the first stop for the swallowed food. Several problems can arise at this point. These can range from mild indigestion to more severe infection or cancerous growths.

Possible causes of stomach problems

- eating too fast
- food intolerance or food allergy
- swallowing non-food items like plastic, rubber or cloth
- drinking or eating chemical poisons
- continuous use of some medications
- stress, fear, anxiety and depression
- too much or not enough production of stomach acid
- infection and disease, feline distemper
- cancerous growths

Typical signs of stomach problems are loss of appetite, vomiting, bloating, pain and crying and weight loss.

All of these and more can by themselves or in combination give our cat problems. Something simple we will be able to correct; for the others we require the help of our veterinarian.

What signs will we see?

- the cat is in pain and discomfort after eating
- the abdomen may be swollen and hard; bloated
- reluctance to move and may stand with hind legs under and with an arch to her back
- may appear to "pray" with front legs kneeling and back legs standing
- usually vomits and may continue to retch
- is excessively thirsty and may drink a lot
- cat has no appetite

Stomach problems usually show more dramatic signs than those further down the digestive system such as the intestines or liver. If we suspect our cat has a stomach problem, our first step is to remove any food that may be left and watch for all the signs. We might want to save any vomited material for later analysis and we should think back to anything that was done or fed differently. This history will help to make a diagnosis.

A sudden irritation to the stomach of the cat will make the cat vomit. This is her natural response. The other is to not eat anything after. Fasting allows time for the stomach and other parts of the digestive system to heal and to avoid any more irritation.

Hair balls are something to consider when dealing with stomach upsets. Cats normally groom by licking themselves which results in hair being swallowed. This accumulation of hair may form into a ball that may cause an intestinal blockage. Prevention involves good nutrition, weight control and frequent grooming, especially for a long-haired individual.

To prevent stomach problems from arising, regular feeding habits and proper nutrition are the first steps. If our cat tends to eat fast and swallow a lot of air, smaller portions given throughout the day in a private area without disturbances will help. Allow at least two hours before and after eating for exercise and keep garbage in covered containers. Play things, balls, toys etc. should be large and durable enough that they cannot be swallowed. Watch kittens that pieces of cloth or plastic are not swallowed.

A typical home treatment for a minor stomach or food related problem could be as follows
- For several days feed only water and broths. A vitamin-mineral supplement should be fed during this time as it is required for healing.
- Next, feed bland foods that are easy to digest such as cottage cheese, cooked eggs, liver and cooked porridge.
- Gradually introduce meat.
- If we thought that the original problem was the brand of commercial cat food that we were using and we want to go back to this type of diet, pick a different one and start with a little at a time so the cat can get used to it.

Refer to Part Two "Commercially Prepared Cat Food" for guidance on selecting a cat food.

FASTING BROTH

A broth for a sensitive stomach while we are fasting the cat. (Avoid fat, milk, sugars, processed and spicy foods)

Warm water	3 cups	750 mL
Beef or chicken bouillon cube	1	1
or fish juice, salmon, tuna,		
sardines	1/2 cup	125 mL
Human Infant Mult-vitamin drops	5 drops	5 drops
Vitamin C, sodium ascorbate		
powder	1/2 tsp.	2 mL
B complex 50 mg tablet (crushed)	1	1

Dissolve the cube in the warm water, then cool and add the other ingredients. Let the cat drink as much as she wants.

Liver Problems

The liver, as we stated in Part One, is the largest and one of the most important organs in the cat's body. It is responsible for taking most of the absorbed nutrients and converting and storing these nutrients for the many needs of the cells. The liver also detoxifies poisons that may be ingested. Because of these various functions, any disorders are serious to the health of the cat. Hepatitis or inflammation of the liver is the usual disorder that can be caused by a viral infection or ingestion of poisonous substances.

Symptoms of liver problems include
- nausea and vomiting
- loss of appetite
- jaundice, a yellowing of the skin due to a back up of bile, that can be seen in the whites of the eyes, gums and skin
- pale, tan, gray or black and sticky looking stools
- an enlargement of the abdomen due to a swollen liver
- urine will be orange

Liver disease not only affects the digestion, absorption and utilization of nutrients but the vomiting and loss of appetite also reduces the intake of important nutrients. The goal is to reduce the liver's work load and to restore liver glycogen.

Fasting with the introductions of foods that will not stress the liver are the treatments. All fats and oils should be restricted to less than four per cent of the total diet; however, the fat soluble vitamins A, D, E and K must be given, probably by injection. Foods such as chocolates, fish meal, shell fish, spleen, thymus, liver and most meat by-products should be avoided as these contain purines and uric acid precursors.

Feed easily digested high Biological Value proteins such as egg, yogurt, cottage cheese and red meat in small portions four to five times a day. Carbohydrates, vitamins and minerals are required to provide adequate nutrition for healing and repair of the damaged tissues at the same time trying not to stress the liver any more than necessary. Be prepared to follow this for a month or more as the healing process takes a long time.

Pancreas Problems

Pancreatitis (inflammation of the pancreas) is a serious problem for the cat. Glandular fibrosis of the pancreas is common in older cats. A condition that also involves the pancreas is diabetes, or a lack of sufficient insulin production. Dietary management for the two are the same. With diabetes, insulin injects may have to be given. The pancreas is involved with digestion and utilization of nutrients as well as the production of insulin. From blood and urine a diagnosis can be made.

The prime suspects are older overweight cats that have a long history of poor nutrition eating a lot of sweet and fat foods. Cats with advancing age that are getting little exercise and extra love in the form of sweet and fat foods are prime targets. The pancreas just becomes overloaded. Watch cat foods with a lot of sugar in them.

Once the pancreas cannot function, the cat will stop eating, vomit often, have diarrhea, be weak and may cry in pain. Have the veterinarian look at the cat and if the pancreas is the problem start the diet and life-style change.

As well as reducing the number of calories fed, avoid fats and oils - not greater than eight per cent - including cod liver oil, as these can irritate the pancreas as it heals. Give twice as much of the fat soluble vitamins, A, D, & E, by injection from the veterinarian which will last up to two months. Give vitamin C (sodium ascorbate 1/4 tsp. 1/2 tsp. per day depending on the size of the cat) as well as the water soluble B vitamins. Eliminate the fiber foods such as cereals, fruits and vegetables as they are especially hard for the cat to digest. As with liver disease give bland, easy-to-digest, high quality animal proteins. Zinc and vitamin D have lately been thought to be important for the pancreas in its production of insulin. The pancreas produces digestive enzymes and it also manufactures insulin for the utilization of blood sugars for energy. Pancreatic problems require a combined effort of treatment and prevention including our veterinarian, diet and exercise.

Yellow Fat Disease or Pansteatitis

This is a condition associated with a deficiency of vitamin E and the cat's body fat. This condition occurs when high levels of polyunsaturated fatty acids, such as from red tuna, are fed with low levels of vitamin E. This leads to a yellow pigment being deposited in the body fat or adipose tissue resulting in fat cell necrosis or death.

Pansteatitis, the inflammation of the fat cells, in the cat's body produces an overall general tenderness and soreness, loss of appetite, depression and fever. The fat under the skin may be lumpy especially around the lower abdomen.

Cats that have an addiction for fish, especially red tuna to the exclusion of other foods, develop this condition. Commercial cat foods that use a lot of fish and fish meal fortify the food with adequate vitamin E.

The best prevention is to not allow a cat to become hooked on fish, or any other food such as liver alone but a variety of foods so that all of the required nutrients are eaten.

Retinal Degeneration and Blindness

Simply put, the cat's retinas degenerate with the cause being the lack of the essential nutrient taurine. This amino acid or protein, that we have discussed in Part One of the book, is only found in animal tissue and must be eaten by the cat. Taurine is also associated with reproductive performance of queens as well as heart problems, specifically dilated cardiomyopathy, in all cats not consuming enough taurine.

Modern commercial cat foods are all fortified with taurine if they have a lot of non-animal ingredients or plant products in their formulation. This is one of the reasons cats cannot be vegetarians in that they must consume taurine.

Vomiting

Vomiting is something that cats can do very easily. This ability to evacuate the stomach is a trait that they have acquired from their wild ancestors. As we have stated in Part One vomiting is an asset. If, in their hurry, they eat harmful fragments of sharp bones or irritating chemical substances, throwing up is a way to get rid of it.

Should our cat occasionally throw up her meal we do not have to become too concerned. However, if this continues with repeated retchings, professional help must be sought. This is also true if our cat vomits after every meal and appears unable to keep anything down.

Causes for vomiting that should arouse our concern

- bacterial or viral infection
- foreign body obstructions
- poisoning, antifreeze
- hairballs
- drug medications
- gall bladder problems
- liver problems
- pancreas problems
- kidney problems
- intestinal problems
- pain, such as after surgery
- excitement and/or stress

Because vomiting is a sign or symptom of something else, we have to get to the root cause and correct it. Once this has been determined, then the treatment can be started. Nutrition plays a part in the recovery but can be difficult if nothing can be kept down. Dehydration and electrolyte (minerals such as sodium and potassium) loss may be to such an extent that intravenous feeding may be necessary. Withholding all food and water giving the cat ice cubes or the popsicles (page 215) can help. Try bland foods as discussed for stomach problems once the cat appears to be able to hold something down. Vitamins may have to be given by injection at this time.

Diarrhea

Diarrhea, the opposite of constipation, is characterized by soft unformed stools. It is comparatively rare in cats. The cat's digestive system is responding to some irritation or disorder. Pushing the contents of the intestines through quickly is the defense mechanism to get rid of the irritant. Because the speed of passage is rapid there is little absorption of water by the large intestine so the stools are not formed and the material is quite liquid. Diarrhea can occur from a simple change in diet or a food sensitivity. Lack of one or more digestive enzymes can produce diarrhea as can excitement or anxiety. If this continues for some time the consequences can be serious. Dehydration and loss of vital minerals, called electrolytes, can be life threatening. This is especially true for young kittens. Several hours of diarrhea for a kitten may be fatal.

Possible irritants include viruses, bacteria, chemicals, worms, spoiled foods, foreign bodies and antibiotics. Foods such as milk, ice cream, vegetables and fruits can also cause diarrhea. As we have said before, adult cats do not have the lactase enzyme for lactose, the milk sugar, and their short intestine is unsuited for ideal plant or vegetable digestion.

Seek a reason for the diarrhea and eliminate the cause rather than treating the symptom. Obtaining a diagnosis will include a history of what the cat has eaten in the last twelve hours and what he or she was in contact with as well as activities or sources of stress. Very fluid feces may indicate bacterial or worm infestation; black, tarry indicates bleeding high up in the gastrointestinal tract or a recent feed of liver.

A simple approach to treatment is to fast the cat of all solid food for at least forty-eight hours. (Nature does this anyway when the cat loses its appetite.) Fasting allows the intestine to rest. Water must not be restricted. Easily digested, bland foods such as soups and broths give some nourishment at this time as well as fluids and electrolytes.

Diarrhea is the mechanism by which the cat is attempting to get rid of an undesirable substance. It is up to us to allow the process to work. If this should continue so that the loss of fluids and other nutrients has gone too far, then we must intervene. Veterinary treatment at this stage is essential.

Identifying what is causing the diarrhea is our first concern. The loss of appetite, or self-induced fast, is the cat's own means of attacking the problem, giving the digestive system a rest and allowing time to heal.

Some old time remedies and holistic type treatments involve giving mineral oil at the first signs of diarrhea. This is to help the cat's body to flush out the irritating substances and offer some protection to the inner walls of the intestine. Producing a diarrhea with this treatment perhaps prevented some damage before it became extensive. Other treatments are kaopectate and activated charcoal. These substances, while absorbing the offending substances, also firm up the stools and reduce the fluid and electrolyte loss. Long term use of these treatments is not advisable in that the digestive process and nutrient absorption can be hindered.

WARM FORTIFIED BROTH

A tasty broth that will not aggravate the intestine but gives water and nutrients that may be lost.

Chicken or Beef bullion cube (Chicken or Beef Broth soup 1 can)	1	1
Water	3 cups	750 mL
Baking Soda	1/2 tsp.	2 mL
Garlic powder or catnip	1/4 tsp.	1 mL

Dissolve the cube in hot water or prepare the soup as directed on the can or package. Cool mix in the baking soda (to replace the bicarbonate lost), garlic powder and serve.

Home Management of Diarrhea

These guidelines are for the adult cat. Kittens require veterinary attention quickly as they are very vulnerable to dehydration and complications.

At the first signs of diarrhea
- be sure that the litter box is handy with fresh litter
- carefully clean up the litter box
- remember some infections can infect us and our family
- ensure that clean drinking water is always available
- start the detective work to find the cause
  - was there a change in diet?
  - did the cat get into something that she shouldn't have?
  - is this more than a food problem, is fever present?
  - when was the cat last tested for worms?
  - did we start medication recently?
  - was there a recent cause for excitement or stress?
- remove food (place in air tight container and keep cool; we may want to have it tested for toxins or bacteria)
- fast from solid foods for 24 to 48 hours
- if our cat wants to eat, start with the soups and broth
- use easily digested quality foods next
- if regular food was not the problem, gradually start back
- reduce the regular proportions and feed more often

Ingredients to use: lean ground meats, liver, cottage cheese, yogurt, eggs and consomme.
Ingredients to avoid: fats, oils, milk, ice cream, breads, cereals and flour, vegetables and fruits. No fiber.

Because the cat is a carnivore we give animal protein source foods and stay away from hard-to-digest plant or vegetable products until her digestive system has settled down.

We may want to try Mom's Chicken Soup and Hospital Gruel (page 229.)

Constipation

Constipation usually means difficulty in passing stools, reluctance to pass stools or hard dry stools. This is common in older cats. There are many causes for these signs so a diagnosis is essential in that the constipation may not be dietary. Some common non-dietary causes could be an obstructed bowel, cancer of the colon, pelvic fractures, bowel infection, illness with fever, dehydration, stress, drug therapy, old age or lack of exercise. Dietary causes may be from poor quality cat food, lack of water, food sensitivity and low fiber diets. There are other things that will look like constipation so have a veterinarian examine the cat.

Things that we can do for constipation concerning the diet

- increase the fiber intake, foods like whole grains, vegetables, fruits and seeds.
- avoid poor quality cat foods
- eliminate fatty refined foods, sugar and salt
- provide regular exercise
- supply good quality water
- try raw meat
- sprinkle 1/2 - 1 tsp. of bran on the food once a day
- add melted butter: 1 tsp. to 1 tbsp. to the food
- add 250 - 500 mg of vitamin C to diet per day

HIGH FIBER - LAXATIVE

Try this raw meat, high fiber recipe if the cat has the need for a simple laxative meal.

Ground beef	1 lb	500 g
All Bran ® (or Bran Flakes ®)	1 cup	250 mL
Butter, melted	2 tbsp.	30 mL
Garlic powder	1/4 tsp.	1 mL
Vitamin C	500 mg	500 mg

Mix all the ingredients, warm to body temperature and serve. Will feed an 8 to 10 lb (4.5 kg) cat three days.

Flatulence

Flatulence is the medical term for the excessive production of gas. This gas is then passed either anally or orally. The production of some gas in the digestive tract is normal; however, when it becomes excessive and foul we become concerned.

Excessive flatulence can result from the type of food eaten or from a malfunction in the digestive system.

Gas production is primarily the result of bacterial fermentation of the various foods eaten. Herbivores tend to have a lot of gases formed in their digestive systems in that they must rely on bacterial activity for digestion of the plant material that they eat. When we feed our cat more vegetable type foods, especially beans, cabbage, and onions, for example, the gas formed may be offensive. Remember onions affect the cat's blood, so no onions.

Increased fermentation can occur if there is an overgrowth of bacteria in the digestive tract due to a slow down in passage of food through the system. Any of the problems of the stomach, pancreas or intestines, including worms, decrease the ability of the digestive system to work. The food stays longer in the system allowing the fermentation to occur.

Food intolerances, constipation, stomach, liver, pancreas and intestinal problems can all lead to excessive gas produced. Again if our cat should have a lot of foul gas, we should try to find the root cause as flatulence is a symptom of something else.

If we are feeding our cat a low quality cat food containing a lot of vegetable material or we are feeding a lot of the same, be prepared for gas. Try experimenting with different foods to see if the culprit food can be identified. Animal proteins and fats are digested quickly by the carnivore so should not produce much flatulence; however, if these foods do, perhaps the problem is not the kind of food but rather a problem with the cat's digestive system.

FOOD INTOLERANCES AND ALLERGIES

"However, regardless of our nutritional sophistication, in my clinic I am increasingly seeing many diseases that are caused by dietary deficiencies and excesses."

Dr. Louis L. Vine, D.V.M.

First, I should explain the difference between a food allergy and a food intolerance. An allergy is a response by the cat's immune system to an antigen, or foreign substance. When the cat came in contact with the antigen, antibodies were made to counteract what the cat's body considered undesirable. If the cat comes in contact with this substance later on an immune reaction occurs. These reactions can vary from runny nose and eyes to reddening and itching of the skin as the cat's body attempts to remove or "wall-off" this undesirable substance.

A food intolerance is basically the inability to digest or utilize a particular food so it is passed out without the cat receiving any benefit. The cat's body decides that it is not going to tolerate this food so it just flushes it on through without much involvement of the other body systems. This differs from an allergy in which the immune system becomes involved with a release of antibodies and histamine resulting in itching and scratching of the skin, a runny nose, diarrhea and congestion.

Itching with or without diarrhea may indicate a food allergy. It is my opinion that food allergies are not as common in the cat as food intolerances. Signs of allergies in cats and dogs primarily show up with skin symptoms such as an itch and scratching, whereas in humans and horses the primary signs are more of the respiratory system such as coughing, sneezing and nasal discharge. This might have something to do with the fact that cats and dogs do not sweat or perspire through their skin like humans and horses. The latter two have many more respiratory problems which may be part of the explanation.

Signs of allergy in our cat may include itching, scratching, hive-like swellings, diarrhea, vomiting, coughing, sneezing, runny eyes and eye rubbing. Even though food allergies are not that common, we should still be on guard and not miss the signs.

Allergies are also referred to as hypersensitivities. Other causes of hypersensitivities include ectoparasites such as fleas and mites, drug sensitivities, contact dermatitis, viral agents, cat bites, feline acne, biotin and fatty acid deficiencies.

One of the cat's reactions to an irritant within its body is to release a substance called histamine. This natural biochemical sets up the sneezing and runny nose which is the cat's body defense mechanism to "wash out" the irritant. We know, with ourselves, if we want to stop a runny nose we take antihistamines which block our body's histamine to dry up our nasal passages. Histamine produces these signs.

Histamines are released in response to three things:
- The natural body's internal mechanism to eliminate an irritant
- Histamine containing foods: fish based, poorly refrigerated mackerel in which histidine is converted to high levels of histamine, also fermented cheeses, dry pork and beef sausages, pig's liver, canned tuna and spinach.
- Common histamine-releasing foods such as egg whites, shell fish, chocolate, fish, alcohol, strawberries and tomatoes.

So any one or all of these mechanisms may be involved when our cat shows signs of itching, sneezing or diarrhea.

Food additives have been attributed, due to the increase in consumption of commercial pet foods, to various hypersensitivity type reactions. These include itching, runny noses, irritable bowel syndromes and behavioral disturbances including hyperactivity. Many veterinarians and pet owners have found that a number of skin problems cleared up when the pets were fed on homemade, additive-free diets. Some people are saying, "If you can't understand the label maybe you should avoid it."

Food additives to question
- monosodium glutamate
- colouring agents: tartrazine and erythrosin
- preservatives: benzoates, sulfur dioxide
- antioxidants: sodium nitrate, butylated hydroxytoluene, ethoxyquin

Allergic responses to food are not always consistent as the response will vary with the amount of the offending food eaten, what form it is in and the presences of other foods in the diet.

A food intolerance typically is seen as just diarrhea as the cat's digestive system cannot "tolerate" a particular food. Diarrhea may result from eating too much or too fast or a change in diet and not necessarily a specific food problem. Often the digestive system and bowel will just need some time to get used to the different diet. When changing cat foods or trying a new recipe, especially those with a lot of vegetables or fruits, start out with small portions then increase over several days to avoid too big a change to the cat's digestive system.

Milk and milk products, such as ice cream, given to an adult cat often result in diarrhea. This we could call an intolerance in that the cat, as we said earlier, does not have the enzymes to digest the milk sugar lactose. Therefore, the undigested milk portions are flushed (diarrhea) out of the system.

With the help of our cat's veterinarian, a record of all foods eaten and any changes in the environment (a new house plant) will help in the diagnosis. Once suspected and by eliminating the culprit foods that cause these reactions, the diagnosis can be confirmed.

Clearly the ideal solution is to eliminate and avoid the offending food. The difficulty is in identifying which one. With the great array of commercially processed cat foods on the market today containing many ingredients from various sources, finding the exact culprit might be impossible. The cat may be reacting not only to a food ingredient but to the hundreds of chemicals and foreign substances that may be present, everything from additives, pesticides, herbicides to colour and artificial flavours. The list could be endless.

The usual approach is to fast the cat of all foods for several days to a week. Do not eliminate water. Then introduce specific fresh foods with close observation so that the offending food may be be identified.

Another method is to totally eliminate all commercial foods and feed only fresh home-cooked diets. This may have to be done for several weeks before the condition improves.

Lately we have seen an increase of lamb and rice preparations in commercial cat foods. The industry is responding to the demand for hypoallergenic type foods. It is my opinion that before we jump to too many diet changes and treatments for food allergies and skin problems, that we get back to the basics. First try to get the "big picture" with regard to the complete home environment. Is the present diet deficient in any of the required nutrients especially vitamins and minerals? What is the quality of the present diet ingredients, sources, additives, preservatives or contaminations in storage. Using fresh home processed ingredients with attention given to the vitamins and minerals might be the final solution. Refer to Skin Problems on page 279 for more information.

To offer our cat a complete diet of homecooking involves a little work but the rewards are not only a contented cat but we become more aware of our pet as we prepare and feed different recipes and watch for purrs of approval or a nose turned up with disapproval. Feeding our cat fresh ingredients and recipes that we have to prepare gets us involved more closely with her well-being and nutritional needs.

LAMB AND RICE

A recipe utilizing lamb and rice with no additives.

Lamb or Mutton, boiled	1 lb	500 gm
Water	2 cups	500 mL
Rice (not instant)	3 cups	750 mL
Vitamin C, sodium ascorbate	1 tsp.	5 mL

Boil the lamb for about 20 minutes, longer for the mutton. Cook the rice. Chop or grind the cooked lamb and mix with the rice. Use the broth and add the vitamin C last. Serve warm, refrigerate the rest. Will feed a 8 to 10 lb (4 to 5 Kg) cat a week. If to be fed continuously add vitamin/mineral mix from pages 196 and 197

We have discussed Food Intolerances and Food Allergies but some foods are actually toxic or poisonous to the cat.

Foods Toxic to Cats

Cats can tolerate most foods but a few are toxic

- A lot of liver, too much vitamin A, see page 59
- Onion poisoning, consumption of onions leads to an increased number of Heinz bodies in the cat's red blood cells which in turn leads to hemolytic anemia and hemoglobinuria.
- Food preservative toxicity, example Benzoic Acid; cats cannot detoxify benzoic acid quickly which leads to aggression, hyperesthesia - an abnormally increased sensitiveness of the skin or of an organ of special sense - and death.
- Propylene Glycol, a preservative in semi-moist cat foods, that decreases red blood cell survival time. (European pet food manufacturers have discontinued use of propylene glycol)
- Chocolate contains methylxantines; caffeine and theobromine, that cats and dogs have difficulty detoxifying, ultimately leading to death.

BEHAVIOR PROBLEMS

Behavior is the way a cat acts, all the time or in certain situations. Behavior problems are abnormal actions for that particular individual. Abnormal behavior may be related to feeding and diet; other causes might be: breeding, individual personality, loneliness, fear, stress, or lack of exercise. Often more than one factor is involved.

Typical behavior changes related to diet would be those related to skin and intestinal changes. An itchy skin with diarrhea may be the first indication of a food sensitivity. The itching and scratching can become self-mutilating and cause severe damage.

Some commercial cat foods tend to use less animal source ingredients and more plant source starches and sugars. To maintain palatability and flavor, additives are introduced as well as preservatives. These additional ingredients might explain some of our cat's behavior problems.

Cats cannot talk so a painful tooth, a headache or perhaps pain from a stomach ulcer may be bothersome enough to alter their normally happy behavior. A good medical examination may be called for. Behavior problems are a large and encompassing topic which can involve many things including our own expectations.

From the nutritional aspect, we should strive for a balanced diet with all known nutrients present. Supplements we may try

- fresh foods, organ meats, meat, animal fats
- fresh raw foods
- a vitamin/mineral supplement
- a vitamin/mineral home recipe supplement
- B complex vitamins and foods
  - B complex tablet/day (with no vitamin A or D)
  - foods: liver, kidney, eggs
- vitamin C: 250 - 1500 mg / day
  - foods: fresh fruits (especially papaya, and cantaloupe),
  - peppers, broccoli and beef liver

SKIN PROBLEMS

The skin is not only the cat's largest organ, it also has the most problems. This soft flexible organ covered with hair serves the cat with protection from the elements, sensation, heat regulation, secretion and elimination. Because of the size of the skin and its complex nature, many things can go wrong. It has been said that ninety per cent of skin problems originate from the inside and ten per cent from the outside. Inside would be such things as improper nutrition, food allergies, hormonal problems, inheritance and disease in other body organs. Outside factors would include parasites, bacteria, chemicals and physical trauma. Skin problems occupy a large part of a veterinarian's small animal practice. I believe that skin problems and obesity are the two main medical concerns in our pet population today and both are strongly associated with nutrition.

There is no set of skin conditions in the cat that we could say typically points to a food sensitivity. Pruritis, itching, characterized by scratching and licking, would be the most often seen. Other signs can range from a scaly and crusty skin, general or localized hair loss to itchy and inflamed ears. These may all be the result of a food sensitivity and all have to do with skin.

Skin problems associated with nutrition can start with the kitten before birth. If the queen has not been fed properly during her gestation, the litter may have redder skin than normal combined with dry hair. Adequate nutrition is important for skin health even before birth, in particular protein and vitamin A.

Nutritional considerations for skin health are an ongoing process as the skin and hair are always growing and at a very rapid rate. This large organ in which the cells are replaced in about three weeks requires a lot of nourishment. Poor nutrition will show up almost immediately, giving us a good indication of the cat's health.

To specifically look at the nutrients involved we have to start with the basics: protein, fat, vitamins and minerals. Hair is ninety-five per cent protein and normal growth of the skin uses up about twenty-five per cent or one quarter of the daily protein requirement of the cat. Adequate, high quality protein obviously is the number one consideration in skin and hair health. Poor quality cat foods or poor quality and low protein home diets will soon show thickened, darker skin and loss of hair colour. Hair may fall out in patches with other hair becoming thin, dry, dull and brittle. We will see this more in growing cats or nursing queens because their demand for protein is much higher.

Fat, or more specifically the three fatty acids, are important for skin and hair growth and health. Fatty acid deficiency causes dry, lusterless hair and fine scaling, thickened skin. Hair loss and itching may develop. Later the skin becomes oily or greasy. This oily secretion or sebum at first slows down than increases to excess. With these changes, bacterial infection can start as well as self-inflicted trauma from the itching and scratching. Poor quality or improperly processed, dry cat foods with inadequate fat combined with poor containers can start a cat on a journey to fatty acid deficiency.

Of the vitamins the fat soluble A and E, especially A, function to maintain a healthy skin. As we said near the beginning of the book, vitamin A is required for the epithelial cells of the cat's body. Insufficient or too much vitamin A, will give the cat a poor hair coat, hair loss, scaling of the skin and an increased susceptibility to bacterial infection. Vitamin E, selenium and the fatty acids work together for healthy skin.

The water soluble vitamins B and C also play an important role is skin and hair health which may explain why a cat fed only processed cat foods responds to B and C supplementation with improved skin and hair health. The heat of processing and long storage depletes these water soluble vitamins.

All the B complex vitamins are given with riboflavin, niacin and biotin being especially important for the skin.

Vitamin C deficiency in man causes scurvy with hemorrhages throughout parts of the body tissues as well as broken "corkscrew" hair and thickening of the skin. Even though we believe our cat can make her own vitamin C - wild cats eat raw adrenal glands and liver - in times of stress and disease she may require more than can be manufactured.

Of the minerals, zinc has been shown to be important for skin health in many animals and man. Some cats have a decreased capacity to absorb zinc as well as cats on high-calcium or high-cereal diets which tie-up or bind zinc. Growing kittens are especially vulnerable and will have reddened skin, followed by hair loss, crusting, scaling and then weeping areas around the mouth, chin, eyes and ears. Their coats will be dull and they may develop thick crusts on the elbows and other joints.

Over supplementation of vitamins and minerals will lead to other problems so do not attempt to treat these conditions without professional help. Concentrate our efforts on prevention with adequate attention to feeding a well-balanced diet containing all of the essential nutrients.

Prevention of skin problems starts with adequate nutrition so that the skin is healthy and can resist any assaults upon it. A balanced diet with all the correct and available nutrients of protein, fatty acids, vitamins A and E, and the minerals zinc and selenium gives this fast growing and dynamic organ a chance to do its job. Refer to Part One, "Nutrition and Nutrients" for a review of how each of the nutrients play their role in the cat's overall health.

In my experience dealing with skin problems in my animal patients I look at the nutritional aspects first; if the skin is to heal and resist further assaults it must be fed properly.

SKIN SUPPLEMENT

Supplements containing polyunsaturated fatty acids, vitamins A, B's, C and E, and zinc.

Dry Supplement (water soluble vitamins)
Brewer's yeast	1 cup	250 mL
Sodium ascorbate powder	4 tbsp.	60 mL
Zinc sulfate 50 mg tablets, crushed	2	2
Kelp powder	1/2 tsp.	2 mL

Liquid Supplement (fat soluble vitamins)
Wheat germ oil	1/4 cup	50 mL
Cod Liver oil	1/4 cup	50 mL
Safflower oil	1/2 cup	125 mL

Mix the dry ingredients together and store in an air tight container in the refrigerator. Give 2 tbsp. every day on top of other foods.

Mix the oils and store in an air tight coloured container. Shake well and give 2 tbsp. every day with the dry supplement. Have enough for a week. Can mix both with regular daily meal. If cat is fussy and not that interested try adding fish oils such as salmon, tuna, sardine or others in place of the safflower oil.

Any recipe using liver, as it is a good source of vitamin A, should be fed on a regular basis such as twice a week or at least 1 tablespoon of liver every second day. This can be any kind of liver, raw or lightly cooked, and this amount will not be enough to cause problems yet will supply the much needed vitamins and fats for healthy skin and hair.

Good quality proteins and fats including the vitamins and minerals are the foundation for healthy skin and hair.

FUS, FELINE UROLOGICAL SYNDROME

FUS, or Feline Urological Syndrome refers to problems associated with the cat's bladder and urethra in particular. The urethra is the tube carrying urine from the bladder to the outside. This problem is primarily seen in neutered males and cats with an alkaline urine. This has arisen with the advent of the commercial cat foods containing less animal products and more plant products. The normal carnivores' diet produces an acid urine and the wild and ancestral cats were not neutered.

These problems usually involve cystitis and/or bladder stones and/or urethral plugs. Cystitis is inflammation of the walls of the bladder and stones are accumulations of mineral crystals. The most common crystals are those of magnesium ammonium phosphate, known as sturvite. Others might be calcium oxalate crystals. Signs often seen will be no urination, difficulty or pain in passing urine, increased frequency of urination and discoloured urine. The condition is most commonly seen in the neutered male, but can occur in the female and intact male.

Any or all of these signs are cause for concern and a trip to the veterinarian for a diagnosis is called for. We shall limit our discussion to bladder stones.

The accumulations of the mineral crystals into bladder stones, or uroliths, may form in the bladder as a result of certain minerals crystallizing around a tiny piece of inner wall that has broken off. The pH, or acidity of the urine, the amount of offending mineral content present in the diet and/or water and the general health of the cat will determine if these stones will form and become large enough to cause trouble. An alkaline or less acidic urine is thought to be a contributing factor from a cereal or vegetable type diet. Cats on high meat diets have acidic urine.

Neutered males tend to have the most problems which I believe is due to the penis remaining smaller than in an intact male. Therefore, I believe it is better to neuter a male cat after he has reached his adult stature rather than too young. If he is neutered at too young an age the penis and urethra remain infantile combined with the lack of testosterone, the male hormone. The smaller urethra then is more prone to blockage. Older cats of both sexes can develop uroliths as well. If the uroliths become too large they cannot be passed and will continue to grow in the bladder or become lodged in the urethra. Large uroliths have to be removed surgically.

Prevention involves having males neutered after they have reached the adult size and avoiding water and foods with high mineral (ash) contents. Some rural water supplies for drinking and crop production contain high levels of the offending minerals that can lead to these problems.

Poor quality dry cat foods, which contain low amounts of animal products and large amounts of plant products, fed over extended lengths of time, may also contribute to this problem as the urine becomes less acidic. A lack of sufficient good quality drinking water may contribute with the cat not drinking enough to flush out any offending crystals and the water may in fact be high in minerals prone to crystallization.

Acidifying the urine also helps. Ascorbic acid or vitamin C supplementation and low ash diets are in order.

The best prevention is to neuter our males after they reach adult stature, feed good quality cat food with adequate animal products and provide fresh good quality drinking water.

If we should suspect a urinary problem, a visit to the veterinarian should be quickly planned so that the problem can be identified and attended to as quickly as possible. If complete blockage is present, the problem is serious.

SUMMARY

I have attempted to explain in this section of Nutritionally-Related Problems those conditions where diet is a consideration in the cause of the problem. By understanding, without over simplifying, we may avoid having these conditions develop in our cat. If we understand what is going on, we should be able to recognize a problem before it gets out of hand. Remember many of the problems discussed may be a combination of several things so the complete "big picture" has to be considered. Seek professional help when necessary.

Feeding our cat is one of the most important things we do as cat owners. Just as important is to watch and listen to our cat and realize what she is telling us. From her appetite and behavior to her breath and coat condition, she is telling or showing us that all is not right. It is up to us to read the signs and act accordingly.

If all is fine, our cat will show it. What we feed and how much goes a long way to preventing many problems. Our cats live in a different environment from their ancestors. Our cats have many advantages when it comes to the supply of food and shelter. However, our modern cats have to do their best when it comes to adapting to our modern pollutants, processed foods, additives and the inability to pick and choose. Many of our cats' problems seen today are not seen in their wild and ancestral cousins. We have changed their environment and their food.

Now and in the future we will have to do our best to understand where our cats are coming from and to supply them with those essentials that will allow them to live happy and healthy productive lives. Be it as a house pet or a cat used for breeding, the total responsibility is ours. This does not have to be difficult and the first place to start is with the food we give them to eat. Good luck; when in doubt do what nature would do.

GOING ON TRIPS

With a mobile society such as ours we often take our pet with us either by car or by airplane. There are a few things we can do to prepare that will make the trip more comfortable for all.

- Visit the veterinarian, well in advance of the trip, and have all vaccinations and health certificates in order. We may want to pick up medication for motion sickness at this time.

- Purchase a good neck or body collar. Attach an identification tag with the pet's name, our name, address and phone number or some other address so if the cat is lost we can be notified.

- If planning to stay in motels or camp grounds ask about pets when making reservations.

- When a long trip is planned and we are not sure how the pet will travel, taking short trips in the neighbourhood will help train the cat and alert us to signs of motion sickness.

- A travel crate or portable kennel may be something we should look into especially if air travel is planned. Using the crate at home before we leave gives the cat some security later.

- Allow at least two hours before car travel and six hours before air travel with no food. Cats can fast for many hours without harm. Do not remove water.

- Take familiar food, toys or blankets as well as a container of water as unfamiliar water can be upsetting.

- Some people claim that an antistatic strap attached to their car helps avoid motion sickness. This could be something to try.

- Stop often to allow exercise and bathroom breaks. Use a leash and beware of dogs that may be loose such as guard dogs around service stations and truck stops.

BOARDING OUR PET

If, rather than taking our cat with us, we decide to board, a few items of note may help.

- Check out the facility before we commit. Ask other pet owners for recommendations and ask for a tour of the facilities. Look at the cleanliness and condition of the cages. Note heating and/or air conditioning facilities as well as the freedom from drafts.

- Are only cats boarded here and if not are they kept separated from the dogs?

- Note smells, noises and condition of food and water dishes.

- What kind of litter is used and how often is it changed?

- Talk to the staff and observe their attitude and cleanliness.

- Ask about supervision as well as night and weekend routines.

- Inquire about after hours delivery and pick ups.

- Get the facilities rules with regard to vaccinations, health certificates and contracts required. Beware of payments in advance and added costs.

- Make a list at home and bring with the cat

  - an emergency telephone number
  - the food currently fed
  - name and telephone number of the cat's veterinarian
  - any special problems, medication, or diet instructions
  - any behavioral habits

- Consider the cost of the services and the distance away.

APPENDIX I

CVMA (Canadian Veterinary Medical Association) Pet Food Certification Program: 339 Booth Street, Ottawa, Ontario K1R 7K1 (613) 236-1162 (see page 125 for standards)

Pet Food Association of Canada, 1435 Goldthorpe Road, Mississauga, Ontario, L5G 3R2, (416) 891-2921 A Canadian pet food manufacturer's Nutrition Assurance Program

United States regulation of pet food labeling:
Agencies involved:
    Food and Drug Administration, FDA
    U.S. Department of Agriculture, USDA
    Federal Trade Commission, FTC

American Association of Feed Control Officials, AAFCO, is made up of all state and federal officials (FDA, USDA, & FTC) responsible for regulating the production, labeling, distribution, and sale of animal food. The AAFCO with recommendations from trade associations such as the Pet Food Industry, PFI, the National Feed Ingredients Association, and the American Feed Industry Association has developed the regulations in the Uniform State Feed Bill. This bill allows monitoring of pet food labels, ingredients, additives, facilities and statements of nutritional adequacy. The bill also describes testing protocols for all animal feeds, label format and statements of guarantees.

AAFCO advises the state feed control officials. Pet food manufacturers must follow FDA regulations and can take legal action but rely upon the various state feed control officials for inspection and enforcement.

APPENDIX II

Comparison of 2% Cow's milk to Goat's milk

nutrient	1 cup 2% Cow milk	1 cup Goat milk
calories	121 cal	168 cal
protein	8.1 g	8.7 g
carbohydrate	11.7 g	11 g
total fat	4.7 g	10 g
saturated fat	2.9 g	6.5 g
mono-unsaturated	1.35 g	2.7 g
poly-unsaturated	0.17 g	0.36 g
cholesterol	18 mg	28 mg
vitamin A	466 IU	456 IU
vitamin C	2.3 mg	3.2 mg
vitamin D	100 IU	5 IU
vitamin E	0.09 mg	0 mg
thiamine	0.1 mg	0.1 mg
riboflavin	0.4 mg	0.3 mg
niacin	0.2 mg	0.7 mg
vitamin B6	0.1 mg	0.1 mg
vitamin B12	0.9 mcg	0.2 mcg
folate	12 mcg	1 mcg
sodium	122 mg	122 mg
calcium	297 mg	326 mg
magnesium	33 mg	34 mg
potassium	377 mg	499 mg
iron	0.1 mg	0.1 mg
zinc	1 mg	0.7 mg

A comparison of the nutrients. Cow's milk for sale in the stores is usually fortified for vitamins A, D, and E

GLOSSARY

Acid: A chemical substance that contains hydrogen atoms. Acids have a pH "power of the hydrogen" of less than 7.0. Examples of acids are vinegar and hydrochloric acid in the stomach.
Acute: Of sudden or rapid onset, as opposed to chronic.
Additive: Substances added to food to affect the characteristics of food such as to stabilize, cure, tenderize, fix color, flavor, season or give aromas without affecting the weight.
Alkaline: A base, opposite of acid, having a pH of more than 7 example; Baking soda.
Allergy: A specific sensitivity which results from exposure to a particular antigen.
Amino Acid: A building block of protein, over 20 known amino acids are utilized in the body to make various proteins, such as muscle, skin, hair, nails.
Anemia: The reduction in the number of red blood cells in the body, thus lowering the ability of the blood to carry oxygen.
Antibiotic: A substance made from a living organism which is capable of killing or inhibiting growth of another organism, especially bacteria, example penicillin.
Anus: The posterior opening of the digestive system.
Antibodies: Proteins made by the cat's immune system in response to a disease organism or vaccine that helps to fight against disease and infection in the future.
Antigen: A substance (usually a foreign protein) that stimulates the cat's immune system to manufacture antibodies.
Antioxidant: A substance that protects other substances or tissues from oxygen fragments by reacting with the oxygen itself. An example is vitamin E preventing rancidity in fats.
Appetite: The desire to eat.
Avidin: A product in raw egg white that binds biotin and limits it's absorption and use by the cat.
Bacteria: Microscopic one-celled organism found in the cat's body, food and on all living matter.
Balanced diet: A diet in which all the known nutrients are present in the correct amounts.

Base: Opposite of Acid, an alkaline compound, pH greater than 7.
Beriberi: A disease caused by a deficiency of vitamin B1, (thiamine) in man.
Beta Carotene: The water soluble form of vitamin A found in dark green, yellow and orange plants example; carrots. Beta Carotene cannot be used by the cat as a source of vitamin A.
Bile: A fluid produced by the liver and stored in the gall bladder that is secreted into the small intestine to aid in the digestion of fat foods.
Calorie: A measurement of heat. One calorie of heat energy will raise the temperature of one gram of water (1 mL) from 14.5^0 C to 15.5^0 C. In nutrition the the calorie actually refers to a kilo-calorie or the amount of heat required to raise the temperature of one kilogram (1 L) of water one degree Celsius.
Chelated Minerals: Chelation links a trace mineral atom to an amino acid forming a compound that is believed by some to be absorbed by the digestive tract more efficiently.
Chronic: A condition that continues or recurs and often lasts a long time, as opposed to one that is acute.
Collagen: Fibers that form scar tissue, tendons and ligaments.
Colostrum: The first milk secreted after queening containing antibodies for the kittens to fight infection and disease.
Colouring Agents: (dyes) Synthetic or natural source substances that are mixed into or applied to various foods in order to retain or change the natural colour.
Congenital: A condition or disease present at birth that may surface in later life. Not necessarily hereditary.
Dehydration: Loss of water from the cat's body. Any loss greater than the normal amount required for the cat to function.
Diabetes: A condition where there is an excess of glucose in the cat's blood stream and an inability of the cat to utilize it due to a shortage of adequate insulin production by the pancreas.
Duct: A tube used for conducting fluid, example bile duct.

Enriched, fortified food: Foods in which nutrients have been added because: precooking, pasteurizing, refining, milling, or bleaching usually destroys all or part of some or all nutrients that were present in the raw form.

Eclampsia: A metabolic disorder in the queen at or near queening seen as general weakness, convulsions and possible coma. Due to a disorder of calcium and vitamin D metabolism.

Electrolyte: A substance or salt that dissolves into positive or negative charged particles, conducts an electrical charge and is essential for the movement of body fluids, examples are: sodium, potassium and chloride.

Ersatz: A substitute, something synthetic, artificial or an article used to replace something natural or genuine.

Energy: The ability to do work.

Enzymes: Are complex organic substances produced by living cells that are involved in the digestion, assimilation and utilization of all nutrients. They are present primarily in raw foods as their effectiveness is destroyed by heat.

Farina: A floury substance usually made from durum wheat after the removal of the germ and bran. Can be used as noodles or as a breakfast cereal cooked in milk.

Fasting: Going without food or water or both for an extended period of time. Helpful in determining food intolerances.

Feline: Pertaining to the cat family, *Felidae*, which includes the domestic cat, lions, tigers, leopards, lynxes and jaguars.

Fiber: The indigestible residue of food. From carbohydrates cellulose, pectin, and hemicellulose are not digested in the dog. Hair and feathers would also be considered fiber.

Fixed formula: A commercial cat food formula in which the ingredients used do not change between manufacturing batches.

Flavouring agents: Substances made either by chemical synthesis or by extraction from natural sources and added to foods to enhance or modify the natural flavour or taste.

Flavour enhancers: Are substances which do not have an inherent flavour but when added to various foods especially with a high protein content intensify the natural taste, example monosodium glutamate (MSG).

Food Intolerance: Inability to digest a food may be due to a chemical idiosyncrasy, food contamination or lack of digestive enzyme, example lactose intolerance.
Gastritis: Inflammation of the stomach.
Glucose: Sugar; blood sugar; the building blocks of starch.
Glycogen: The storage form of glucose in the cat's body. Formed and stored in the liver and muscles and is converted back to glucose when energy is needed.
Gram: A unit of weight. 28 grams = 1 ounce.
Hairballs: Accumulations of hair in the cat's digestive system.
Hard Water: Water with a high concentration of calcium, magnesium or other substances.
Hepatitis: Inflammation of the liver.
Hereditary: A disease or condition present at birth that can be traced back to ancestors or parents. It can surface later.
Hormones: Biochemical substances produced by ductless glands that are secreted directly into body fluids exerting specific and vital effects on other organs.
Humectants: Ingredients in soft-moist pet foods that take up water and do not allow bacteria to use it, preventing bacterial growth and spoilage; examples are propylene glycol and sorbitol.
Hydrogenation: The process in which hydrogen is added to the molecule of an unsaturated compound, such as vegetable oil. This process condenses the oil to solid texture, allowing storage without refrigeration. Most vitamins and minerals are lost in this process. The fat form is also changed from the cis to the tran.
Immune System: A complex system of organs and substances that protect the cat against disease and infection.
International Unit (IU): A unit of measurement that signifies biological activity for the fat soluble vitamins A, D, and E.
Jaundice: A yellowing of the skin due to the appearance of bile in the blood, indicating liver disease.
Keratin: A form of protein found in hair, skin, and feathers.
Lactose: The sugar in milk made up of glucose and galactose. A carbohydrate present only in the milk of mammals. Aids in absorption of calcium and phosphorus. Adults may have difficulty digesting lactose.

Lecithin: A colourless compound found in brain, nerves, egg yolk and soybean. Is a combination of fatty acids and is an important source of choline and inositol. Used to metabolizes fats, and treatment of skin disorders.
Malignancy/malignant: Descriptive term(s) used to describe a cancer that can spread (metastasize) to other parts of the body.
Megadose: A large intake of a nutrient.
Muzzle: The nose and jaw of the cat.
Neoplasia: Abnormal cell growth; tumour or cancer.
Nutrient: A substance in food providing energy, helping in the regulation of metabolism, or building, maintaining or repairing tissues.
Nutrition: The process by which animals and plants take in and utilize food material. Also the study of the nourishment of humans, animals or plants.
Obese: Over weight, obesity: body fat weight more than 20% above ideal body weight.
Oncology: The study of tumours.
Organic: A substance that contains carbon.
Oxidation: The combining with oxygen. Spoilage and rancidity of carbohydrates and fats. Prevented by antioxidants or hydrogenation.
Pasteurization: A process in which a food is heated for a determined time to destroy pathogenic organisms. Also lessening the nutrient values of proteins, vitamins, minerals and enzymes.
Pad: Sole of the foot.
Pancreas: An organ within the abdomen that produces and secretes various digestive enzymes and the hormone insulin.
Photosynthesis: The process whereby plants, utilizing the sun's energy manufacture carbohydrates in their chlorophyll-containing tissues.
Phytate: A substance in unleavened whole grains that binds to minerals in the cat's intestines and inhibits their absorption.
Pica: The practice of eating non-food items; feces, dirt, wood.

Preservatives: Chemical substances added to foods to protect against: spoilage, discoloration, and decay by destroying or inhibiting the growth of microorganisms.
Prides: Groups of female lions that live together for life and usually include from one to six mature males.
Pruritis: Itching.
Queen: The brood cat or female used exclusively for breeding.
Queening: The act of giving birth to kittens.
RDA's: Recommended Dietary Allowances are guidelines for humans to the quantities of nutrients that should be eaten every day.
Rectum: Last portion of large intestine extending to the anus.
Refined: The process in which the coarse parts are removed, for example, the refining of whole wheat removes the bran and the germ leaving the endosperm or white flour.
Rendering: Process were fat is separate from livestock carcasses
Requirement: The amount of a nutrient needed by the cat to prevent deficiency symptoms.
Respiratory Tract: The lungs and their airways.
Retinol: Vitamin A
Retinol Equivalents (RE): A unit of measurement for vitamin A; 1 RE = 1 mcg or 3.33 IU of vitamin A as retinol.
Riboflavin: Vitamin B_2
Rickets: Abnormal bone development due to a lack of vitamin D.
Salt: common salt, or sodium chloride.
SDA: specific dynamic action, is the increase in metabolism over the basal rate brought on by the ingestion and assimilation of food, varying from 4 to 6 % for fats and carbohydrates to 30 % for protein.
Sebum: An oily secretion from the sebaceous glands of the skin.
Sweetbread: Packing house term for pancreas.
Tannin: Tannic acid. A yellowish, astringent compound in tea.
Tocopherol: Vitamin E.

Toxic: Poisonous.
Toxicity: The ability of being poisonous.
Trace Mineral: Minerals required by the cat in very low amounts.
Tripe: Packing house term for the rumens of cattle and sheep.
Ulcer: Damage to the outside layer of the skin or the lining of the stomach appearing as an erosion with inflammation and pain.
Uremia: Build up of poisons in the blood due to kidney failure.
Vegan: A strict vegetarian who eats no food of animal origin.
Variable formula: A commercial pet food formula in which a number of ingredients are listed. Those used will depend on availability, cost and will change between batches.
Whey: The watery part of milk left after the protein-rich curd (casein) is separated in the process of making cheese. Rich in lactose and lactalbumin, some fats and minerals.
Whole Grain: An unrefined grain that retains it's edible outside layers (bran) and it's highly nutritious inner germ.
Xerophthalmia: A condition of the eye producing a dry and lusterless eyeball, due to a deficiency of vitamin A.
Yeast: The common name of the fungi, Saccharomyces, used for leavening bread and producing alcoholic fermentation. Brewer's yeast is yeast obtained as a by-product in the brewing of beer.
Zinc: A blue-white metal, required by the cat in minute amounts but toxic in high levels.
Zoonosis: Diseases of animals that may be transmitted to man.

INDEX

AAFCO 105, 114, 120, 123, 190, 288
Absorption 27, 31, 95
Additives 79, 122, 129, 156, 160, 189, 194, 274, 275
Additive free 190
Adrenal gland 196, 281
Adrenalin 53
Aging 57
Albinism 89
Allergy 90, 273-277, 279
Aluminum 94
Amino acids 44
Ammonia 45
Anemia 70, 86, 88, 90, 163, 231, 277
Ancestral cat 154
Antibiotics 68, 70, 228, 268
Antibodies 33, 40, 46, 68, 69, 236, 273
Antioxidants 57, 63, 73-74, 89, 94, 101, 122, 129, 202, 275
Antistatic strap 286
Anus 34
Appetite 46, 59, 227, 228, 248, 257-258, 261
Arachidonic acid 49-50
Arthritis 73
Ash 284
Avidin 70, 162
Bacteria 53, 159, 160, 272, 279
Balance 21, 22, 43, 124, 157, 171, 183, 278, 281
Behavior 135, 278
Beriberi 56, 66
Beta carotene 57, 59, 180
BHA 74, 120
BHT 64, 74, 120
Bile 32, 36, 264
Biological value 46, 180, 239, 248, 264
Biotin 70, 162, 184
Bladder stones 283
Blood sugar 35-36, 54, 89, 90
Boarding 287
Bones 62, 77, 79, 80, 82, 84, 155, 156
Botulism 133, 204
Bowls feeding 140
Breeds 252
Butter 202
By-products 103, 107, 156
Cadmium 94
Calcium 62, 79, 80-83, 157, 232
Calorie 42, 51, 221, 223, 265
Caloric density 234
Cancer 102, 261
Canned cat food, see Commercial cat food
Carbohydrates 21, 52-55, 100, 180, 260
Carbon 77
Cardiomyopathy 266
Carnivora 16
Carnivores 12, 41, 47, 60, 154, 167, 175, 180, 191, 194, 258, 270
Carron 155
Catnip 171

Cecum 34
Cellulose 53, 79
Choline 85
Chocolate 55, 163, 218, 277
Chromium 89
Chyme 31
Cobalt 90
Collagen 72, 88
Colostrum 235, 236, 240, 242
Commercial cat food 13, 19, 102-150, 126, 158, 181, 263, 274
    canned 104, 110, 132, 142
    dry 110, 131, 141, 157
    semi-moist 110, 132, 277
Complete food 21, 105, 124, 150
Containers 131
Constipation 248, 271
Convalescing 228
Cooking 178
Copper 78, 88
Cornea 88, 89
Cost of cat food 130, 137
CVMA 105, 114, 125, 288
Cyanocobalamin (B_{12}) 70, 90
Cysteine 91
Cystitis 283
Dandruff 89, 100
Deficiency 43, 46, 56, 64, 66, 70, 71, 75, 133, 171, 246, 256, 280
Dehydration 39, 228, 241, 246, 267, 268
Dental 259
Diabetes 36, 98, 265
Diarrhea 39, 52, 65, 157, 159, 228, 231, 268, 273, 275
Dieting 224
Digestibility 136
Digestion 27, 28, 95
Digestive system disorders 255-272
Diuretics 85
DNA 57
Dogs 16, 17, 44, 117, 191, 286
Dog food 191, 203
Domestication 16, 19, 147, 252
Eating habits 19
Eclampsia 62, 82, 233
Eggs 162
Electrolytes 267, 268
Empty calories 43
Energy 27, 41, 45, 48, 52, 58, 78, 176, 223, 233
Enzyme 30, 31, 35, 77
Epithelial tissue 59, 280
Epileptic type convulsions 69
Equipment, cooking 161
Esophagus 29, 30
Ethoxyquin 64, 74, 120, 129
Exercise 51, 147, 158, 246, 265
Extruded 120
Fasting 143, 224, 257, 258, 262, 264, 268, 276
Fat 21, 48, 54, 100, 154, 180, 183, 264, 265

Fat soluble vitamins 51, 59, 62, 63, 65, 180, 280
Fatty acids 36, 48, 248, 280
Feces 34
Felis domestica 16
Feline Urological Syndrome see FUS
Fermentation 272
Fever 98, 255, 271
Fiber 21, 52-53, 136, 163, 223, 249, 271
Fight or Flight 55
Fixed formula 121
Flatulence 52, 272
Flavor 108, 120
Fleas 71
Fluorine 91
Folic acid 69
Food intolerance 98, 272, 273-277
Food poisoning 159
Free choice 141
Free radicals 57, 63, 73, 94, 101
Fresh foods 75
FUS 39, 256, 283-284
Genetic potential 236
Glucagon 35
Glutathione reductase 73
Gluten enteropathy 47
Glycerol 49-50
Glycogen 36, 54
Glucose 30, 36, 45, 54
Goat's milk 244, 289
Goiter 89
Gourmet 211-218
Grooming 18, 28, 243, 262
Guaranteed analysis 118
Habits 20, 25
Hair balls 18, 79, 262
Hair depigmentation 88
Hairlessness 90
Hair loss 67, 87, 89, 137, 231, 233, 279
Halitosis 261
Hard keepers 227
Harmony 78
Hemoglobin 90
Hepatitis 264
Herbivores 17, 18, 272
Histamine 273, 274
Holistic 269
Hormones 35, 44
Humectants 110, 120
Hydrochloric acid 30
Hypersensitivities 274
Hypervitaminosis 62
Hypoallergenic 276
Hypoglycemia 55
Immune system 68, 71, 84, 87, 236, 258, 273
Iodine 90
Ingredients 162-173
Ingredients commercial cat food 119
Insulin 35-36, 55, 67, 89, 90, 265
Intestine 31-34
Iron 86, 88
Itching 137, 273, 278
Jacobson's organ 29, 152
Jaundice 264
Kitten 28, 39, 60, 62, 65, 83, 86, 99, 143, 231, 235, 236-244
Kitty bag 142, 157, 185
Labels 113, 114-125
Lactase 35, 268
Lactation 231
Lactic acid 54
Lactose 35, 98, 162, 268, 275
Laws cat food 114
Lead 94
Linoleic acid 49, 162
Linolenic acid 49
Lite salt 215
Liver 36, 44
Liver as food 60, 282
Liver problems 264
Lymph 33
Lymphatic system 33
Maintenance 138, 142, 176, 177
Macrominerals 77
Magnesium 80, 83, 84
Manganese 89
Margarine 202, 248
Mastitis 241
Meat 162
Medication 92
Mercury 94
Metabolism 40, 41, 55, 56, 78, 142
Methione 91
Metric 174
Metritis 241
Microminerals 77
Minerals 21, 77-93, 101, 122, 249
Mineral oil 65, 269
Mold 132, 160
Molybdenum 88
Motion sickness 286
Mouth 28, 259
Mucus 30, 34
Natural 80, 122, 129, 143, 189-202, 208, 224, 235, 258, 260
Neutered 92, 284
Niacin 67
Nickel 90
Night blindness 59
Nitrogen balance 45
NRC, National Research Council 124, 149, 238
Nutrients 14, 97, 253
Nutrition 14, 16, 95, 234, 236, 255
Nutritionists 113
Obesity 43, 50, 51, 141, 158, 221-226, 237, 246, 248, 253
Olfactory cells 152
Omnivore 191
Orphans 241-244
Organic 189
Osmotic equilibrium 77
Osteoporosis 81, 221, 245
Oxalic acid 157
Oxydation 40, 48, 63, 73
Oxygen 57, 70, 73, 77, 86, 88, 147, 158
Palatability 48, 100, 119, 123, 126
Pancreas 35-36
Pancreatitis 265

Pansteatitis 63, 266
Pantothenic acid 68
Parasites 178, 192, 220, 227, 257, 274, 279
Parathyroid hormone 82
Pellagra 67
Peridontal disease 260
Perspire 40, 154
Pet food industry 102
Pharynx 29
Phosphorus 62, 80, 83-84, 232, 249
Phytates 81
Phytic acid 83
Pine needles 98
Placenta 233, 236
Polyunsaturated 49
Potassium 85, 215
Prescription diet 112, 127
Preservatives 57, 108, 156, 194
Propylene glycol 110, 120
Prostaglandins 49
Proteins 21, 44-47, 99, 180, 228, 279
Prothrombin 65
Proximate analysis 118
Pruritis 279
Purines 264
Pyridoxine 69
Queen 82, 86, 143, 170, 177, 227, 231-235, 279
Rancid 48, 58, 63, 73, 111, 132
Raw 178, 179, 191
Recipes 175-251
Rectum 34
Regulations 105, 114
Retinal degeneration 266
Retinol 59
Riboflavin 67
Rickets 62, 81
Saccharides 53
Saliva 29
Salmon poisoning 163
Salmonella 165
Salt 85, 154, 249
Saturated fats 49
Scheduled feeding 142
Scurvy 72, 281
Selenium 63, 89, 280
Seniors 246
Shelf life 108, 109, 123, 129
Sick 228-230, 255
Silicon 88
Skin 133, 253, 279-282
Smell 152
Snacks 124, 126, 143
Sodium 85
Spaying 92
Specific dynamic action 247
Spices 155, 156, 163
Starches 53
Starvation 43, 46, 54
Steatitis 63
Stomach 30, 144, 261
Stools 135
Storage 137
Stress 30, 219-220, 237, 268, 281
Sturvite 283

Sugars 52, 110, 111, 154, 163, 265
Sulfa drugs 65, 68, 69, 70
Sulfur 91
Sweat 154
Table scraps 103, 107, 137, 156, 181
Taste 107, 152
Taste buds 28, 153
Taurine 19, 46, 193, 266
Teeth 29, 62, 77, 80, 84, 91, 259
Testosterone 284
Texture 152, 199
Theobromine 218, 277
Thermoregulation 247
Thiamin 56, 66
Thiaminase 66, 163
Thyme 202
Thyroid gland 89
Tocopherols 63
Tongue 28, 153
Tonsillitis 259
Toxins 70, 94, 160, 277
Toxoplasma gondii 178
Trace minerals 77
Trans fatty acids 202
Triglycerides 49
Underweight 227
Urethra 283
Uric acid 36, 264
Urine 40, 45, 71, 134
Uroliths 283
Vaccinations 220, 236, 286
Vanadium 88
Variable formulas 121, 128
Vegetables 193, 198
Vegetarian 47, 193, 266
Veterinarian 20, 105, 124, 233, 240, 244, 245, 249, 253, 255, 261, 265, 271, 275, 283, 286
Villi 32
Vitamins 21, 56-76, 101, 122, 249, 265
 A 59-61, 180, 193, 279, 280
 B 66-71, 83, 90, 259, 278, 280
 C 72, 78, 196, 214, 171, 278, 280, 284
 D 62, 80
 E 63-64, 89, 266, 280
 K 65
Volatile fatty acids 48
Vomernasal organ 29, 152
Vomiting 18, 159, 262, 264, 267
Warfarin 65
Water 16, 21, 38, 98
Water soluble vitamins 56, 66-72
Weaning 234, 238, 243
Worms 179
Yellow fat disease 63, 266
Yogurt 35
Zinc 87, 94, 249, 265, 281

RECIPE INDEX

BARNABY'S BISCUITS	201
BEAR'S BREAKFAST	208
BEEF TONGUE	226
BIG FAMILY DISH	205
BIRTHDAY PARTY CAKE	217
BUDGET STRETCHER	186
CASPER'S CLAM CHOWDER	211
CHICKEN LIVER DELIGHT	200
CHOU CHOU'S DELIGHT	213
CHRISTMAS CASSEROLE	214
CHUMLEY'S MEAT LOAF	216
CLEOPATRA SALAD	211
COMING HOME FROM SURGERY	245
COUGAR AID	215
CREAM AND VEGETABLE SOUP	201
DEEP FRIED GIZZARDS OR LIVERS	213
DRY VITAMIN & MINERAL SUPPLEMENT	197
EBENEZER'S SPECIAL	250
ECONO MIX	207
FELINE FEAST	205
FELIX'S FISH WITH MILK SAUCE	202
GET BETTER SOON	230
GRANDMA'S CHICKEN SOUP	229
GRANDMA'S VITAMIN MIX	251
HANNIBAL'S HAM & PEA SOUP	212
HEARTY BREAKFAST	184
HIGH FIBER LAXATIVE	271
HOBART'S HAMBURGER HASH	251
HOSPITAL GRUEL	229
JOAN HARPER'S KITTY CRUNCHIES	210

KITTY CRUNCHIES	199
KITTY TREATS	239
KITTY SQUARES	209
LAMB & RICE	277
LEFTOVER OMELET	185
LINUS'S LAMB & RICE	201
LIQUID VITAMIN & MINERAL SUPPLEMENT	197
LIVER MORSELS	230
LOW FAT HIGH FIBER	226
MILK REPLACEMENT RECIPES	244
OCTAVIUS CASSEROLE	250
OSCAR'S DEEP FRIED OYSTERS	212
PANTHER PIZZA	187
PRINCESS'S PASTA PIE	187
PUSS'S POPSICLES	215
RED "WINE" FELINE STYLE	215
RESTAURANT, KITTY BAG, LEFTOVERS	185
SAMBO'S SHRIMP SALAD	200
SARDINES ON TOAST	217
SARDINE SALAD	200
SIR VIVER SALAD	206
SKIN SUPPLEMENT	282
SOUP A LA SAMBO	207
SOUR CREAM SAUCE	188
SYLVESTER'S SALMON PATTIES	216
THANKSGIVING FEAST	214
VITAMIN & MINERAL FOODS	196
VITAMIN & MINERAL GRAVY	188
VITAMIN / MINERAL SUPPLEMENTS	278
WHITE WINE	215

ADDITIONAL READING FOR CAT OWNERS

Good Food For Your Cat by Jean Powell, Citadel Press, 120 Enterprise Ave., Secaucus, NJ 07094, 1980

Holistic Animal News, PO Box 9384, Seattle, WA, 98109

Native Nutrition, Eating According to Ancestral Wisdom, by Ronald F. Schmid, N.D. Healing Arts Press, One Park Street, Rochester, Vermont 05767

Natural Health for Dogs and Cats by Richard H. Pitcairn DVM, Ph.D. and Susan Hubble Pitcarian, Rodale Press, Emmaus, Pa. 1982

Natural Pet, Editor-in-Chief/Publisher: Charlene Smith, Pet Publications, Inc. Box 351, Trilby, FL 33593-0351

Nutrient Requirements of Cats, National Academy of Sciences, 2101 Constitution Ave., N. W., Washington, D.C. 20418, 1986

Pet Care, by A.T.B. Edney and I.B. Hughes, Blackwell/Year Book Medical Publishers, Inc.

The Cat Lover's Cookbook by Franki B. Papai, St. Martin's Press, 175 Fifth Ave., New York, NY 10010, 1993

The Healthy Cat and Dog Cook Book by Joan Harper, Pet Press, Richland Center, Wisconsin 53581, 1988

The Revolution in Cat Nutrition by Jane R. Bicks, D.V.M., Rawson Associates, 115 Fifth Ave. New York, NY 10003

The Complete Herbal Handbook for the Dog and Cat by Juliette de Bairacli Levy, Arco Publishing, Inc. New York, 1986

HOW TO ORDER ADDITIONAL BOOKS AND PRINTS

Our Pet's INC.

Our Pet's Inc.
P.O. Box 2094,
Fort Macleod, Alberta,
Canada TOL OZO

___***Let's Cook For Our Cat***
  @ **$ 19.95** Canada **$ 16.95** United States **£ 9.95** United Kingdom =___
___***Let's Cook For Our Dog***
  @ **$ 19.95** Canada **$ 16.95** United States **£ 9.95** United Kingdom =___
___***Watercolour Dog Prints***
  @ **$ 24.95** Canada **$ 19.95** United States **£ 12.95** United Kingdom =___
              (GST included)
     Watercolour prints are 11"/17" on 100# stock
     Prints will be signed and dated by the artist
     Canada and U.S. Add Shipping and Handling $ 2.50
     Total amount of order Books & Prints $ _____

NAME _____
   (please print)
Street/P.O. Box _____

City/town _____

Province/State _____**Postal code/Zip**_____

Make cheque or money order payable to: **Our Pet's Inc.**, P.O. Box 2094, Fort Macleod, Alberta TOL OZO

Orders outside of Canada: paid in U.S. funds by cheque or money order drawn on a Canadian or U.S. bank. Allow several weeks for delivery. **Thank You**

GIFT GIVING

I would like to send
___***Let's Cook For Our Cat***
  @ **$ 19.95** Canada **$ 16.95** United States **£ 9.95** United Kingdom =___
___***Let's Cook For Our Dog***
  @ **$ 19.95** Canada **$ 16.95** United States **£ 9.95** United Kingdom =___
___***Watercolour Dog Prints***
  @ **$ 24.95** Canada **$ 19.95** United States **£ 12.95** United Kingdom =___
              (GST included)
     Watercolour prints are 11"/17" on 100# stock
     Prints will be signed and dated by the artist
     Canada and U.S. Add Shipping and Handling $ 2.50
     Total amount of order Books & Prints $ _____

to the following person.

A GIFT FOR YOU

NAME _____
   (please print)
Street/P.O. Box _____

City/town _____

Province/State _____**Postal code/Zip**_____

AUTHOR PROFILE

Dr. Edmund R. Dorosz has been a practicing veterinarian and college instructor to Animal Health Technicians for many years. After receiving his Bachelor of Science in Agriculture (B.S.A.) in 1966 and his Doctor of Veterinary Medicine (D.V.M) in 1971 he was engaged in veterinary practice as well as instructing Animal Health Technicians.

In his many years of dealing with animal health and animal feeding, nutrition was an important component. Always attempting to be practical with animal owners and their animals, he strived to educate his clients and students to look at the big picture. He asked them to understand and always question what they were doing with respect to the welfare of their animals.

Seeing the need for a practical approach to pet nutrition and feeding in our changing world inspired the books: Let's Cook For Our Dog and Let's Cook For Our Cat.

Dr. Dorosz continues with his interests in pet nutrition and writes regularly in many national and international pet publications as well as appearing on local and national radio and television.

"Dr. Ed" has always had an interest in art, drawing and painting, since childhood. The watercolour painting of a kitten on the cover and the illustrations in the book are some of his latest works.